The Michigan model, named after the institution where it originated and was first articulated in *The American Voter* (Campbell et al. 1960), has been used successfully to explain voting behavior in North American and western European democracies. In this book, experts on Latin America join with experts in electoral studies to evaluate the model's applicability in this region. Analyzing data from the AmericasBarometer, a scientific public opinion survey carried out in 18 Latin American nations from 2008 to 2012, the authors find that, as do democratic voters elsewhere, Latin Americans respond to long-term forces, such as social class, political party ties, and political ideology. At the same time, Latin Americans pay attention to short-term issues, such as the economy, crime, and corruption. Of course, Latin Americans differ from other Americans, and among themselves. Voters who have experienced left-wing populism may favor government curbs on freedom of expression, for example, while voters enduring high levels of economic deprivation or instability tend to vote against the party in power.

The authors thus conclude that, to a surprising extent, the Michigan model offers a powerful explanatory model for voting behavior in Latin America.

**Richard Nadeau** is Professor of Political Science at the University of Montreal.

**Éric Bélanger** is Professor of Political Science at McGill University (Canada).

**Michael S. Lewis-Beck** is F. Wendell Miller Distinguished Professor of Political Science at the University of Iowa.

**Mathieu Turgeon** is Assistant Professor of Political Science at the Universidade de Brasília (Brazil).

**François Gélineau** is Research Chair on Democracy and Parliamentary Institutions and Professor of Political Science at Université Laval (Canada).

# Latin American Elections

*Choice and Change*

Richard Nadeau, Éric Bélanger, Michael S. Lewis-Beck,
Mathieu Turgeon, and François Gélineau

University of Michigan Press
Ann Arbor

Published in the United States of America by the
University of Michigan Press
Manufactured in the United States of America
♾ Printed on acid-free paper

2020   2019   2018   2017      4   3   2   1

A CIP catalog record for this book is available from the British Library.

Library of Congress Cataloging-in-Publication Data

Names:  Nadeau, Richard, author.
Title:  Latin American elections : choice and change / Richard Nadeau, Éric Bélanger, Michael S. Lewis-Beck, Mathieu Turgeon and François Gélineau.
Description:  Ann Arbor : University of Michigan Press, [2017] | Includes
    bibliographical references and index.
Identifiers:  LCCN 2016028267| ISBN 9780472130221 (hardcover : alk.
    paper) | ISBN 9780472122523 (ebook)
Subjects:  LCSH: Elections—Latin America. | Voting—Latin
    America. | Latin America—Politics and government.
Classification:  LCC JL968 .N34   2017 | DDC 324.98—dc23
LC record available at https://lccn.loc.gov/2016028267

# Acknowledgments

Many individuals, institutions, and encounters have made this book possible. First are the scholars in Latin America and North America who have inspired and encouraged us. Numerous colleagues in Argentina, Brazil, Ecuador, Mexico, Peru, and Uruguay have commented, in whole or in part, on this work. Foremost, we wish to thank our dear friend and fellow professor, María Celeste Ratto (CONICET Argentina), for her tireless practical assistance and intellectual support. Also, from Argentina, we want to mention the precious help of María Laura Tagina, Universidad Nacional de San Martín, and the comments and encouragement received from Raúl Jorrat, Universidad de Buenos Aires; Carlos Gervasoni and Germán Lodola, Universidad Torcuato Di Tella; Marcelo Escolar, Universidad Nacional de San Martín; Mariano Montes, Instituto Nacional de la Administración Pública. In Brazil, the aid of Lucio Rennó, Universidade de Brasília, stands out, as does that of Felipe Burbano and Jorge León, both of FLACSO in Ecuador. With respect to Mexico, we are happy to acknowledge Gerardo Maldonado and Allyson Benton, each at CIDE México, as well as Alejandro Moreno and Juan Pablo Micozzi, each at ITAM México. At least three Peruvian scholars have supported us, namely Stéphanie Rousseau, Arturo Maldonado, and Jorge Aragón, all of the Pontificia Universidad Católica del Perú. Finally, in Uruguay, we benefited from an excellent discussion with Santiago López Cariboni, Juan Ariel Bogliaccini, and Diego Hernández, all from Universidad Católica del Uruguay.

In North America, there are influences, direct and indirect, from various scholars. Most of all, however, we want to thank the team of Ryan E. Carlin, Matthew M. Singer, and Elizabeth J. Zechmeister, who together edited an emerging classic—*The Latin American Voter*. Ryan, Matt, and Liz have pushed forward our volume in countless ways, by their insights, approaches, criticisms, and abiding support. They set before us a worthy goal—write something that would stand on the shoulders of their seminal work. We have engaged in a struggle similar to theirs: how to make sense of the complex world of Latin American elections and public opinion. Our answers are in some ways the same, in some ways different. Both volumes shed new light on the vitality and challenges of democratic politics in this important region of the world.

This research would not have been possible without the financial support of the Social Sciences and Humanities Research Council of Canada and the Fonds de recherche du Québec—Société et culture. These monies sustained travel to the region, as well as funding the field research, including purchase of selected items in the AmericasBarometers, carried out by the Latin American Public Opinion Project (LAPOP), housed in Vanderbilt University under the leadership of two fine directors, Mitch Seligson (past) and Elizabeth Zechmeister (current). The data analyzed here come from AmericasBarometer surveys in 18 Latin American nations conducted in three waves—2008, 2010, 2012. We would have nothing of value to say without these datasets, so ably processed by our three excellent research assistants, El Hadj Touré (at the University of Montreal) and Thomas Didier and Chris Chhim (both at McGill University).

With pride, we publish this book under the banner of the University of Michigan Press, long a leader in election studies. Melody Herr, PhD and Senior Acquisitions Editor, has never wavered in her attention to this project, always working hard to make it better, helping it fulfill its purpose. In these efforts, Danielle Coty, Editorial Assistant, has been an excellent set of eyes and hands. An obvious related mention is the extended, thoughtful, and helpful comments of the anonymous reviewers selected by the University of Michigan Press. These comments made for a much better book, and of course the errors that remain are ours. Turning to the question of broad intellectual acknowledgment, the Michigan imprimatur evokes the name of the research model we have followed. Angus Campbell, Phillip Converse, Warren Miller, and Donald Stokes were all professors at the University of Michigan when they wrote *The American Voter* (1960). In that pathbreaking book, they put forward a theoretical paradigm for explaining the act of voting in democracies. That paradigm, now commonly referred to as the Michigan model, serves to guide our discussion of vote choice in Latin America. As the reader will see, it works well, even managing to offer critical insight when it does not.

Last, but not least, we want to thank the citizens of Latin America whom we have come to know, especially those in the countries of the region where we have worked and lived, sometimes for years, namely Argentina, Brazil, Colombia, Guatemala, Mexico, and Peru. You have taught us much.

# Contents

# Introduction

The notion that national elections in Latin America are, or should be, democratic now forms part of the ordinary discourse regarding the region's politics. It was not always so. Throughout the twentieth century, governments were often selected (or deselected) by *golpes del estado*, coups where typically a military leader forcefully overthrew the seated rulers, installing himself as dictator. This pattern can be traced back at least to the beginnings of that century, and the era of militarism and caudillismo—the rule of ironfisted leaders (Johnson 1964). The caudillo was a strongman who exacted obedience by fear, patronage, and a powerful personality. Such authoritarian leaders often came from the military, a dominant institution, given the relative weaknesses of its supporting political institutions. The governing role of the armed forces, well into the 1960s, has been documented by various historians (Lieuwen 1967; McAlister et al. 1970). Military, as opposed to civilian, government stood as an accepted way of life. A leading political science observer of the period drew the following conclusion: "Military coups are a regular, recurrent, normal part of the Latin American political process" (Silvert 1961).

Today, traditional military coups, with their pattern of ensuing dictatorship, have essentially disappeared. However, nontraditional coups continue (Loveman 1993). In the 1990s, the phenomenon of the *autogolpe* (self-coup) arose, highlighted by the Guatemalan and Peruvian experiences. In this sort of coup, the seated executives themselves suspended rights and Congress, and called for new affirming elections. Another form of current coup can be labeled the *constitutional coup* (a coup technically within the limits of the constitution). Here the army, out of legal obligations written into many Latin American constitutions, foremost to maintain internal order, steps in. The outstanding case in point saw the army overthrow President Manuel Zelaya of Honduras in 2009. Clearly, the army remains a force to be reckoned with in the formulation (or dissolution) of Latin American governments. In a special report, one noted team of analysts recently concluded: "One can hope that they [coups] have gone away, but they likely have not, and the international community has to deal with this fact realistically" (Wiarda and Collins 2011, 10). This assessment must be based, in part, on the lingering effects of caudillismo, a sort of charismatic leadership style that some current political chiefs find difficult to resist.

The Latin American legacy of coups, and caudillismo more generally, do not mean that meaningful elections have not occurred. For one, military rule has always been an exception in certain of these nations, with Mexico as an outstanding example. Moreover, some nations of the region have had an extended democratic practice, namely Colombia, Costa Rica, and Venezuela, with a fifty-year tradition of democratic alternation in power. Further, since the so-called third wave of democracy in Latin America, beginning around 1980, about three hundred more or less reasonably free and fair elections (presidential or legislative) have taken place (Carlin et al. 2015, 1). Indeed, some have suggested that Latin America has lived through a period of democratic consolidation (Mainwaring 1999).

Nevertheless, the consolidation may be incomplete (Diamond 2008). In their recent examination of presidential elections in Latin America, Hartlyn et al. (2008) decide that at least 18 contests from 1980 to 2003 were flawed or unacceptable, in terms of democratic criteria. More generally, worry exists over the fragility of democratic institutions in the region, which perhaps comes no surprise given its long history of coups. Freedom House, in its 2012 evaluation, rated 20 nations there. It found one-half Free (i.e., a score of 70 or more on its 100-point scale), one Not Free (i.e., Cuba), and the remaining nine only Partly Free (i.e., a score of less than 70). (See Puddington 2014a, 2014b.) Moreover, the general trend of the Freedom House scores over the previous five years (2007 to 2011) was one of decline.

Contemporary scholarship on Latin America's "authoritarian drift" offers a fresh explanation, one that might be applied to these declining democracy scores (Weyland et al. 2013). In certain countries, a populism from the left has taken hold, with hegemonic leaders such as Hugo Chávez

(Venezuela), Evo Morales (Bolivia), and Rafael Correa (Ecuador) attempting to implement what has been called a "competitive authoritarianism" (Levitsky and Way 2010). The influence of this populism has spread to Nicaragua, Honduras, and Argentina, posing "a new threat from the left [that] emerged during a time of what appeared to be democratic consolidation" (Weyland, de la Torres, and Kornblith 2013, 31). In their thoughtful essay on the problem, Weyland et al. (2013, 32) conclude that "the end of the authoritarian trend in Latin American is not in sight."

The documented fragility of Latin American democracy in something like half of its nations stands out as a concern, especially since so much public and political faith has been placed in democratic elections as a social remedy for the region. In this delicate, but demanding, context, it behooves us to know how these elections work. But we know embarrassingly little about what makes them tick. This book aims to help fill that knowledge gap. We start that discussion by a review of the extant literature on Latin American elections. Then, we explore, in a general way, theories of electoral behavior in Latin America, and why they may be different from other democratic regions. We decide that the application of the "Michigan model" of voting has merit, and develop that line of argument. Our introduction concludes with an outline of the theoretical organization of the book, which closely follows the "funnel of causality" laid out in *The American Voter* (Campbell et al. 1960).

## Literature on Latin American Elections

Democratic elections, as widespread routine phenomena, are barely a generation old in Latin America. Therefore, relevant research literature is scarce, especially work touching on the individual-level behavioral mechanisms of vote choice, as opposed to system-level aggregate characteristics of electoral outcomes and policies. The larger nations have been studied more, as witness survey-oriented studies in Brazil and Mexico (for Brazil, see Ames 2001 and Baker, Ames, and Renno 2006; for Mexico, see Domínguez and McCann 1996 and Moreno 2003). In the smaller nations, a select number of vote intention investigations have been conducted. For Venezuela, two stand out, those of Weyland (2003) and Nadeau, Bélanger, and Didier (2013). Each offers a rather complete explanation of the Chavez vote. Most of the other single-nation studies have had to make do with one published analysis, generally appearing post-2000 (see the papers reviewed in chapter 5).

In addition to a growing, but still spotty, collection of individual-level, single-nation voting studies, there have been some cross-national election studies within the region. The kickoff was the seminal paper by Remmer (1991), which researched 21 presidential elections in the region that took place from 1982 to 1990. This work was updated and lengthened by Benton (2005), to cover 39 presidential elections. Since then, other scholars have pursued a similar set of questions on more current data pools (Johnson and Schwindt-Bayer 2009; Johnson and Ryu 2010). Singer (2013), in an effort to be definitive about emerging debates, looked at the biggest dataset yet (18 countries and 79 elections, 1982–2010).

These efforts have suggested that considerable structure underlies the presidential vote. However, all the conclusions rest on macrodata, rather than microdata. In that regard, relatively few comparative political behavior investigations have come out of the region. The first was the effort by Echegaray (2005), who fitted essentially the same theoretical model to preelection vote intention data from Argentina, Peru, and Uruguay. A second, more recent, effort was by Lewis-Beck and Ratto (2013), analyzing an individual-level survey pool from 12 Latin American nations. That investigation is limited, however, by its narrow focus on the economic voting question. Most recently, the edited volume by Carlin et al. (2015) has been assembled. That fine collection contains contributions from 20 scholars of Latin American elections, each with their specialties, and makes extensive use of datasets we also explore. However, no scientifically unified, book-length cross-national survey investigation of the political behavior of voters in Latin America as a whole has yet appeared. That is the ambitious task we have set for ourselves in this book.

## Theories of Electoral Behavior: Is Latin America Different?

We have known little, overall, about why Latin American voters behave the way they do. Certainly, elections have been investigated, as the above discussion makes clear. But these studies have not been guided by overarching theories of vote choice in the region. Instead, specific variables, which constitute the research focus of the scholar, have been pursued. For example, it might be election quality (Baker, Ames, and Rennó 2008), incumbency advantage (Boas and Hidalgo 2011), political corruption (Dominguez and

McCann 1998), political violence (Arce 2003), retrospective voting (Benton 2005), or vote buying (Brusco, Nazareno, and Stokes 2004). These are variables worthy of study in any democracy; but they are not explicitly embedded in a theory of Latin American political behavior.

What might such a theory look like? An expectation could be that it differs from theories applied to national elections in the advanced industrial democracies. Although Latin America is changing, it still can be characterized as a region where incomes are modest, with large pockets of grinding poverty. (According to the World Bank data for fiscal year 2016, 14 of the 18 Latin American countries we examine have a Gross National Income per capita of less than $12,736 annually. Of this group, 5—Bolivia, El Salvador, Guatemala, Honduras, and Nicaragua—have a GNI per capita of less than $4,126. For comparison, in the United States GNI equals $55,200.) Moreover, considerable ethnic diversity persists, a result of the mingling of the indigenous peoples with migrants of African and European descent. Religiously, the Catholic Church remains a hegemon, although it has been losing ground to Protestant Evangelical movements. Also, the educational system has great weaknesses, which means less fertile ground for the growth of a healthy democracy. Further, because democracy is relatively new in the region, political parties do not often have deep roots, allowing independent charismatic leaders to mobilize a mass following seemingly out of nowhere. These are examples of conditions that could make the Latin American voter look "different," when compared to voters from, say, North America.

But we do not think that, in fact, they are fundamentally different from voters in other, full-fledged democracies. Like democratic voters everywhere, they respond to a set of stimuli, or variables, that together make up known, or discoverable, laws of political behavior. Different elections scholars have offered different explanations of the vote choice in democratic systems. None have offered a more comprehensive theory than that of the authors of *The American Voter* (Campbell et al. 1960, chap. 2). They located central variables influencing voters, and grouped them into long-term and short-term forces, operating along a time line. The long-term forces, such as social class, occur earlier, and tend to be fixed. The short-term forces, such as issue preferences, occur later, and tend to be fluid. All these forces move through what they call a *funnel of causality*, with the vote choice itself at the tip of the funnel (see also Miller and Shanks 1996). A recent replication and update of this classic study offers a sketch of the funnel of causality. The groups of variables, moving from long-term to short-term forces, are as follows: sociodemographics, party identification, issues, candidates (Lewis-Beck et al. 2008, chap. 2). These authors, after analyzing the American presidential elections of 2000 and 2004, conclude: "to state it simply . . . the original theories and interpretations still serve" (Lewis-Beck 2009, 521).

## Exporting the Funnel of Causality:
## Will the Michigan Model Go South?

This funnel of causality model, tied together by principles of social psychology, has been referred to as the Michigan model. Our question concerns whether the Michigan model serves for Latin America as well. The idea—exporting the model to other democratic shores—is not new. The first efforts were carried out in Britain, by Butler and Stokes (1969), and centered on the abiding role of party identification. However, that effort soon met with considerable resistance from other European electoral scholars, who urged that voting research move "beyond" party identification (Budge, Crewe, and Fairlie 1976). The Dutch and French cases, especially, seemed to offer a poor fit to the model (see, respectively, Thomassen 1976 and Haegel 1990). However, work on the place of party identification in European election studies persisted. Particularly influential was the major book by Converse and Pierce (1986), on the controversial French case.

More contemporary comparative work has strengthened the case for the exportability of the Michigan model, at least with appropriate country-specific modifications. In *Political Choice in Britain*, the authors assert that "a core, stable element in public political psychology, Michigan-style party identification constitutes a powerful long-term force on voting behaviour" (Clarke et al. 2004, 20). The Michigan model has also recently been applied to a system quite different from British parliamentary elections—that of French multiparty, presidential elections (1988–2007). Those authors wish to know if "in the French case, over a period of time both recent and with essential political transformations, the hypotheses and principal conclusions of the model are still pertinent"; they answer in the affirmative (Nadeau et al. 2012, 45).

The list continues. Take the Irish case, with its peculiar electoral system of a proportional representation–single transferable vote. In their seminal work, Marsh et al. (2008, 161) claim "everything fits together . . . by adapting the classic 'funnel of causality' framework pioneered by . . . *The*

*American Voter.*" Another European case, complicated in different ways, is the Austrian. Currently, in the first survey-based study of Austrian national elections, Kritzinger et al. (2013, 26) stress that "we organize the work around the funnel of causality, first introduced by Campbell [et al.] (1960)."

One characteristic of all the foregoing studies is that they have been single-country. Can the Michigan model stretch across a set of countries from a large geographic region? That question is of special importance here, as we propose to apply it to a set of Latin American countries. Fortunately, there is at least one baseline of comparison—the Nordic countries. In a sophisticated new investigation of the national election studies of Denmark, Finland, Norway, Sweden, and Iceland, the authors make the following statement about theoretical organization: "The general idea behind the sequencing of chapters is well known to most students of electoral behaviour: the 'funnel of causality.' . . . We begin with stable and long term features of electoral behavior . . . then shift focus to the more short term determinants of political behavior" (Bengtsson et al. 2013, 10). Furthermore, even though they analyze these countries together in this way, they argue that "the five countries are less homogeneous than many think. We need to revise the image of Nordic exceptionality and similarity" (Bengtsson et al. 2013, 3).

That is to say, studying the nations of a region through one theoretical lens does not mean that, for these voters, "one size fits all." Instead, the funnel of causality approach allows for a recognition of country similarities, while permitting at the same time the presence of certain county differences. This flexibility, inherent in the Michigan model, means that we may be able to draw out generalizations about Latin American voting behavior without neglecting evident country-by-country differences. Of course, a fascinating question is the following: To what extent are the voters in the various Latin American nations alike? We devote a special chapter to answering this question.

## The Theoretical Organization of the Book

We test the funnel of causality, or the Michigan model, against political behavior data gathered in national probability surveys of the AmericasBarometer, from 18 Latin America nations over the period 2008–12. Geographic coverage of the region, while not total, remains comprehensive.

The nations of Meso-America (Mexico) and Central America (Costa Rica, El Salvador, Guatemala, Honduras, Nicaragua, Panama) are represented. The Andean nations of Bolivia, Ecuador, and Peru are included, as are the nations of the Southern Cone (Argentina, Chile, Paraguay, Uruguay). Three of the nations (Colombia, the Dominican Republic, Venezuela) have a Caribbean shoreline. Hence, almost all of the former colonies of Spain are covered, plus Brazil, at one time Portugal's colonial prize. There are exclusions, such as Cuba, Suriname, or Haiti, but exclusions are few. (Cuba must be excluded, because no AmericasBarometer data are available there. While the data from Suriname and Haiti are available, Latin American scholars typically omit them, along with other non-Spanish-speaking Caribbean countries).

Chapter 1 explains the evolution of public opinion research in Latin America, especially as it tracks public support (or its lack) for sitting governments. It ends with an explication of the AmericasBarometer data that form the empirical basis of this volume. Chapters 2–5 form the core of the book, and follow closely the funnel of causality framework. Chapters 2 through 4 examine long-term forces, while chapter 5 examines short-term forces. The sequence commences with chapter 2 and its treatment of demographic forces, in particular the variables of age, gender, religion, region, and race. Chapter 3 continues the sociological theme, exploring the socioeconomics of class, material goods, education, unemployment, property ownership, and clientelism. Chapter 4 turns to long-term anchoring forces that are more psychological than social, specifically party identification and ideological identification. Chapter 5 brings the reader, at last, to the short-term forces of issues, in particular state intervention, authoritarianism, corruption, democratic rights, crime, and the economy. Chapter 6 bears down on the question of cross-national similarities and differences, in an exploration of how far our generalizations can carry. The text ends with a conclusion that mulls over, among other things, the comparative weight of long-term versus short-term forces, the Latin American "difference," and the prospects for explaining Latin American voting behavior in future elections. While we do not wish to give away this conclusion, we can affirm the following analogy: the Michigan model, during its drive south, sometimes hits bumpy spots along the way, but manages to cross the finish line pretty much intact.

CHAPTER 1

# Voting Behavior and Public Opinion in Latin America

The research on Latin America politics is impressive and covers much ground. Scholars have developed genuine explanations for a variety of phenomena, such as the pioneer work on state development (Cardoso and Faletto 1979) and military rule (Collier 1979; Malloy 1976; Schmitter 1973; Remmer 1991). More recent contributions have examined the specifics of presidential regimes (Mainwaring and Shugart 1997), legislative politics (Morgenstern and Nacif 2002), or party systems (Kitschelt et al. 2010; Di Tella 2005; Scully 1995). Others, for their part, have explored democratic transition and consolidation, more broadly, in the region (Agüero and Stark 1998; Diamond, Plattner, and Brun 2008; Hagopian and Mainwaring 2005; Camp 1996; Smith 2012). Still others have assessed the impact of neoliberalism on political institutions (Wise and Roett 2003; Stokes 2001; Oxhorn and Ducatenzeiler 1998) and, even more recently, the rise of the political left (Cameron and Hershberg 2010; Castaneda and Morales 2008; Levitsky and Roberts 2011; Weyland, de la Torres, and Hunter 2010). To be sure, these constitute only a few examples of recent comparative work on Latin America. What emerges from all of these endeavors is that Latin America has been the object of study by many social scientists examining many different questions.

Closer to what is of interest here, we can say that the scholarship on elections and voting behavior in Latin America is also extensive. But the great bulk of this scholarship is single-country studies. Very few studies have attempted to treat the region as a whole or, at the least, consider a sufficiently large number of countries, in order to draw conclusions about elections and voting behavior in Latin America. This is particularly true of individual-level voting behavior studies, which are quite rare.

The main barrier to producing comparative analysis of individual-level electoral behavior in Latin America has to do with data availability. Before the early 1980s, only a handful of countries in the region had experience with public opinion polling. But with the return of democracy in the 1980s, the polling industry began to survey people more systematically about issues of public interest. Finding comparable survey data from the 1980s and 1990s, however, proves to be quite a hazardous endeavor. The Roper Center made a great effort to gather public opinion surveys from Latin America for that period. However, in the face of important variations in sampling techniques, interviewing modes, and, more important, question wording, the conduct of rigorous comparative analysis of vote choice was a daunting task.

Multinational efforts at generating truly comparable survey data in the region are quite recent. Among these initiatives, we count the Comparative Study of Electoral System (CSES), the World Values Survey, the Latinobarometer, and the AmericasBarometer. Acting as a consortium of academics already running postelectoral studies in their respective country, the CSES planned for the administration of a common module of survey questions. The first module of the CSES (1996–2001), however, only included three countries from Latin America. The last module (2006–11) only saw the addition of two more countries, making it hard for anyone to draw inferences about Latin America as a whole. The World Values Survey is another multinational survey initiative that started its work in the mid-1990s. It has conducted surveys in some 10 countries of the region. Yet, despite aspiring to study "social and political change," its questionnaires lack most of the variables needed to study voting behavior. The Latinobarometer, for its part, began to employ a unique questionnaire administered by different survey firms in several countries of the region. Although the Latinobarometer has had the necessary questions to study voting behavior, the quality of its national samples has been a constant source of concern among scholars in the area, especially in the earlier years.

The latest initiative is that of the AmericasBarometer, launched in 2004 with coverage of 11 countries of the Americas (North, Central, and South). By the second round of the study in 2006, 22 countries were included in the study, and four more were added in its third wave in 2010.

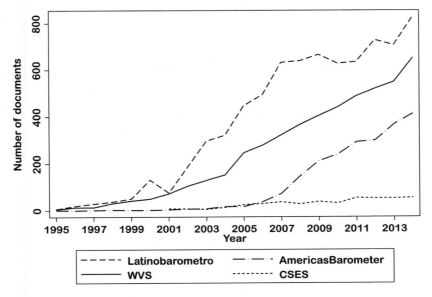

Fig. 1.1. Number of documents found by Google Scholar by year

Note: Individual searches were performed for each year/dataset. For the different datasets, the search included the following keywords: (1) latinobarometro OR "latin barometer" OR latinbarometer OR "latin barometro"; (2) americasbarometer OR "americas barometer" OR "barometro de las americas" OR "latin american public opinion project"; (3) "latin america" OR "latinoamerica" OR "america latina" AND "World Values Survey"; and (4) "latin america" OR "latinoamerica" OR "america latina" AND "Comparative Study of Electoral System" and "Latin America". The searches were performed at http://www.scholar.google.ca on April 2, 2015.

In 2012, the total number of surveyed countries reached 26. In 2014, 28 countries were included. This survey of the voting-age population is specifically designed to measure democratic values and political behavior in the Americas.

Many scholars have exploited these newly available sources of data in order to analyze different dimensions of Latin America's public opinion. A quick search on Google Scholar allows us to illustrate that point in figure 1.1. Since 1995, documents making reference to the four datasets previously described have increased exponentially. Yet, despite the availability of comparable data for over 15 years, systematic attempts to offer a complete and exhaustive profile of the Latin American voter are only beginning.

The most recent contribution is *The Latin American Voter*, a 2015 volume by Ryan Carlin, Matthew Singer, and Elizabeth Zechmeister. This book presents a collection of voting behavior studies divided into stand-alone chapters, ranging from an examination of the decision to vote, to the evaluation of a smorgasbord of notable determinants of vote choice, such as class, ideology, partisanship, and issue valence. The contribution by Carlin and colleagues is important because it explores in great detail how theories of voting behavior, developed in more established democracies, also apply to Latin American countries. The book is ambitious and well executed, examining 18 countries in the region. It seriously considers how context, appropriate to the region as a whole, as well as to each country under analysis, affects the theories being evaluated. They conclude, not surprisingly, that we cannot speak of a single "Latin American Voter"; however, they successfully extract some important characteristics that define voters in the region, and within their unique context.

Our aim in the current book is similar to what the authors of *The Latin American Voter* have achieved, but it is also different in important ways. It is similar in scope, in that we consider the same 18 Latin American countries over more or less the same time period. Moreover, we also make use of the AmericasBarometer data to examine the individual-level voting behavior of Latin Americans. But the similarities stop here. Our contribution is primarily distinct in that we approach the study of vote choice in a more integrative way. Specifically, we propose the evaluation of a *single model* of vote choice, one inspired by the pathbreaking work by Campbell et al. (1960) in *The American Voter*. Using the Michigan Model, we examine the long-term and short-term determinants of vote choice as they operate through a funnel of causality, with vote choice at the tip of the funnel. The remainder of the book highlights other notable differences between our work and theirs. We believe both contributions have merits of their own and should be viewed as complementary, with equal value to students of Latin America.

## Explaining Vote Choice in Latin America

Scholars have proposed different theories for explaining vote choice in democratic elections. Several explanations value certain determinants of vote choice over others, and every explanation is conditioned, to some degree, by varying electoral and societal contexts. Admittedly, explaining vote choice is not an easy task, so it is not surprising to find many explanations of the same phenomenon. Very few of these explanations, however, offer such a comprehensive, generalizable framework of analysis as that proposed by *The American Voter* (Campbell et al. 1960, chap. 2).

These authors identify long-term and short-term forces that operate through a funnel of causality to explain vote choice (see also Lewis-Beck et al. 2008, chap. 2). The long-term forces found at the wider end of the funnel are more remote from vote choice and less variable over time, if not constant. These forces include the demographic and socioeconomic characteristics of voters. Many of those, such as gender and race, are indeed given determinants of vote choice, in that there are no prior factors defining them. Moving along the funnel, we encounter slow-changing determinants of vote choice like partisanship and ideology and, as we arrive closer to the tip of the funnel, some truly malleable determinants like issue stances, on both economic and noneconomic matters, and evaluations of candidates and parties. Together, these determinants form the funnel of causality, moving from early or long-term forces to late or short-term forces. In the end, these forces culminate into explaining the tip of the funnel, i.e., vote choice.

There are many ways in which vote choice could be operationalized, but, for the purpose of this book, we decided to examine support for the incumbent. More precisely, we rely on a vote intention question that asks respondents who they would vote for "if a presidential election were held tomorrow." Respondents are given the option of choosing between voting for the incumbent candidate or voting for a party or candidate opposing the current administration. We recognize that this vote intention question is hypothetical, and may not always completely reflect the final electoral reality. But the wording has the advantage of being explicit, inviting the respondent to fully express his or her vote intention.

In our explanation of vote choice in Latin America, we consider four groups of determinants, those related to social structure (demographics), class and material belongings (socioeconomics), partisanship and ideology (political anchors), and issues. Thus, the model of vote choice we propose takes the following general form, from the wider to the narrower end of the funnel, in that order:

Vote = $f$ (demographics, socioeconomics, political anchors, issues)

In the model, demographic variables reflect social cleavages like religion and race; socioeconomic variables measure education, employment, income, and wealth; political anchors represent social-psychological characteristics of voters like partisanship and ideology; and issue variables embody preoccupations of the day, such as the economy, crime, or corruption.

The first group of variables, consisting of the demographic characteristics, specifically considers age, gender, religion (affiliation and church attendance), race, and the rural-urban divide. These characteristics are either given, like race and gender, or near-constant, like religious affiliation. We consider them as long-term forces, since they operate both directly and indirectly, through the other forces found closer to the tip of the funnel, where vote choice occurs.

These determinants were once at the center of studies on voting behavior (e.g., Lazarsfeld, Berelson, and Gaudet 1948) and have received renewed interest in recent years (e.g., Ansolabehere, Persily, and Stewart 2010), including in Latin America (e.g., Boas and Smith 2015; Morales 2015; Morgan 2015). We believe these forces to be important in explaining vote choice in Latin America given the region's deep religious roots,[1] high ethnic/racial diversity,[2] aging population,[3] and changing gender roles.[4] Admittedly, Latin America has seen an important growth in its urban population over the past decades, but there are still today large portions of its people living in rural areas.[5] These forces undoubtedly shape people's interests and values, and should affect the way they form political opinions and preferences. For these reasons, we believe it is justified to include them in our model of vote choice.

Next, we consider socioeconomic status, defined as a function of one's education level, income level, employment status, occupation (private or public sector), and relative wealth. These factors are slow-changing forces, but should exert, just like demographics, both direct and indirect effects on vote choice. Although socioeconomic status is found not to have much of an effect nowadays on vote choice in the developed world (e.g., Lewis-Beck et al. 2008), much less is known about its effect in Latin America. The earlier studies in the region found only weak effects (e.g., Dix 1989; Torcal and Mainwaring 2003). However, a recent account has shown a growing effect for class on voting (Mainwaring, Torcal, and Sommá 2015), especially in countries that experienced leftist governments, e.g., Argentina (Lupu and Stokes 2009), Brazil (Hunter and Power 2007), and Venezuela (Handlin 2013). There are good reasons to believe that socioeconomic forces have nonnegligible effects on vote choice in Latin America, given the region's high levels of inequality in income, wealth, and education, coupled with the recent rise of leftist governments in the region.

The third group of forces explaining vote choice, labeled political anchors, consists of two social-psychological variables, namely party identification and ideological orientation. These two variables, especially party identification, contribute to reinforce voters' loyalty to political parties over time. Attachments to a particular party and ideological orientation are frequently developed early in life, but prone to change over time. These two factors are closer to the tip of the funnel than demographic and socioeconomic characteristics and are generally found to significantly affect how people vote. We believe that they also matter in Latin America. Recent research in the region has shown that many Latin American citizens do indeed develop attachments to political parties (Lupu 2012, 8), and that many are capable of placing themselves on a left-right ideological scale (Zechmeister and Corral 2013). Admittedly, though, party identification and ideological orientation may not play as strong a role as they do in older established democracies, in part because parties in many Latin American countries have not been around long enough for strong party attachments and ideological cleavages to develop.

Fourth, our explanation of vote choice would not be complete without a group of variables that accounts for short-term forces like issues. Our treatment of issues is divided into economic and noneconomic factors, and valence and positional evaluations. The valence issues are the national economy, crime, corruption, and democracy. The positional issues are state intervention in the economy and authoritarianism (as expressed in a desire to limit opposition party free speech). Even on the face of it, these six issues would appear to have considerable saliency for Latin American publics.

As we will see, the four groups of factors we just described go a long way toward explaining how Latin Americans vote. Still, this general model does not completely account for the influence of all possible electoral forces in the region. Outstanding examples of other forces are personalism and clientelism. To be sure, some voters may respond to the personal characteristics of the candidates, rather than to the party itself (Mainwaring and Torcal 2006). It is very unlikely, however, that most voters base their vote on this sole characteristic. But more important for present purposes is the question of clientelism. Admittedly, given the region's general lower level of income, some voters may be tempted to alter their vote choice in exchange for material benefits, in the traditional clientelist pattern (Roberts and Wibbels 1999). We address this issue head-on in chapter 3. Our analysis of clientelism there indicates, first, that it is not as widespread as is frequently believed, being mostly confined to rural areas and to unemployed voters. Second, our estimate of its effect on vote choice suggests it has only a small impact.

We acknowledge that select other considerations remain outside of the scope of this book. Some scholars have explored how the electoral system design affects the behavior of individual voters (e.g., Norris 2004). Others have studied the effect of political campaigns and money on vote choice (e.g., Holbrook 1996; Jacobson 1978). Still others have assessed the moderating role of the media, and of the elites, in providing cues for voters when they decide how to cast their vote (Bartels 1993; Popkin 1994). One thing these studies have in common is looking at exchanges between voters and their broader environment. While we do not wish to discard these important contributions, we made the decision to limit our analysis to factors that are closest to the individual voters. We leave it to future research to broaden the scope of this already challenging task.

## Data, Measurement, and Estimation Strategy

In order to test our proposed vote choice model, we use survey data from the AmericasBarometer. More specifically, we use the data from three recent available AmericasBarometers, the 2008, 2010, and 2012 waves.[6] All three waves include the questions needed to perform the evaluation of our vote choice model in all 18 Latin American countries. The countries retained for analysis are Argentina, Bolivia, Brazil, Chile, Colombia, Costa Rica, the Dominican Republic, Ecuador, El Salvador, Guatemala, Honduras, Mexico, Nicaragua, Panama, Paraguay, Peru, Uruguay, and Venezuela. Questionnaires are pretested in each country, and probability samples are employed to ensure the representativeness of national samples. The survey is administered in the local language in face-to-face interviews using handheld electronic systems.[7]

The AmericasBarometer questionnaire includes the usual battery of questions about the respondents' demographic and socioeconomic characteristics, their ideological orientation, opinions on various issues, evaluations of the economy and political institutions, and a vote intention question to be used as our dependent variable, as discussed above. The full details about the operationalization of our independent variables are given in the following chapters, as the groups of variables are presented. A few technical points, however, are worth highlighting. Recall that respondents were asked a vote intention question that required them to choose between voting for the incumbent candidate or party (coded 1) or voting for a party or candidate opposing the current administration (coded 0) "if a presidential election were held tomorrow." A crucial characteristic of the incumbent candidate, however, concerns his or her ideological orientation (or at least, the ideological orientation driving his or her administration). Thus, vote intention for the incumbent candidate refers to a left-wing incumbent candidate in some countries and to a right-wing incumbent candidate in others. But recall too that our model examines how demographic and socioeconomic characteristics, ideology, partisanship, and issues affect vote choice. For some of these determinants, there are clear theoretical expectations, and their impact on vote choice depends on the ideological orientation of the incumbent candidates considered.

To arrive at coefficient signs equally interpretable across countries, some of our independent variables require adjustments. For example, in a country in which the president is right-leaning, we expect wealthier respondents to be more likely to vote for the incumbent. In that case, the wealth variable remains unchanged, with higher values indicating wealthier respondents. In a country in which the president is left-leaning, we expect lower classes to be more likely to vote for the incumbent. In such a case, we invert the scale of the wealth variable, for higher values to identify poorer respondents. All in all, we adapt the scale of some variables to the ideological position of the incumbent president. In doing so, a positive coefficient always indicates support for our hypotheses.[8]

The classification of the ideological orientation of incumbent candidates was performed based on information about the candidate and his or her party, but also on the way the incumbent president was governing the country at the time of the survey. Some candidates were easily classified and others less so. Easy classifications include Brazil, Chile, and Venezuela, for example. In Brazil, President Lula da Silva (known as Lula) and his successor, Dilma Rousseff, are coded as leftist governments. Both Lula and Dilma are from the center-left Workers' Party (PT). Lula's mandates (2003–6, 2007–10) are defined in great part by the implementation of important social policies like the well-known Bolsa Família that helped reduced Brazil's poverty and inequalities. Rousseff (2011–) continued and expanded some of these policies. In Chile, President Michelle Bachelet from the Socialist Party of Chile (2006–10) was coded as leftist. Her tenure is characterized by the implementation of pro-poor policies, like the reform of the pension system to benefit poorer workers and the introduction of equal pay for women in the private sector. Bachelet's successor, Sebastián Piñera from the liberal conservative party National Renewal, was coded as rightist. Piñera clearly governed to the right. One notable illustration of Piñera's ideological thinking is his support of for-profit activity in education, a program that led to important student protests in 2011. Venezuela is another understandable classification. For the entire period considered, the president in office was Hugo Chávez from the United Socialist Party. Chávez's "socialism for the 21st century" was inspired by both Bolivarianism and Marxism, and many of the public policies his government put forward promoted wealth redistribution. His coding as a leftist president comes as no surprise.

Other cases, however, were not as easily classified. For example, Alan Garcia in Peru was elected on the basis of a center-left political party (APRA, or Alianza Popular Revolucionaria Americana), but his government mostly ruled on the center-right, signing several new foreign trade agreements and giving continuity to the neoliberal economic policies put in place by his predecessor Alejandro Toledo. We thus coded President Garcia on the right. Another notable example is that of the Dominican Republic. For all three studies considered, the president in office was Leonel Fernández from the Dominican Liberation Party. Although the PLD was initially considered a party from the left, with Fernández in office the party clearly adopted policies of the center-right. To be sure, we recognize the daunting task of classifying some candidates; but overall we feel very confident about our classification.[9]

Table 1.1 below presents the details about our dependent variable, including the name of the presidents and their party affiliation at the time of the survey, the beginning and ending dates of their tenure, the date of the survey, the number of months the survey stands from the beginning of the presidents' terms, and the ideological classification of said presidents. The table presents information for all 18 countries and three study waves.

The information about the number of months the survey stands from the beginning of the presidents' terms is important to consider. Recall that the AmericasBarometer studies are not electoral studies per se, in that they are not purposefully conducted during an election or right after it. On the contrary, the studies are conducted every other year, independent of electoral cycles. Consequently, some of the country surveys are conducted shortly after presidential elections, others at midterm, and still others toward the end of presidential terms. This could cause concerns, given what we know about the popularity of presidents during a typical mandate. Indeed, recently elected incumbents generally benefit from greater popularity than incumbents at the end of their mandate.

We do see a correlation of –.10 between our dependent variable and the Months variable, implying a mild time decaying function. But, perhaps surprisingly, when comparing the actual vote share received by the incumbents and their support as measured by our dependent variable, we find them to be very close. Specifically, the average vote share of all incumbents, as measured by the vote share they received in the first-round election (or in the second round when one was needed) is 52.4%. Our measure of incumbent support, i.e., the voting intentions for the incumbents at the moment of the surveys, averages 51.6%. Thus, our measure of incumbent support is very close to the real support incumbents have received in the previous election (with an error of less than 1 percentage point). Still, we recognize the importance of time in office and so consider this factor in our analysis of vote choice.

As mentioned earlier, the data we consider in our analysis are those from the 2008, 2010, and 2012 AmericasBarometer, covering a total of 18 countries. When combining these studies, we have a total sample of a little over 90,000 observations. But, because not all respondents were willing to express a preference in our vote intention question, the size of the analyzed sample shows attrition. Nearly 40,000 respondents abstained, refused, or did not indicate a vote intention. While this is a large number, it closely tracks key sociodemographic characteristics of the total sample from which it was taken.[10] Thus, the analysis we present below, based on some 50,000 vote intention respondents, appears effectively representative of the larger sample from which it was taken.

We conclude this section with a few words about the estimation strategy we adopt in order to evaluate our vote choice model. We start by proposing a baseline model that includes dichotomous variables for all countries considered (except for Mexico, our country of reference) and one other independent variable: Months, i.e., the number of months the respondent stands from the beginning of the president's term. As men-

TABLE 1.1. Additional Information about the Dependent Variable, by Survey Year

| Country | 2008 | | | 2010 | | | 2012 | | |
|---------|------|---|---|------|---|---|------|---|---|
| | President and tenure | Survey date (month) | Ideology | President and tenure | Survey date (month) | Ideology | President and tenure | Survey date (month) | Ideology |
| Argentina | C. Fernández de Kirchner (PJ-FPV) 2007/12–2011/12 | 2/1/2008 (3) | Left | C. Fernández de Kirchner (PJ-FPV) 2007/12–2011/12 | 4/1/2010 (29) | Left | C. Fernández de Kirchner (PJ-FPV) 2011/12– | 4/1/2012 (5) | Left |
| Bolivia | E. Morales (MAS) 2006/01–2009/12 | 3/1/2008 (27) | Left | E. Morales (MAS) 2010/01–2014/12 | 3/1/2010 (3) | Left | E. Morales (MAS) 2010/01–2014/12 | 4/1/2012 (28) | Left |
| Brazil | L. da Silva (PT) 2007/01–2010/12 | 5/1/2008 (17) | Left | L. da Silva (PT) 2007/01–2010/12 | 4/1/2010 (40) | Left | D. Rousseff (PT) 2011/01–2014/12 | 4/1/2012 (16) | Left |
| Chile | M. Bachelet (PS) 2006/03–2010/03 | 2/1/2008 (23) | Left | S. Piñera (RN) 2010/03–2014/03 | 5/1/2010 (2) | Right | S. Piñera (RN) 2010/03–2014/03 | 5/1/2012 (26) | Right |
| Colombia | A. Uribe (PC) 2006/08–2010/08 | 2/1/2008 (18) | Right | A. Uribe (PC) 2006/08–2010/08 | 5/1/2010 (45) | Right | J. M. Calderón (PSUN) 2010/08–2014/08 | 4/1/2012 (20) | Right |
| Costa Rica | O. Arias (PLN) 2006/05–2010/05 | 2/1/2008 (21) | Right | O. Arias (PLN) 2006/05–2010/05 | 2/1/2010 (45) | Right | L. Chinchilla (PLN) 2010/05–2014/05 | 2/1/2012 (21) | Right |
| Dominican Republic | L. Fernández (PLD) 2004/08–2008/08 | 3/1/2008 (43) | Right | L. Fernández (PLD) 2008/08–2012/08 | 3/1/2010 (19) | Right | L. Fernández (PLD) 2008/08–2012/08 | 2/1/2012 (42) | Right |
| Ecuador | R. Correa (Alianza PAIS) 2007/01–2009/08 | 3/1/2008 (14) | Left | R. Correa (Alianza PAIS) 2009/08–2013/08 | 3/1/2010 (7) | Left | R. Correa (Alianza PAIS) 2009/08–2013/08 | 2/1/2012 (30) | Left |
| El Salvador | A. Saca (ARENA) 2004/06–2009/06 | 3/1/2008 (45) | Right | M. Funes (FMLN) 2009/06–2014/06 | 3/1/2010 (9) | Left | M. Funes (FMLN) 2009/06–2014/06 | 5/1/2012 (35) | Left |

| Country | President (2008) | Date (n) | Orientation | President (2010) | Date (n) | Orientation | President (2012) | Date (n) | Orientation |
|---|---|---|---|---|---|---|---|---|---|
| Guatemala | A. Colom (UNE) 2008/01–2012/01 | 3/1/2008 (2) | Left | A. Colom (UNE) 2008/01–2012/01 | 3/1/2010 (26) | Left | O. P. Molina (PP) 2012/01– | 4/1/2012 (3) | Right |
| Honduras | M. Zelaya (PLH) 2006/01–2009/06 | 2/1/2008 (25) | Right | P. Lobo Sosa (PNH) 2010/01–2014/01 | 2/1/2010 (1) | Right | P. Lobo Sosa (PNH) 2010/01–2014/01 | 2/1/2012 (25) | Right |
| Mexico | F. Calderón (PAN) 2006/12–2012/11 | 2/1/2008 (15) | Right | F. Calderón (PAN) 2006/12–2012/11 | 2/1/2010 (39) | Right | F. Calderón (PAN) 2006/12–2012/11 | 2/1/2012 (63) | Right |
| Nicaragua | D. Ortega (FSLN) 2007/01–2012/01 | 2/1/2008 (13) | Left | D. Ortega (FSLN) 2007/01–2012/01 | 2/1/2010 (37) | Left | D. Ortega (FSLN) 2012/01– | 2/1/2012 (1) | Left |
| Panama | M. Torrijos (PRD) 2004/09–2009/07 | 2/1/2008 (41) | Right | R. Martinelli (CD) 2009/07–2014/07 | 2/1/2010 (7) | Right | R. Martinelli (CD) 2009/07–2014/07 | 3/1/2012 (32) | Right |
| Paraguay | N. Duarte (ANR-PC) 2003/08–2008/08 | 2/1/2008 (54) | Right | F. Lugo (APC) 2008/08–2012/06 | 2/1/2010 (18) | Left | F. Lugo (APC) 2008/08–2012/06 | 2/1/2012 (42) | Left |
| Peru | A. García (APRA) 2006/07–2011/07 | 2/1/2008 (19) | Right | A. García (APRA) 2006/07–2011/07 | 2/1/2010 (43) | Right | O. Humala (PNP) 2011/07– | 2/1/2012 (7) | Left |
| Uruguay | T. Vázquez (FA) 2005/03–2010/03 | 5/1/2008 (38) | Left | J. Mujica (FA) 2010/03–2015/03 | 4/1/2010 (1) | Left | J. Mujica (FA) 2010/03–2015/03 | 3/1/2012 (24) | Left |
| Venezuela | H. Chávez (PSUV) 2007/01–2013/01 | 2/1/2008 (13) | Left | H. Chávez (PSUV) 2007/01–2013/01 | 2/1/2010 (37) | Left | H. Chávez (PSUV) 2007/01–2013/01 | 3/1/2012 (62) | Left |

tioned above, this variable works as a control variable and accounts for the differing times the country elections were conducted in relation to the survey. Specifically, it captures the dynamic proper to the time in office for the incumbent candidate. The country dichotomous variables, for their part, are included in the estimation to account for all the country-specific characteristics that our model does not measure already.[11] Next, we employ a "block-recursive" specification strategy in which we successively add to the baseline model the variables pertaining to the four blocks of determinants, in the following order: demographics, socioeconomics, anchor variables, and issues.[12] This strategy evaluates the contribution of each of the four blocks as we approach the tip of the funnel of causality, that is, vote choice.[13] Finally, note that the sample sizes of the 18 countries considered in our analyses are very similar (with a few exceptions) and thus no region-wide weight was applied.[14]

## Overview of the Main Findings

We offer here a summary of this book's main findings, to guide the reader through the thicket of data that must be absorbed. Recall that our vote choice model operates as a funnel of causality where we examine first the role of long-term forces like demographic and socioeconomic characteristics. These determinants are explored in chapters 2 and 3, respectively. In chapter 4, we get closer to the tip of the funnel (i.e., vote choice) and evaluate the effects of ideology and partisanship. Finally, in chapter 5, we take a look at issues (economic and noneconomic ones) as short-term determinants of the vote. In the following paragraphs, we summarize the important findings uncovered in these four chapters. This section concludes with a discussion about the country differences examined in chapter 6.

Chapter 2 looks at age, gender, religion (Catholic affiliation and church attendance), community type (urban or rural/small town) and race (measured by degrees of whiteness), as demographic determinants of vote choice. The results indicate that all six determinants, except community type, have some influence on vote choice. Admittedly, the effects of these factors on the probability of voting for an incumbent candidate are small, as one would expect given how remote they are from vote choice; but these findings are consistent with the extant literature. More particularly, we find that older and whiter voters, women, Catholics, and churchgoers are more likely to vote for a right-wing incumbent candidate. The result for women might seem surprising at first; however, it is not. Women in Latin America mimic the behavior of women in the developed world before they received more educational and work emancipation. The strongest demographic result is that for race. White voters are much more likely to vote for a right-wing incumbent candidate than mestizos, mulattos, blacks, and indigenous voters. Mestizos and mulattos, for their part, are also more likely to vote for a right-wing incumbent candidate than are blacks and indigenous. To be sure, degrees of whiteness constitute an important determinant of vote choice in Latin America. As a group, however, the demographic characteristics of voters do not explain much of the vote choice overall, as testified to by the very small improvement in the model's fit.

Chapter 3 examines the socioeconomic determinants of the vote. It explores how class structure (measured by unemployment status, public sector employment, and education) and material comfort (measured by income and property) affect vote choice in Latin America. The overall contribution of these determinants on the vote choice model is modest. But four of the five socioeconomic variables appear to drive vote choice to some extent: unemployment status, public sector employment, household income, and property. The results presented in chapter 3 suggest that the patterns of class voting in contemporary Latin America are related in good part to the emergence of a strong and viable political left, one that has been able to politicize class issues and mobilize significant support from the most disadvantaged groups of society—in particular, the unemployed and the poor. The chapter also examines how clientelism impacts voters. What we find is a limited role for clientelism on voters' decision.

Chapter 4 discusses the effect of two anchor variables on electoral behavior in Latin America: party identification and ideology. About one-third of voters in Latin America readily identify with a political party, and more than 80% among them are able to position themselves on a scale going from the extreme right to the extreme left. The results show the very clear dominance of anchor variables, over the preceding two blocks of variables, in explaining electoral behavior in Latin America. The results also show that the effect of party ID on vote choice is stronger and systematic, when compared to ideology. Two patterns emerge among Latin American countries. In about half the countries, party ID has a large impact on vote choice, but ideology still holds significant sway over voters. In the other half, party ID completely dominates and the effect of ideology is comparatively weak. That said, while partisanship does play a key role in explaining voting in Latin America, the impact of this variable remains lower in this region than in most established democracies. As for ideology, the conclusion is even clearer. This explains why the Michigan Model does not perform quite as well in Latin America, compared to the more established democracies.

Chapter 5 examines the role of issues as short-term determinants of vote choice. Four valence issues and two positional issues are examined, and they are divided along economic and noneconomic lines. The valence issues are the national economy, crime, corruption, and democracy. The positional issues are state intervention in the economy and authoritarianism (as measured by support for curbing the freedom of expression of the opposition). The valence findings show a strong effect. The positional findings are much weaker, but suggest interesting interaction effects, related to economic hardship and left-wing populism. In the end, chapter 5 concludes that issues matter, a lot, in Latin America. The increase in the model's fit provided by the inclusion of issues is substantial and supports this conclusion quite strongly.

Finally, chapter 6 presents and discusses the results for vote models across 18 countries in comparative perspective. Four main conclusions are drawn. First, the explanatory power of the Michigan Model for Latin American countries is similar to what has been observed in emerging democracies, but lower than what has been observed in the more established democracies. Second, the dispersion in the performance levels of the model, across Latin American countries, largely resembles what has been seen when other groups of countries are simultaneously studied. Third, the gap between the overall performance of the Michigan Model in Latin America and the more established democracies is due to the weaker effect of social-psychological variables, such as party identification and ideology. Fourth, the results also highlight some interesting variations in voting behavior among the Latin American countries, which we further develop in our later discussion in the final chapters.

## CHAPTER 2

# Demographics and the Vote

The very first individual-level studies of voting behavior (e.g., Lazarsfeld, Berelson, and Gaudet 1948; Berelson, Lazarsfeld, and McPhee 1954) gave particular attention to demographic characteristics, like age, gender, and religiosity, as determinants of vote choice. Early contributions on voting behavior in Latin America also gave demographic determinants an important place (e.g., Soares 1961). Following these original studies, demographics have been relegated to a second-tier role in subsequent studies of vote choice, although we know party systems (in some parts of the world more than others) have developed around important social cleavages (Lipset and Rokkan 1967). In recent decades, some of these determinants, most notably race, religion, and gender, have received renewed attention (e.g., Ansolabehere, Persily, and Stewart 2010; Broughton and Napel 2000; Studlar, McAllister, and Hayes 1998), including in Latin America (e.g., Bohn 2007; Madrid 2005a; Morgan and Buice 2013).

Voting behavior research in the United States, for example, noticed the emergence of a gender gap in the early 1980s as a product of important changes in sex roles (Abzug 1984). Women, as compared to men, tended to be more supportive of presidential Democratic candidates and expressed more liberal policy preferences (Baxter and Lansing 1983). A similar phenomenon also appeared to be occurring in other established democracies like the United Kingdom and Australia (Studlar, McAllister, and Hayes 1998). The systematic preference for the Democratic Party and its candidates among African American voters since the Voting Rights Act in 1965 is also noteworthy (Handley and Grofman 1994). The role of race in shaping American elections is today undeniable (Ansolabehere, Persily, and Stewart 2010). Finally, despite the growing secularization of the developed world, religion still plays an important role (directly and indirectly) in voting (Broughton and Napel 2000). Certainly, demographic characteristics exert strong and persistent effects on vote choice, at least in the advanced industrial world. Should we expect demographics to also influence the vote choices of Latin Americans?

There are good reasons to believe that gender, race, and religiosity, for example, also influence the voting behavior of many Latin Americans. As compared to the developed world, Latin Americans are deeply religious[1] (in most countries in the region 90% of the people have declared to be Catholics or Protestants), are profoundly divided ethnically[2] (most countries in the region have large Afro-descendant, e.g., Brazil, or indigenous populations, e.g., Peru, or both). As compared to the developed world, Latin American countries exhibit relatively young populations, but aging nevertheless.[3] Although women in Latin America have not as profoundly integrated the workplace, nor gained as much access to higher education, as women have in the developed world,[4] their overall conditions have improved and today they occupy considerably more space in politics. Moreover, the recent (re)democratization of many of the Latin American countries have opened opportunities for new parties to emerge, some taking advantage of the social and racial structure defining the region (Madrid 2005a). What are we expecting for demographic effects on the vote choices of Latin Americans? This is the question we propose to address in this chapter.

## The Demographic Determinants of the Vote

Let us begin our examination of age, gender, religiosity, race, and the rural-urban divide as demographic determinants of the vote. As discussed in the previous chapter, these factors come early in the "funnel of causality" and are treated as long-term forces of the vote. In what follows, we present each demographic characteristic, discuss what effect we expect it to exert, and indicate how it is operationalized.

### Age

Age is the omnipresent independent variable of any vote choice model, although it is frequently included as a mere control. But some studies have given it more attention. There are two ways in which age can influence political behavior (Braungart and Braungart 1986). First, age tells us about life-cycle development (young, middle-aged, and old). Different phases of life set the stage for different life experiences that can influence the way we see and think about politics. Second, age also tells us about generations or cohorts, that is, about particular age groups in history. For example, military coups and first democratic elections are important events that can have effects of their own on people's political thinking. Important events of that nature, however, are not likely to affect everyone equally. They can leave more impressionable and long-standing effects on some age groups. When examining age, it becomes nearly impossible to disentangle the effects of life-course and cohort on political behavior. Generational effects, certainly, would be hard to identify in a comparative context, given that countries experience different events in different times. Therefore, the emphasis here is given to the life-course effects of age on the vote.

The life-course approach to the study of political behavior relates to biopsychological processes—like changes in physiology, needs, cognitive capacities, and interests—that people go through as they grow older. These changes are believed to be sequential and nearly universal. The bulk of the research about age and political behavior has focused on youth (ages 15–24). At that age, young adults come to possess the necessary cognitive abilities to make sense of the political world. Moreover, they strive for independence and seek to form an identity (Adelson 1980). As a result, the young are believed to develop political attitudes more orthogonal to those held by older people. Empirical evidence generally supports this theory. Specifically, young American adults, as compared to older people, are more critical of politics and society and tend to identify in larger proportions with the center and center-left (e.g., Yankelovich 1974). Interestingly, age has not received much attention as a determinant of vote choice in Latin America. In the most recent account of voting behavior in the region, age appears as a mere control variable, with no specific hypothesis about how it should affect vote choice (Carlin, Singer, and Zechmeister 2015).

The above discussion suggests that younger people should have a stronger preference for center and center-left parties and candidates, as compared to older people. We expect Latin American voters to be no different. To account for the effect of age, we include a continuous variable that indicates the respondents' age. The age variable is rescaled from 0 to 1. We expect the variable's coefficient to show a positive sign, as older people should be more likely to support right-wing incumbent candidates.[5]

## Gender

Differences in political behavior between men and women received increased attention in the early 1980s in the United States. Wirls (1986) identifies four gender gaps: (1) the participation gap; (2) the policy opinion gap; (3) the electoral gap; and (4) the partisan gap. In the 1980s, women closed the gap in voting participation (Poole and Zeigler 1985) and now actually vote in greater numbers (Center for American Women in Politics 2011). The Center for American Women and Politics (CAWP) has tallied data documenting differences between men and women. Their results show that women tend to be more supportive of liberal policies than men, vote in larger proportion than men for Democratic presidential candidates, and identify more strongly with the Democratic Party than men (CAWP 2012a, 2012b, 2013). These findings are not confined to the United States. Indeed, Studlar, McAllister, and Hayes (1998) show similar patterns for Australia and Britain. This is what is referred to as the "modern gender gap" as opposed to the "traditional gender gap," when women participated less in elections and were generally more supportive of candidates and parties defending conservative policies (Morgan 2015).

Several theories have been advanced to explain this important change in gender differences. Among them, the developmental theory of the gender gap has received substantial attention (Inglehart and Norris 2000). In short, the theory stipulates that the important change in sex roles in postindustrial societies has had an important effect on women's values. Women in these societies have entered the workforce in large numbers and attained levels of education undreamed of before. These changes have opened new opportunities beyond the traditional roles of women as housekeeper and nearly sole child caretaker. Women's more liberal preferences would be the product, in part, of their work experience. Specifically, women frequently occupy low-paid jobs providing public sector services in education, healthcare, and welfare. These experiences would make them more sympathetic to liberal policies and candidates/parties.

Iversen and Rosenbluth (2006) offer a different explanation. According to these authors, it is the prospect of divorce that produces the gender gap in political preferences. When divorce is not an option, the family works as a unit and the preferences of men and women should be more similar. In such circumstances, it is the traditional division of family labor that would prevail with the women working in the home. But, when divorce is an option, members of the family have to be treated as individuals with potentially distinct preferences. The threat of divorce forces members of the family to explore opportunities outside the family to guarantee one's long-term welfare. This threat, coupled with women's fewer and lower prospects for advancement, and their larger share of unpaid work in the household, explain women's general preference for more liberal policies, e.g., those related to child and elderly care, unemployment benefits, and public employment.

The above discussion about gender carries important implications for understanding the voting behavior of women in Latin America. First, Latin America's political and economic development has not reached the same levels as in postindustrial societies. Women have entered the workplace but not in as large numbers as in the developed world.[6] Consequently, women in Latin America are also more involved with housekeeping and child-rearing duties. Divorce is also much less frequent in Latin America than in the developed world.[7] To be sure, the status of women in the region today is starkly different from that of women in the developed world. But women in Latin America have gained greater access to political positions traditionally occupied by men. Recent examples are Dilma Rousseff in Brazil (2008–), Michelle Bachelet in Chile (2006–2010, 2014–) and Cristina Fernández de Kirchner in Argentina (2007–2015), all three occupying the presidency in their respective countries. This illustrates well the increasing role of women in politics.

But the balance of the evidence suggests that women in Latin America should not be more liberal than men, as found in postindustrial societies. Indeed, recent studies in the area suggest that the "traditional gender gap" remains in the developed world (Arana and Santa Cruz 2005; Inglehart and Norris 2003). The latest account by Morgan (2015) finds that women in Latin America have closed part of the gap, but that they remain more ideologically conservative than men and tend to also be more supportive of candidates and parties of the right. Thus, according to that author, the "traditional gender gap" persists in the region.

To account for the effect of gender on vote choice, we include in our equation a dummy variable coded 1 for women and 0 for men. We expect the effect of this dummy variable to be positive, indicating support for a right-wing incumbent.

## Religion

Latin America has historically been heavily, if not exclusively, Catholic. In recent decades, however, the Catholic Church has lost its nearly monopolist position, with the significant growth of Protestants (mainline, Evangelicals, and Pentecostals) and individuals with no religious affiliation (Chesnut 2009; Garrard-Burnett 2009). Still, today, most of Latin America's population is Catholic. Religion has always played an important role in shaping elections and politics, both in established democracies and in other parts of the world, including Latin America. Although the developed world and Latin America have become more secularized over recent decades, the role of religion in politics remains undeniable (Broughton and Napel 2000; Chesnut 2003).

In many European countries, the link between religion and voting is direct, deriving from the establishment of parties based on religious principles (e.g., the many Christian Democratic parties). Deeply Christian voters in Europe tend to overwhelmingly support such parties. In other places, however, the relationship between religion and voting is rather indirect, as in Canada (Blais et al. 2002) and the United States (Lewis-Beck et al. 2008), where some parties tend to attract more religious voters than others, although the parties were not originally founded on religious principles. Such parties attract voters instead by adopting positions on issues like abortion and same-sex marriage, positions that are in line with mainstream religious beliefs.

Most parties in Latin America were not originally founded on religious principles. The one notable exception is Venezuela's COPEI, a party founded in 1946 to promote Catholic social principles and to offer an alternative to leftist parties; but they went from a dominant party in Venezuelan politics (1948 to 1998) to a marginalized one today (Crisp, Levine, and Molina 2003). That is not to say that religion does not exert any effect on voters' decisions in Latin America. Rather, its effects there are indirect. Religiosity in the region generally affects voters by emphasizing the importance of some social issues frequently debated in the public sphere and, more particularly, in religious communities. An interesting example is the 2010 Brazilian presidential election, where candidate Marina Silva from the Green Party drew important votes from Evangelical voters, hurting mostly Dilma Rousseff from the Workers' Party, who has been portrayed as wishy-washy over the issue of abortion. Obviously, it is not Silva's Green Party affiliation that mattered to voters, but her clear opposition to abortion, from being Evangelical.

The most recent and complete account of religiosity on vote choice in the region is the work by Boas and Smith (2015). According to the authors, there are two important religious cleavages in Latin America. First, religious voters and those that attend religious services more frequently, as compared to those with no religious affiliation, tend to be more supportive of candidates and parties on the right. This first cleavage, however, is concentrated in countries where party systems are polarized and programmatic. Second, Protestant voters are influenced by the religious identity of candidates, independently of their ideological orientation. Specifically, they have a stronger preference for Protestant, or at least non-Catholic, candidates. No such behavior is observed among members of other religious groups.

Building on the above discussion, we believe too that voters with a religious membership should prefer parties and candidates of the right, because they tend to hold more conservative positions toward social issues like abortion, euthanasia, and same-sex marriage. We recognize the growth of Protestantism and secularism in Latin America, but Catholicism is still the dominant religion in the region. Moreover, the Catholic Church has more or less constantly held conservative positions on social issues, positions that most Latin Americans embrace (Seligson and Morales 2010; Valenzuela, Scully, and Somma 2007; Patterson 2004). Thus, we account for the role of religion by creating a dichotomous variable, indicating whether respondents are Catholic (1) or not (0). We expect the variable to show a positive coefficient, as Catholic voters should be more likely to support right-wing incumbent candidates.[8] Moreover, as in Boas and Smith (2015), we believe that the frequency of attendance at religious services, independently of religious affiliation, should also affect vote choice. Specifically, we believe that voters that attend religious services with greater frequency should also have a stronger preference for right-wing incumbent candidates. Consequently, we include a 5-point-scale church attendance variable that runs from never or almost never attend religious services (0) to attending such services more than once per week (5). The scores of this church attendance variable are then rescaled from (0) to (1).

## Race

The racial composition of Latin America is unique in many regards. Some countries in the region have very large indigenous populations (e.g., Bolivia), others large contingents of Afro-descendants (e.g., Brazil), and still others are intensely mixed (e.g., Colombia) or very much white (e.g., Uruguay). Being nonwhite in Latin America carries important implications. Specifically, nonwhites in Latin America are generally poor, less educated, have a short life expectancy, and generally are less represented politically (De Ferranti et al. 2004; Hall and Patrinos 2006). Interestingly, very few parties in the region have sought actively to represent nonwhite interests, like the Democratic Party has done in the United States for African Americans. Indeed, the emergence of significant ethnic parties like the Movimiento al Socialismo (MAS) in Bolivia is a very recent development (Madrid 2005a; Van Cott 2005; Yashar 2005). Up to the end of the 1990s, there existed no significant ethnic party in Latin America (Madrid 2005b).[9] Since then, ethnic parties have grown significantly in some countries, including most notably in Bolivia, Ecuador, Guatemala, and Nicaragua. These new parties seek to represent the interests of indigenous populations that have long been ignored by major parties. No similar party movement, however, has been observed to cater to the votes of Afro-descendants.

Given the lower socioeconomic status of nonwhites, ethnic-based parties in Latin America, like the MAS or the Pachakutik Plurinational Unity Movement in Ecuador, generally tend to advocate leftist reforms and greater redistribution for nonwhite voters, including most notably indigenous voters (Madrid 2012). Other parties in the region like the Workers' Party in Brazil have not deliberately sought the votes of nonwhites, but many of the recent social policies they have pushed forward, like the Bolsa Família and racial quotas for university admissions and public service, have greatly benefited nonwhites indirectly or directly. In a recent account examining 18 Latin American countries, Morales (2015) finds that both whites and indigenous vote very slightly to the right of mestizos, but that mulattos themselves also vote slightly to the left of mestizos. His findings about indigenous voting can hardly be explained, as they defy common wisdom and, more important, previous empirical findings like those from Madrid (2012). Moreover, his separate classification of mestizos and mulattos is difficult to justify on theoretical grounds.

We hold race to be a potentially consequential determinant of the vote. However, racial classification in Latin America is not straightforward, because whites, Afro-descendants, and indigenous have engaged extensively in interracial mixing. We follow here the recommendation of Telles (2004), by first differentiating whites from nonwhites. According to that author, this is the racial distinction that matters because whites, as compared to nonwhites, are privileged. Nonwhites, for their part, have suffered extensively from discrimination and exclusion. But, nonwhites are not all treated equally. Mulattos, mestizos, or mixed-race people alike, although also discriminated against, are generally better treated than blacks and indigenous people. To capture these subtleties, we created a three-category variable that identifies whites (coded 1), mestizos/mulattos (coded .5), and blacks/indigenous (coded 0).[10] (Note that Asians, which represent only a very small fraction of the Latin American population, were coded as whites. Asians, contrary to blacks, indigenous, mulattos, and mestizos, have not suffered extensively from discrimination and exclusion. Moreover, their social status is much more similar to that of whites than it is to nonwhites.)

Based on the above discussion, we expect white voters to be the most supportive of right-wing incumbent candidates because these candidates and their parties are generally more favorable to them. On the other hand, we expect blacks and indigenous to be the least supportive of right-wing incumbent candidates, and mulattos and mestizos also less supportive, but to a lesser degree.[11]

### Rural-Urban

As a last demographic characteristic, we consider the distinction between rural and urban voters. There is some evidence in the literature suggesting that rural voters are generally more conservative than urban voters, at least in the developed world (e.g., Johnston et al. 2001). Some of these differences can be associated with other socioeconomic characteristics like income and education, all of which tend to be lower in rural areas, and the greater propensity of urban areas to be secularized. To our knowledge, the rural-urban divide on politics has not been looked at very closely in Latin America. We have no particular reason to expect rural voters in Latin America to be any different than those found in the developed world. Thus we expect rural voters to also be more favorable to conservative candidates and their parties. To account for possible differences in voting behavior between rural and urban voters, we include a dichotomous variable labeled Region in our model of demographic determinants, where rural or small-town voters (= 1) and urban (medium and large cities or metropolitan areas) voters (= 0).

Table 2.1 below presents some descriptive statistics about each of these demographic variables for all 18 countries and for all three waves of the Latin American Public Opinion Project, or LAPOP (2008, 2010, and 2012), considering only those respondents who indicated a vote preference. Specifically, table 2.1 shows the minimum and maximum values of each variable, together with its mean and standard deviation. Table 2.1 also indicates which country exhibits the highest and lowest mean values. Table 2.1 reveals that the average age of the Latin American voter is about 40, that half of them are women (50%), that 69% declare themselves as Catholics, that most attend religious services with a certain frequency, and that a little less than half (44%) live in rural areas or small towns. There are voters as young as 16 and others as old as 101. Chile has the oldest population and Nicaragua the youngest; Chile's population also has the largest share of women and Paraguay the smallest; Paraguay shows the largest proportion of Catholics and Uruguay the smallest; Salvadorans attend the most religious services and Uruguayans the least; and Honduras has the largest proportion of its population living in rural areas or small towns and Uruguay the smallest.

The bottom part of table 2.1 presents the region's racial distribution. We find that 32% of the population declares itself as white, 57% as mestizo or mulatto, and 11% as either black or indigenous. The population with the most whites is Uruguay and the one with the least is Guatemala. The population with the most mestizos or mulattos is Ecuador and with the least is Venezuela. Finally, Guatemala's population has the largest share of blacks or indigenous and Argentina has the least. Together, the descriptive statistics presented in table 2.1 exhibit rather clearly the heterogeneity of the Latin American population.

TABLE 2.1. Descriptive Statistics of the Demographic Determinants

| Variable | Min. | Max. | Mean | St. dev. | $N$ | Country with lowest mean | Country with highest mean |
|---|---|---|---|---|---|---|---|
| Age | 16 | 101 | 39.8 | 15.8 | 52,341 | Nicaragua | Chile |
| Women | 0 | 1 | .50 | .50 | 52,489 | Paraguay | Chile |
| Catholics | 0 | 1 | .69 | .46 | 52,489 | Uruguay | Paraguay |
| Church attendance | 0 | 1 | .53 | .34 | 51,537 | Uruguay | El Salvador |
| Region | 0 | 1 | .44 | .50 | 52,489 | Uruguay | Honduras |
| *Race:* | | | | | | | |
| Whites/Asians | 0 | 1 | .32 | .46 | 50,094 | Guatemala | Uruguay |
| Mestizos/Mulattos | 0 | 1 | .57 | .49 | 50,094 | Venezuela | Ecuador |
| Blacks/Indigenous | 0 | 1 | .11 | .31 | 50,094 | Argentina | Guatemala |

## Demographic Determinants of the Vote: Bivariate Relationships

As a starting point, we look first at the bivariate relationship between vote choice and each of the six demographic variables presented above: age, gender, religion, church attendance, race, and region (rural/urban divide). Table 2.2 presents these measures of association. The measure used, tau-b, takes a value close to 0 when the relationship between two variables is weak and approaches 1 when the relationship is strong. The sign of the measure tells us about the direction of the relationship.[12] The results presented in table 2.2 show weak relationships between vote choice and demographic characteristics. That is, all six demographic characteristics (except age) show a very small association with vote choice. We find, as expected, that older voters are more inclined to vote for right-wing incumbent candidates (tau-b = .05). Women, Catholics, churchgoers, and whiter voters, for their part, are only very slightly more likely to vote for right-wing incumbent candidates, at .02, .01, .03, and .03, respectively. Contrary to expectations, rural area and small town voters are very slightly less inclined to vote for right-wing incumbent candidates (tau-b = −.01). All these associations reach a conventional level of statistical significance ($p < .01$). Thus, while some relationships may be there, these are generally very limited in strength, at least at the bivariate level. To confirm (or disconfirm), we need to present a multivariate analysis of vote choice, including all six demographic characteristics.

## Demographic Determinants of the Vote: Multivariate Analysis

Conceptually, our multivariate model, for the first block of our recursive system of equations, can be expressed as follows:

TABLE 2.2. Demographic Variables and Vote Intention in 18 Latin American Countries: Bivariate Relationships (2008, 2010, 2012)

| Independent variables | Tau-b |
|---|---|
| Age | .05** |
| Gender (women = 1, men = 0) | .02** |
| Religion (Catholics = 1, others = 0) | .01** |
| Church attendance (1 = More than once per week; 0 = Never or almost never) | .03** |
| Race (Whites/Asians = 1; Mestizos/Mulattos = .5; Blacks/Indigenous = 0) | .03** |
| Region (rural/small town = 1, others = 0) | −.01** |

Number of observations: 51,394
**Relationship is statistically significant at $p \le .01$.

Vote = $f$(demographics)                                                    (2.1)

In terms of the specific variables, it reads

Vote = $f$(age, gender, religion, church attendance, race, region)   (2.2)

Recall that in chapter 1 we mentioned that our baseline model includes a Months variable to account for the length of time in office. This variable measures the number of months respondents stand from the beginning of the incumbent's mandate. This control variable effectively holds constant the time the vote intention is expressed. Importantly, it allows the other coefficients to be interpreted "as if" they were measured at the same election time. Our baseline model also includes 17 dichotomous variables, one for all countries considered in our analysis but Mexico, our reference country. This constitutes our baseline model.[13] As a first step, we simply regress vote intention on Months and the country dichotomous variables. The results for this baseline model are presented in the first column of table 2.3, under Model 1. Although the country dummies were included in all our analyses, we do not present the estimated coefficients and standard errors, in order to save space. As expected, Months has a negative effect on vote choice, i.e., the farther the respondent stands from the beginning of the incumbent's mandate, the less likely he or she is to be supportive of the incumbent candidate. But let's now move on to the other determinants of greater interest, the demographic characteristics of the voters noted in Equation 2.2.

The second column of table 2.3, under Model 2, shows the unstandardized logistic regression coefficients from this multivariate analysis of vote choice, with standard errors in parentheses. In addition to the six demographic characteristics discussed above, it includes the Months variable and the country dummies. The results are presented for all 18 countries pooled together and for all three waves of LAPOP (2008, 2010, and 2012). They are interesting in many regards. First, note that the model fit is not very high, with a Nagelkerke pseudo-$R^2$ equal to .10. The inclusion of the demographic characteristics does not improve the model's fit from the baseline model, also at .10. The percentage of cases correctly predicted, however, is slightly improved, at 63.0%, a small increase from the baseline model at 61.5%. More important for present purposes, we find that five of the six demographic determinants exert a statistically significant effect on the vote and in expected ways. The only independent variable here that does not statistically affect vote choice is the rural/small town dummy, labeled Region.

We examine next the effect of each of the independent variables on vote choice. Because the logistic coefficient estimates are less interpretable, we calculate the change in probability of voting for an incumbent candidate, when the independent variable of interest is changed from its lowest to its highest value (holding the other independent variables at their mean). Table 2.4 shows these changes in the probability of voting for a right-wing incumbent candidate for each of the six demographic variables.

Starting with age, we find that, as expected, the variable has a positive and statistically significant effect on the probability of voting for a right-wing incumbent candidate. Older voters in Latin America are, on average, more supportive of right-wing candidates. Specifically, the entry in table 2.4 indicates that the typical oldest voter (aged 101), as compared to the typical youngest voter (aged 16), is 3 percentage points more likely to vote

TABLE 2.3. Logistic Regression Models for Voting Intentions in 18 Latin American Countries by Demographic Characteristics (2008, 2010, 2012)

|  | (1) | (2) |
|---|---|---|
| Months | −1.03** | −1.11** |
|  | (.04) | (.04) |
| Age | — | .13** |
|  |  | (.04) |
| Gender (women = 1, men = 0) | — | .06** |
|  |  | (.02) |
| Religion (Catholics = 1, others = 0) | — | .17** |
|  |  | (.02) |
| Church attendance (1 = More than once per week; | — | .22** |
| 0 = Never or almost never) |  | (.03) |
| Race (Whites/Asians = 1; Mestizos/Mulattos = .5; | — | .37** |
| Blacks/Indigenous = 0) |  | (.03) |
| Region (rural/small town = 1, others = 0) | — | .04 |
|  |  | (.02) |
| Constant | .28** | −.22* |
|  | (.05) | (.06) |
| Nagelkerke pseudo-$R^2$ | .10 | .10 |
| % correctly predicted | 61.5% | 63.0% |
| N | 52,489 | 51,394 |

**$p \le .01$; *$p \le .05$ (two-tailed tests). Entries are unstandardized logistic regression coefficients, with standard errors in parentheses. Country dummies are not shown (Mexico is the reference case). See appendix 4 for variable's specification.

for a right-wing incumbent candidate. The effect, although statistically significant, is not substantively very strong.

Gender exerts a very small effect on vote choice, but in the expected way. Women in Latin America are 1 percentage point more likely than men to vote for a right-wing incumbent candidate, holding all the other demographic characteristics constant. This result contrasts with that found in most of the developed world, where women generally hold more progressive views of politics and are more supportive of left-wing candidates and parties, as compared to men. As we discussed earlier in this chapter, women in Latin America are not as emancipated as women from the developed world. What we find is that women in Latin America exhibit a behavior more similar to that of women in the developed world, when in the past they were too more financially dependent on men, i.e., the "traditional gender gap." Certainly, women in Latin America still lag behind men in educational attainment and in the workforce. But the difference is very small, meaning that women are closing the gap. If Latin America follows a similar path to that of countries from the developed world, it is likely that we will observe a "modern gender gap" in that region too in the near future.

We argued earlier that Catholic voters should be more supportive of right-wing candidates. Table 2.4 indicates that Catholic voters, as compared to non-Catholics, are indeed more supportive of right-wing incumbent candidates. But, again, the effect of being Catholic is substantively

TABLE 2.4. Change in Probabilities for Voting Intentions in 18 Latin American Countries (2008, 2010, 2012)

|  | (1) | (2) |
|---|---|---|
| Months | –.24** | –.25** |
| Age | — | .03** |
| Gender (women = 1, men = 0) | — | .01** |
| Religion (Catholics = 1, others = 0) | — | .04** |
| Church attendance (1 = More than once per week; 0 = Never or almost never) | — | .05** |
| Race (Whites/Asians = 1; Mestizos/Mulattos = .5; Blacks/Indigenous = 0) | — | .08** |
| Region (rural/small town = 1, others = 0) | — | .01 |
| N | 52,489 | 51,394 |

**$p \leq .01$; *$p \leq .05$ (two-tailed tests). Entries represent change in probabilities. Country dummies are not shown. See appendix 4 for variable's specification.

small. More specifically, Catholic voters, as compared to non-Catholics, are 4 percentage points more likely to vote for a right-wing incumbent candidate, all else being equal. Although small, this finding is consistent with what is found in other parts of the world, where Catholic voters generally favor more conservative candidates and parties. Similarly, church attendance increases the probability of voting for a right-wing incumbent candidate. That is, voters who attend religious services more than once per week are 5 percentage points more likely to vote for a right-wing in-cumbent candidate, compared to those voters who never (or almost never) attend such services.

The strongest effect on vote choice among the demographic variables is that of race. White voters, as compared to nonwhites, are significantly more supportive of right-wing incumbent candidates. Whites, as com-pared to blacks and indigenous voters, are 8 percentage points more likely to vote for a right-wing incumbent candidate, and this change in prob-ability is statistically significant. Recall that we expected white voters to be more supportive of right-wing candidates and parties because these parties have generally better protected their interests. With the exception of re-cent ethnic-based parties in Latin America, very few parties and candidates have defended vigorously the rights and interests of indigenous, blacks, mestizos, and mulattos, and those that have done so have generally been from the left.

Finally, we find no difference between rural/small town and urban vot-ers. Our results thus suggest that there exists no rural/urban divide of the vote in Latin America, unlike other parts of the world, where the rural voters are usually more conservative.

Admittedly, the pooled analysis presented above hides potentially im-portant differences between the countries considered in our analysis. For example, the racial composition of Brazil is very distinct from that of Uru-guay. Similarly, some countries have large rural populations, while others are mostly urban. Women are also more emancipated in some countries, as compared to others. Some countries have ethnic parties, and some do not. Although the region exhibits a fair amount of homogeneity, there are noticeable differences between certain countries. These questions will be addressed more fully in chapter 6, but some differences are worth high-lighting here.

First, it is worth noting that demographic characteristics play a more important role in certain countries (see column 2 in the relevant country tables in appendix 2). For example, in Bolivia and Colombia five of the six demographic characteristics considered here exert a statistically significant change in probability on vote choice and some of these effects are large. In Paraguay, on the other hand, none of the six demographic variables have a statistically significant effect on vote choice.

An examination of the pseudo-$R^2$ is also indicative of how demographic variables matter in some countries and not in others. To calculate the contribution of the demographic variables, we compute the difference in the pseudo-$R^2$ between our demographics model (Model 2) and that with our baseline model (Model 1). The largest difference is found in Bolivia, where the addition of the demographic variables increases the pseudo-$R^2$ by .10. It is also large in Uruguay at .09. On the other hand, demographic variables do not explain much of the variation in vote choice in countries like Ecuador and Paraguay, where the difference in the pseudo-$R^2$ is nearly zero.

Bolivia stands as *the* country in the region where demographic determinants matter most. Indeed, all six determinants but gender reach a conventional level of significance, and the change in the pseudo-$R^2$ is the largest. That demographic determinants matter so much in Bolivia, as compared to the other countries in the region, could possibly be explained by the recent surge of the MAS and its charismatic leader Evo Morales. The party built its support from grassroots efforts, by reaching out first to peasant organizations and later to the urban middle classes. The party's platform and its adopted policies since it came to power in 2006 have promoted wealth redistribution, and have been particularly popular among poor and indigenous voters. To be sure, the MAS stands as a recent case of a political party in Latin America that was able to successfully exploit important social cleavages. Not surprisingly, demographic determinants of the vote matter more in Bolivia than in other countries in the region.

Another way to denote country differences is to compare the role of each of the demographic variables individually. The country comparison for age, for example, indicates that older voters are, as expected, more supportive of right-wing candidates in five countries (Colombia, Costa Rica, the Dominican Republic, Panama, and Uruguay), but surprisingly less supportive in three others (Argentina, Bolivia, and Nicaragua). In the other 10 countries, age has no effect on the vote. Some of the effects are noticeably large. In Costa Rica and Uruguay, for example, the oldest voters, as compared to the youngest ones, are 30 and 23 percentage points more likely to vote for an incumbent right-wing candidate in these electorates, respectively. On the other hand, the oldest voters in Argentina and Bolivia are 21 and 20 percentage points less likely to vote for an incumbent right-wing candidate, respectively, as compared to the youngest voters in these electorates. Certainly, the effect of age on the vote in Latin America is not uniform. But the results for Costa Rica and Uruguay are telling. Indeed, Costa Rica is the oldest democracy in the region (its constitution dates back to 1949). Uruguay, excepting a comparatively short dictatorship (1973–85), has a party system that is among the oldest and most stable in the region. The greater political stability found in these two countries may well explain the greater importance of the age variable, and in expected ways.

Gender exerts no effect on the vote in 11 of the countries considered. In five of them, women are more supportive than men of right-wing incumbent candidates (Colombia, Costa Rica, the Dominican Republic, El Salvador, and Mexico) and in two they are less supportive (Chile and Panama). Although there are some notable country differences, the effect of gender on vote choice is generally very small. The one exception is the Dominican Republic, where women are 12 percentage points more likely than men to vote for right-wing incumbent candidates. Overall, we can say that gender does not have much of an effect on vote choice in Latin America.

Being Catholic has no effect on vote choice in 8 of the 18 countries. But, when it has an effect, it is more consistent than what we have found for both age and gender. Indeed, Catholics are, as expected, more likely to vote for a right-wing incumbent candidate in all but one of the countries where it has a statistically significant effect. The effect of being Catholic is also quite large in some countries like in Uruguay, where Catholics are 15 percentage points more likely to vote for right-wing candidates. Only in Chile are Catholics less likely to support a right-wing incumbent. The effect for Uruguay is noteworthy, since Uruguay also has the largest percentage of its population with no religious affiliation. The strong effect in Uruguay illustrates the gap between Catholics (who prefer the right) and those with no religion affiliation (who prefer the left).

Church attendance exerts a statistically significant effect in one-third of the countries (Bolivia, Chile, Costa Rica, Mexico, Panama, and Uruguay). The effect in these countries is strong and all are in the expected direction. The strongest effect is found in both Uruguay and Bolivia, where frequent churchgoers are 15 percentage points more likely to vote for incumbent right-wing candidates, as compared to voters who never (or almost never) attend religious services.

We find that rural and small-town voters are more likely to vote for a right-wing incumbent candidate, as expected, in 5 of the 18 countries (Argentina, Bolivia, Brazil, Ecuador, and Guatemala). The effect on the vote is generally small, but substantively significant in Bolivia (15 percentage points) and Argentina (11 percentage points). In four of the other countries, rural and small-town voters are less likely to vote for right-wing candidates (Colombia, Costa Rica, El Salvador, and Uruguay). The effect is particularly strong in Colombia (–15 percentage points). Note, however, that this variable does not show any effect when all 18 countries are considered together. Interestingly, it is not because it does not matter. In fact, it matters in half of the countries under analysis; it is just that the effects are in one direction in five of them, and in the other direction in the other four, so tending to cancel out in the aggregate.

Finally, race, just like being Catholic, also plays a more consistent role for vote choice in Latin America. Whites are more likely to vote for an incumbent right-wing candidate, as expected, in 8 of the 18 countries (Argentina, Bolivia, Brazil, Colombia, the Dominican Republic, Guatemala, Peru, and Venezuela). It has no effect in the other 10 countries. In some countries, the effect of being white is substantial. In Bolivia, for example, whites are 33 percentage points more likely to vote for a right-wing incumbent candidate. As mentioned earlier, important parties like the MAS have developed around ethnic divisions and in defense of indigenous voters' interests. Finally, whites are also much more likely to vote for right-wing incumbent candidates in Brazil and Guatemala, by some 19 and 20 percentage points, respectively. In Brazil, the Workers' Party has seen an impressive growth in the poorer and more nonwhite-populated states of the Northeast. The South and Southeast, where most of the whites live, has tended to be more favorable to the center-right Brazilian Social Democratic Party in recent elections.


## Conclusion

In this chapter, we have examined the role of demographic characteristics on the vote. Overall, we find that most demographic variables exert effects on vote choice that are in line with expectations: that is, older and whiter voters, and Catholics and churchgoers, are all more likely to vote for right-wing incumbent candidates. Women, in general, are also slightly more likely to be supportive of right-wing incumbent candidates. This finding is not surprising, given that women in Latin America, as compared to women in the developed world, still show lower levels of educational attainment and a much more limited participation in the workforce. Women's voting behavior resembles that of women in the developed world in former times, when they were more financially dependent on men. The rural/urban divide does not show an effect on vote choice in the aggregate. But, the country-level analysis reveals that the variable does play a role in some countries.

We have also identified some important country differences. Indeed, for some determinants the effect on vote choice is more uniform (e.g., frequent churchgoers and being Catholic, white, or women), but for others much less (e.g., age, and particularly living in a rural area or a small town). Overall, we cannot say that demographic characteristics are strong determinants of vote choice in Latin America, as the generally low model fits reveal. But demographic characteristics still exert some effect on vote choice. In the aggregate, five of the six characteristics considered showed a statistically significant effect. True, their effect on the probability of voting for a right-wing incumbent candidate is small, but it is not null. Among them, we can stress the role of race. Whites, for example, are systematically more likely to support right-wing incumbent candidates. This finding is important given the significance of race in Latin America.

CHAPTER 3

# Socioeconomics and the Vote

Several studies carried out in well-established democracies have shown that variables indicating socioeconomic status have less of an impact on vote choice nowadays (see notably Blais et al. 2002 for Canada; Lewis-Beck et al. 2008 for the United States; Clarke et al. 2009 for Great Britain; Nadeau et al. 2012 for France; and Franklin, Mackie, and Valen 1992 for Europe in general). However, we must consider whether a similar conclusion is applicable to contemporary Latin American countries. Some could argue that the situation in emerging democracies and transitional economies today shares traits with the situation in developed Western countries from a few decades ago, when socioeconomic status still played a significant role in structuring voter behavior (see notably Butler and Stokes 1969). Another factor to consider is the recent rise of the political left in the Latin American region. The electoral success of these new leftist forces may be attributable, at least in part, to their ability to heighten the salience of class issues in these countries and hence to mobilize class voting (Mainwaring, Torcal, and Sommá 2015).

In this chapter we explore the relationship between socioeconomic status and presidential voting intention in Latin America by looking at two of its dimensions. The first dimension of socioeconomics that we focus upon is class, which we operationalize in this book by using indicators of educational attainment, employment status, and employment sector. The second dimension of socioeconomic status that we examine relates to an individual's material condition. We look at both a traditional indicator of wealth (level of income) and a nontraditional one (ownership of material goods). As will be seen, taking these two indicators into consideration provides for a much more complete picture of the actual relationship between material conditions and voting behavior in the Latin American context.

Any examination of the relationship between socioeconomic conditions and presidential support in the Latin American region raises the question of whether this relationship is truly exogenous or simply the result of clientelistic practices. We know that clientelism is present in Latin America, and that some Latin American politicians attempt to secure voter support in exchange for material benefits. In doing so, they tend to target some specific socioeconomic segments of society, in particular the less well-off. The electoral support that these socioeconomic groups give them may thus be a mere reflection of clientelism. We will consider the issue of clientelism in some detail at the end of this chapter, trying to assess the extent to which this phenomenon may affect the conclusions drawn from our analysis.

## Class Voting in Latin America

Earlier studies examining the extent of class voting in Latin America have reported only weak effects (Dix 1989; Dominguez and McCann 1995; Roberts 2002; Torcal and Mainwaring 2003). More recent investigations of class voting in the Latin American region have tended to show that it has become stronger over the past two decades (Mainwaring, Torcal, and Sommá 2015). This phenomenon has been especially apparent in the countries that experienced the rise of viable leftist presidential candidates and parties, such as in Venezuela (Heath 2009; Handlin 2013), Brazil (Hunter and Power 2007; Zucco 2008; Singer 2009), and Argentina (Lupu and Stokes 2009; Cataife 2011). What is more, class voting in Latin America since the mid-1990s has been found to be strongest among highly disadvantaged groups, such as the poor and the unskilled workers (Mainwaring, Torcal, and Sommá 2015), and not necessarily among the organized working class, as the historical experience of Western democratic societies may lead one to expect (e.g., Lipset 1960; Butler and Stokes 1969).

The main reason for the surge in class voting, and for its particular nature in the Latin American region, appears to lie with the context of the rising political left during the past two decades or so (Mainwaring, Torcal, and Sommá 2015). When in power, leftist Latin American presidents and governments have implemented a number of progressive public policies aimed at improving the social and economic conditions of the disadvantaged. In addition, and perhaps more important, their campaign rhetoric has tended to emphasize, to an even greater extent than in the past, issues of class solidarity and economic redistribution—and this has been particularly true of the most radical leftist leaders such as Hugo Chávez, Evo Morales, and Ollanta Humala (see Hawkins 2010). In other words, leftist politicians have been able to mobilize class support by politically activating class issues, thus making them more salient to voters' decision making.

If such is the case, then we should observe a significant association between indicators of socioeconomic class and presidential vote intention in our Latin American survey data. We look at three indicators of class in our analysis. The first is educational attainment. Everything else being equal, Latin Americans with lower levels of education should be more inclined to support a leftist presidential candidate as opposed to a rightist one, on the general idea that the less privileged derive more utility from leftist candidates' policies. To account for the effect of education, we include a variable coded as a three-point scale going from 0 (none to 6 years of schooling) to 1 (12 years and more). This simple coding is necessary because of the vast difference in national educational systems across the Latin American region. We expect that variable to show a positive relationship with our dependent variable (vote intention in favor of a rightist candidate). Such a result for the schooling variable would be congruent with recent ones reported for Venezuela (Nadeau, Bélanger, and Didier 2013) and Bolivia (Moreno Morales 2015).

A respondent's employment status and employment sector should also matter, and these characteristics constitute our two other indicators of socioeconomic status. Support for a rightist presidential candidate should be weaker among the unemployed and among public sector workers. Unemployed individuals should have less preference for laissez-faire government, which for example should lead them to cast a more policy-oriented type of economic vote (e.g., Kiewiet 1983). Public sector employees should be more sensitive to the development and impact of social policies as advocated by the political left, and their job situation and prospects are also more likely to be affected by the ideological orientation of the government. To account for these respective effects we include two dummy variables in our presidential vote intention model. The first one takes on the value of 1 for individuals out of a job (whether they are actively seeking a new job or not, but excluding students and retirees) and the value of 0 otherwise.

The second dummy variable measures whether an individual is a salaried employee of the government (coded 1) or not (coded 0). We expect both variables to show a negative association with our dependent variable.

## Material Comfort and Latin American Voting Behavior

A second aspect of socioeconomic status that is worthy of investigation relates directly to an individual's level of material comfort. The level of wealth can first be ascertained via household income. How can we expect income to influence voting behavior? The classic hypothesis, formulated within the context of economically developed Western democracies, was proposed by Lipset (1960, 223–24): "the most impressive single fact about political party support is that . . . the lower-income groups vote mainly for parties of the left, while the higher-income groups vote mainly for parties of the right." As explained by Lipset, this influence of income on vote choice is the direct result of class conflict being transposed into the party competition arena.

There is no clear reason to expect that this relationship between income and right-leaning vote choice ought to be different in the emerging economies of Latin America, especially given the heightened salience of class issues and conflict in many of these countries in the contemporary period. For example, income was recently found to be negatively associated with support for President Hugo Chávez (Nadeau, Bélanger, and Didier 2013). That said, the relationship may be weaker overall in Latin America than in advanced Western democracies since economic development remains uneven across the region. To test the general hypothesis of a positive association between wealth and rightist presidential vote intention, we first include the variable of household income in our model. Household income is measured with a five-point scale (going from 0 to 1) based on quintiles. Relying on income quintiles is necessary if we wish to make a meaningful comparison across all Latin American countries.

Income is certainly a good indicator of a voter's socioeconomic location and level of material comfort; but it is also an incomplete one. Recent work on voting behavior in Western democracies—especially in the French context—has highlighted the important influence of a nontraditional socioeconomic variable, that of property ownership, based on the number of assets that an individual owns. The greater the number of assets owned, the greater the likelihood of supporting a right-wing candidate in a presidential election. This relationship has been well established in France (Le Hay and Sineau 2010; Foucault, Nadeau, and Lewis-Beck 2011; Nadeau, Foucault, and Lewis-Beck 2011; Nadeau et al. 2012; Bélanger et al. 2014) although property (also referred to as "patrimony") in this case refers more to the ownership of capital income, especially capital income of a high-risk type such as stocks. The accumulation of capital income is certainly a less common behavior among Latin Americans, if only because the state of the economy in these countries, compared to economically developed ones, does not allow for as much accumulation. Therefore, if we are to take property into account in the Latin American context, it makes more sense to consider ownership of material assets (as opposed to capital income) as constituting another form of affluence in addition to income.

Thus, our fifth and last socioeconomic indicator is a measure of property. The variable is a 12-point scale that counts the number of household assets, or material goods, being owned out of a total of 11 (with the variable rescaled to run from 0 to 1). The list of material assets includes the following: indoor plumbing, indoor bathroom, refrigerator, microwave oven, washing machine, landline telephone, cellular telephone, television, computer, vehicle/car, and motorcycle. Like income, we expect property to be positively related to our dependent variable of right-leaning presidential support. This finding would be consistent with that of Mainwaring, Torcal, and Sommá (2015) who report a strong property effect in Argentina, Bolivia, and Brazil based on a similar indicator—and note that the property effect for Argentina has been confirmed by Nadeau et al. (2015a).

## Modeling Socioeconomic Effects

Our assessment of the relationship between socioeconomic variables and presidential vote intention in Latin American countries is based on the results from our second block model, which takes on the following conceptual form

$$\text{Vote} = f(\text{demographics, socioeconomics}) \tag{3.1}$$

Operationally, the model for the current chapter thus includes the number of months from the beginning of the presidents' terms, country fixed effects, and the block of demographic (SDEM) variables whose effects we analyzed in chapter 2, to which we now add a block of the five different socioeconomic (SECN) variables. Because the countries are pooled together in the analysis, we need to take into account the ideology of the incumbent candidate. To arrive at coefficient signs that pull in the same direction in every country, we have thus inverted the scales of all our socioeconomic variables when the incumbent is left-leaning. As a consequence, a positive coefficient sign in our regression model indicates support for a rightist incumbent candidate. All five independent variables from our socioeconomic block have been inverted that way since we have theoretical expectations that their impact depends on the ideological orientation of incumbents. Educated, employed, and non-public-sector respondents will tend to vote for the right; so will respondents who are wealthy or who own more material goods. For example, we expect the wealthier respondents to be more likely to vote for the right. Therefore, we sort respondents by income (in quintile groups coded from 0 to 1), where the wealthiest respondents are coded 1 in countries with rightist incumbents and coded 0 in countries with leftist incumbents. In both cases, we expect a positive coefficient for the income variable.

Are these five socioeconomic variables related to presidential vote intention? In a preliminary step, we can answer this question via bivariate tests. The values of the tau-b measures of association for the five bivariate tests are reported in table 3.1. They indicate that each of the five independent variables is significantly associated with presidential support, and that each relationship is in the expected direction: positive for schooling, income, and property; negative for unemployment status and public sector employment. In other words, all five of our hypotheses are supported in a bivariate setting. Of course, these relationships need to be assessed

TABLE 3.1. Socioeconomic Variables and Vote Intention in 18 Latin American Countries: Bivariate Relationships (2008, 2010, 2012)

|  | Tau-b |
| --- | --- |
| Schooling | 0.02** |
| Income | 0.03** |
| Unemployment | −0.06** |
| Public sector | −0.06** |
| Property | 0.03** |

**All relationships are statistically significant at $p \leq .01$.

in a multivariate environment that controls for the influence of the demographic characteristics from our previous block of independent variables—a task to which we now turn.

## General Overview of the Multivariate Results

The first important thing to assess is the extent to which these socioeconomic variables contribute to an overall explanation of the variation in presidential vote intention in Latin America. In other words, how much do our five socioeconomic measures contribute collectively to an increase in the models' coefficient of determination (pseudo-$R^2$) across the whole region? Table 3.2 provides a summary of this information. The short answer to this question is as follows: not very much. In fact, for the model estimated across all 18 Latin American countries pooled together, the pseudo-$R^2$ only moves by 0.01, keeping almost the same value as in the previous model, which included only the first block of demographic variables.

Nevertheless, there is some cross-country variation in the overall con-

TABLE 3.2. Global Contributions of Socioeconomic
Variables (2008, 2010, 2012)

| | Pseudo-$R^2$ change |
|---|---|
| All countries | 0.01 |
| Venezuela | 0.08 |
| Chile | 0.08 |
| Bolivia | 0.05 |
| Brazil | 0.05 |
| Argentina | 0.05 |
| Colombia | 0.04 |
| Dominican Republic | 0.03 |
| Paraguay | 0.02 |
| Guatemala | 0.02 |
| Honduras | 0.02 |
| Nicaragua | 0.01 |
| Peru | 0.01 |
| Panama | 0.01 |
| Ecuador | 0.01 |
| El Salvador | 0.01 |
| Uruguay | 0.00 |
| Costa Rica | 0.00 |
| Mexico | 0.00 |

tribution of the socioeconomic block. As the table also shows, while two-thirds of the countries display an increase of 0.03 or less in pseudo-$R^2$ value, the remaining third do show a noticeable increase. In particular, Venezuela and Chile both show a change of 0.08 when moving from the previous (SDEM only) model to the current one (SDEM plus SECN). Bolivia, Brazil, Argentina, and Colombia are not too far behind them, with an increase in pseudo-$R^2$ that varies between 0.04 and 0.05. It is worth noting that Venezuela is the only country for which we observe a statistically significant relationship for all five socioeconomic indicators.

Which ones of our five socioeconomic dimensions seem to matter the most to presidential vote intention in Latin America? As can be seen in table 3.3, three of the variables actually have a statistically significant relationship in the pooled model, namely household income, unemployment status, and the number of material goods owned. This is an interesting finding in the sense that the first two of these variables are usual, if not to say standard, socioeconomic variables while the third is a less traditional variable. It is also interesting to note that the nontraditional indicator, property, has a larger influence on vote intention than the traditional ones—including income. Everything else being equal, going from the minimum category (lowest quintile) to the maximum category (highest quintile) of the income variable yields an increase in the probability of

TABLE 3.3. Change in Probabilities for Voting Intentions in 18 Latin American Countries (2008, 2010, 2012)

|  | (1) | (2) | (3) |
|---|---|---|---|
| Months | -.24** | -.25** | -.26** |
| Age | — | .03** | .03** |
| Gender | — | .01** | .02** |
| Catholic | — | .04** | .04** |
| Church attendance | — | .05** | .06** |
| Region | — | .01 | -.01** |
| Race | — | .08** | .06** |
| Schooling | — | — | -.00 |
| Income | — | — | .04** |
| Unemployment | — | — | -.03** |
| Public sector | — | — | -.01 |
| Property | — | — | .08** |
| N | 52,489 | 51,394 | 45,332 |

**$p \leq .01$; *$p \leq .05$ (two-tailed tests). Entries represent change in probabilities. Country dummies are not shown (Mexico is the reference case). See appendix 4 for variable's specification.

supporting a rightist presidential candidate of 0.04. Being unemployed decreases this probability by 0.03. The comparative effect for the property variable (i.e., going from owning no assets to owning all of the 11 assets in the list) is more substantial, increasing the probability of voting for a rightist presidential candidate by 0.08. The fact that property has a greater total influence on vote intention than the income variable suggests that income may be an incomplete indicator of electorally salient socioeconomic cleavages in Latin America, at least when it comes to explaining presidential voting behavior.

The logistic regression results obtained for each of the 18 countries individually (see the relevant tables in appendix 2) tend to confirm that property and income are the most important determinants of presidential support. The effect of the property variable is statistically significant and of the expected positive sign in more than a third of the cases (7 of the 18 countries). Household income is significant and of the expected positive sign in six of the countries. (The education variable has a significant effect in 11 of the 18 Latin American countries but is not of the expected positive sign in about half of these cases, which helps explain its lack of significance in the pooled model of table 3.3.)

## A Closer Look at Socioeconomic Variables Individually

We can assess the extent of cross-national variation in the socioeconomic dimension of presidential voting behavior in more detail, starting with the unemployment variable. Figure 3.1 reports the probability changes associated with an individual being unemployed for each of the 18 countries, while controlling for the influence of the sociodemographic variables already discussed in chapter 2. (We provide figures only for the independent variables that proved to be statistically significant in table 3.3's pooled multivariate analysis.) Recall that the theoretical expectation for this measure is that it ought to correlate negatively with rightist presidential voting intention. Three countries significantly display such a relationship: Chile (–0.15), Venezuela (–0.12), and Ecuador (–0.06). None of the other effects are statistically significant, however (except one counterintuitive result for the Dominican Republic). This examination of individual country effects confirms that unemployment status constitutes a rather negligible socioeconomic cleavage in Latin American voting behavior.

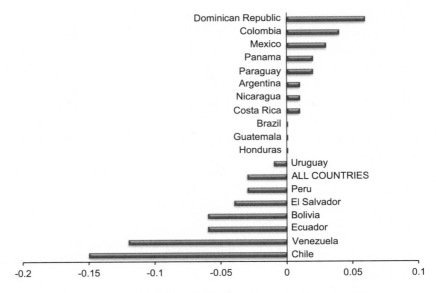

Fig. 3.1. Impact of Unemployment Status among Latin American countries (probability changes)

Note: Entries in the figure are changes in probability adjusted for other variables in the same model (LAPOP 2008, 2010, and 2012 data).

While the pooled results for the public sector employment variable indicate that it has the expected relationship with voting intention (although it is not statistically significant), the cross-national findings call for a more nuanced interpretation. For this variable, we hypothesized a negative effect: public sector employees should be less likely to support a rightist presidential candidate. This expectation is met, in statistical significance terms, in 3 countries only: the Dominican Republic (–0.23), Panama (–0.09), and Uruguay (–0.06). On the other hand, 4 countries show a statistically significant positive (unexpected) relationship. Like for the unemployment variable, these rather underwhelming findings tend to confirm the marginal influence of public sector employment as a predictor of vote intention.

Recall that among our three indicators of class, educational level also did not display a significant association with presidential support in our pooled multivariate analysis. The cross-national comparative effects tend to confirm this conclusion. The expected sign of this relationship is positive: as one moves from low to high educational attainment, the probability of voting for a right-leaning presidential candidate should increase. Only 6 of the 18 countries display a significant positive impact of schooling on the probability to support a rightist incumbent president (or a rightist opposition candidate). From this group, Venezuela and Brazil clearly stand out with the highest probability change (0.15 and 0.14, respectively). The other 12 countries show either a nonsignificant relationship or an impact in the unexpected direction (negative). These contradictory findings provide further evidence that schooling does not appear to be a systematic determinant of presidential vote choice in Latin America, at least in this multivariate context. Indeed, the relationship between schooling and vote intention is found to be statistically significant (with a probability change of 0.03) only when the variables of property and income are removed from the model, suggesting that schooling may in fact be a mediating variable caused by material conditions.

Cross-national differences in the influence of income on presidential vote intention can be summarized briefly and easily. The hypothesized relationship is positive, since the wealthy should be more inclined to express a rightist voting intention than the poor. As figure 3.2 shows, 6 countries display a positive and statistically significant effect of income. We can note that 3 of the countries where the hypothesis is most strongly confirmed were led at the time of the surveys by presidents from the radical left: Bolivia (0.22), Venezuela (0.10), and Peru (0.10). Finally, only 2 countries reveal an unexpectedly negative and significant impact, with Honduras being a clear outlier.

Results associated with our fifth and last socioeconomic variable, that of property, are visually presented in figure 3.3. To recall, the theoretical expectation is that the more household assets owned, the more likely an individual will be to support a rightist candidate in a presidential election. More than a third of the Latin American countries (7 out of 18) show such a positive and significant relationship between property and presidential vote intention. The change in predicted probability yielded by the property variable ranges from 0.11 in Ecuador to as much as 0.44 in Argentina. In other words, the probability that an Argentine supports a rightist presidential candidate increases by almost 45% if he or she owns all 11 assets on the list as opposed to none—although this effect needs to be assessed in light of the fact that Argentina is one of the countries where the mean number of assets owned is the lowest (0.30 on the 0–1 scale). Property has no significant relationship to vote intention in any of the 11

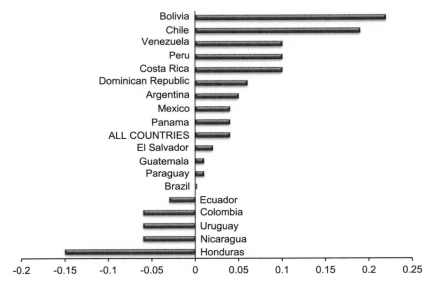

Fig. 3.2. Impact of Household Income among Latin American countries (probability changes)

*Note:* Entries in the figure are changes in probability adjusted for other variables in the same model (LAPOP 2008, 2010, and 2012 data).

remaining countries. In short, property, as a relatively novel indicator of socioeconomic cleavage, reveals itself to be a strong predictor of presidential vote intention in the Latin American region—stronger than income, and even the strongest among our block of five socioeconomic variables.

Note the four countries that find themselves at the top of figure 3.3: Argentina, Venezuela, Brazil, and Bolivia. These same four countries are also among the top five in table 3.2; that is to say, they are among those for which we observe the greatest influence of socioeconomic variables on presidential incumbent support. Without a doubt, these are the Latin American countries where the most electorally influential socioeconomic variables have the most important impact on presidential vote intention.

## The Question of Clientelism

So far, chapters 2 and 3 have focused on identifying the various demographic and socioeconomic constituencies of incumbents across the Latin

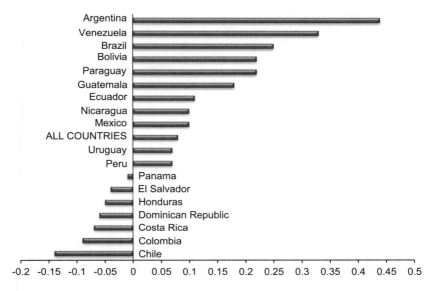

Fig. 3.3. Impact of Property among Latin American countries (probability changes)

*Note:* Entries in the figure are changes in probability adjusted for other variables in the same model (LAPOP 2008, 2010, and 2012 data).

American region. Yet, since the practice of clientelism is relatively frequent in emerging democracies such as those of Latin America, the question of whether these constituencies really support the incumbent government because of its actual policy performance is open to debate. Clientelism ranks among the top institutional or contextual characteristics that may alter the reward/punishment mechanism. Because clientelism revolves around a web of direct relationships between citizens and politicians, generally involving the exchange of targeted goods for support, overall government performance may not be what determines incumbent support. In clientelistic settings, voters may not base their evaluation of the incumbent government on broad policy issues, but may rather focus on the personal benefits they obtain from supporting it. In contexts where clientelistic practices are widespread, one should fail to observe a strong relationship between broad policy performance and incumbent support. If this is true, clientelism would be said to lessen electoral accountability.

The literature on clientelism provides supporting evidence of its detrimental effect on democratic governance (Hicken 2011). First, clientelism has been said to run counter to democratization. It obstructs the development of political institutions (Graziano 1973); it undermines democratic consolidation by limiting the exercise of citizenship (Fox 1994); it is mostly practiced in more volatile and fragmented political party systems (Kitschelt et al. 2010); and it jeopardizes the secrecy of the vote (Stokes 2005; Lyne 2007). Second, clientelism has been associated with corruption (Keefer 2007; Kitschelt et al. 2010; Persson, Tabellini, and Trebbi 2003; Singer 2009). It implies illegal practices (e.g., vote buying), it fosters a culture of impunity, and it increases the incentives of politicians to adopt illegal fundraising strategies (Singer 2009). Third, clientelism is detrimental to good governmental policy performance. It is associated with the politicization of the bureaucracy and the lack of administrative control and oversight (Golden 2003; Cruz and Keefer 2010), with significantly larger public sector employment and expenditures (Calvo and Murillo 2004; O'Dwyer 2006), and with less efficient and effective use of public resources (Keefer 2007; Remmer 2007).

For clientelism to affect the reward/punishment mechanism that is being examined in this book, the phenomenon needs to be relatively widespread among the population. It also needs to alter the voters' decision to support or reject the incumbent. Let us first assess the extent to which Latin American citizens report having been offered material benefits in exchange for their vote. The 2010 wave of the AmericasBarometer contains one item that precisely measures this dimension. As per column 1 of table 3.4, it is possible to conclude that the scope of the phenomenon, at least according to these survey respondents, is rather limited. A little over 1 out of 10 individuals report having been offered material benefits in exchange for their vote. What is more, the phenomenon is not evenly present across the Latin American region. The percentage of citizens having been offered

TABLE 3.4. The Scope of Clientelistic Practices in Latin America (2010)

|  | (1) Were you offered material benefits in exchange for your vote? | (2) Did it make you more likely to vote for the candidate/political party? |
|---|---|---|
| Overall | 12.8% | 17.8% |
| Minimum | 5.5% | 7.6% |
| Maximum | 22.2% | 25.8% |
| $N$ (countries) | 17 | 17 |
| $N$ (individuals) | 29,513 | 3,692 |

*Note:* Honduras is excluded.

material benefits for their vote varies from as low as 5.54% in Chile to as high as 22.21% in the Dominican Republic. In 11 of the 17 countries surveyed here,[1] this percentage is below 15%. In 5 of 17 countries, it is below 10%. (Of course, it must be recognized that the AmericasBarometer question used here does not ask which party offered the material incentive, or whether it was in the last presidential election or in a subnational election. Although one might expect that it is typically the incumbent party, with the most access to state-subsidized resources, that offers material incentives, opposition parties could still engage in clientelistic practices. In addition, survey respondents may be underreporting these practices or may not be honest in claiming that they resisted them. Hence, the findings reported here must be interpreted with these caveats in mind.)

The question of whether the offer of material benefits had any impact on the voter's decision is debatable. One cannot assume that such an offer systematically affects one's behavior. It is possible for many to be approached by a candidate or political party, but abstain from complying with the request. The 2010 AmericasBarometer also asked whether the offer increased the likelihood of voting for the candidate or political party. Column 2 of table 3.4 indicates that the material offer had only a small impact on the voting decision. Of the 12.8% who reported being offered material benefits in exchange for their vote, 17.8% of them claimed that it increased their likelihood of voting for that candidate or party. Overall, this represents 2.3% of the total respondents. Once again, the response to that question varies from country to country. Chileans had only 7.6% report that it made a difference, while Colombians had 25.8% claiming that the offer influenced their choice.

Beyond assessing the scope of the phenomenon, it is worth exploring which citizens are more likely to be exposed to that practice. Column 1 of table 3.5 presents the results of a multivariate logistic regression, using a number of demographic and socioeconomic variables to predict whether a citizen reports having been offered material benefits in exchange for his or her vote. The results suggest that men, church attendees, non-Catholics, nonwhite citizens, better educated voters, the unemployed, public sector employees, and those with less property are more likely to report having been offered material benefits for their vote.[2] Column 2 of table 3.5 assesses which voters are more likely to be influenced by the practice of clientelism. The results initially suggest that only voters who are less educated declare that the material benefits they were offered influenced their vote.

(But note that the coefficient for the unemployment variable is also correctly signed [i.e., positive, meaning that the vote of the currently unemployed is more susceptible of influence from the offer of material benefits] and is statistically significant at the .05 level using a one-tailed test.) These findings are perfectly consistent with the literature on clientelism—a phenomenon that most often targets those who are more vulnerable and who are less likely to detect the fraudulent nature of the offer.

For clientelism to alter democratic governance, it has to affect voters in such a way that it alters their preference. The change has to be large enough that it can alter the aggregated outcome. In order to verify that possibility,

TABLE 3.5. Predictors of Exposure to Clientelism and of Its Influence on Vote Choice in Latin America (2010)

|  | (1) Being exposed to | (2) Being influenced by |
|---|---|---|
| Gender | −.15** | −.09 |
|  | (.04) | (.09) |
| Catholic | −.18** | .19 |
|  | (.04) | (.10) |
| Church attendance | .21** | .21 |
|  | (.06) | (.15) |
| Region | .07 | −.09 |
|  | (.04) | (.09) |
| Race | −.14* | .00 |
|  | (.06) | (.16) |
| Schooling | .23** | −.27* |
|  | (.05) | (.14) |
| Income | .09 | .04 |
|  | (.07) | (.17) |
| Unemployment | .17** | .27 |
|  | (.06) | (.14) |
| Public sector | .17* | .01 |
|  | (.07) | (.17) |
| Property | −.62** | −.45 |
|  | (.11) | (.26) |
| Constant | −1.23** | −1.70** |
|  | (0.11) | (0.28) |
| Nagelkerke pseudo-$R^2$ | .05 | .03 |
| % correctly predicted | 86.7% | 83.2% |
| N | 26,071 | 3,470 |

**$p \leq .01$; *$p \leq .05$; (two-tailed tests). Country dummies are not shown. Honduras is excluded. See appendix 4 for variable's specification. Entries are unstandardized logistic regression coefficients, with standard errors in parentheses.

we calculate the predicted probability of supporting the incumbent using our fully specified model (first introduced conceptually in chapter 1 and to be empirically tested in chapter 5). We first estimate this probability using the full sample of voters.[3] This result serves as our baseline. In a second step we estimate the predicted probability of supporting the incumbent using only those voters who were not offered material benefits in exchange for their vote. In other words, we are calculating the probabilities on the basis of voters that were not exposed to clientelism. If clientelism affects voting behavior, we should find some difference between the two sets of predicted probabilities.

These estimates are presented in table 3.6. They suggest that clientelism has only a marginal effect on voting in Latin America. The absolute change in predicted probability is well below 1 percentage point in 12 of the 17 countries examined. In four of the five other cases, it remains below 1.7 percentage points. The only deviating case is Panama with a change in probability of 5.1 points.[4] Note also that the model's pseudo-$R^2$ value hardly moves when we exclude voters who were offered material benefits for their vote. All in all, the effect of clientelism appears to be quite marginal according to these analyses.

One final observation is worth making. In some countries, the effect is positive. That is, clientelism seems to work in favor of the incumbent party. In other countries, the effect is negative, thus suggesting that the presence of clientelism actually diminishes incumbent support. This is not too surprising since, as noted above, clientelism is not necessarily restricted to the incumbent party. Other political parties can practice clientelism. In doing so, they can even outperform the incumbent party. That may well be one reason why we find a weak effect of clientelism overall, since the null impact observed may be due to clientelistic efforts from incumbent and

TABLE 3.6. Does Clientelism Make a Difference to Incumbent Support? (2010)

| | Mean predicted incumbent support | Excluding voters who were offered material benefits for their vote | Difference |
|---|---|---|---|
| Full model | 52.6% | 52.9% | 0.3% |
| Nagelkerke pseudo-$R^2$ | .541 | .549 | — |
| $N$ (countries) | 17 | 17 | — |
| $N$ (individuals) | 12,679 | 10,891 | — |

*Note:* Honduras is excluded.

opposition parties cancelling each other out. This may be true as much in a cross-country comparison as within some countries.

To sum up, this section's analysis indicates that clientelism in Latin America is not as widespread as one might think, at least according to the survey responses from LAPOP's AmericasBarometer. It is not generally effective in altering electoral preferences. As per common expectations, clientelistic practices mostly target those voters who are in need, like the unemployed or those who have fewer material goods. But most important, the presence of clientelism does not seem to affect incumbent support in the aggregate.

## Conclusion

Generally speaking, in terms of their overall contribution to a vote choice model, socioeconomic cleavages do not seem to matter much to presidential voting behavior in Latin America. That said, three of the five socioeconomic variables examined in this chapter appear to drive voting intentions to some extent: unemployment status, household income, and property. And this seems to be especially true in 4 of the 18 countries: Argentina, Brazil, Bolivia, and Venezuela. The latter particularly stands out since it is the only country for which we find a significant relationship between presidential support and all five of our socioeconomic indicators. These main findings suggest that the patterns of class voting in contemporary Latin America are related in good part to the emergence of a strong and viable political left, one that has been able to politicize class issues and mobilize significant support from the most disadvantaged groups of society—in particular the unemployed and the poor. The possibility of an interaction between the presence of a radical leftist leader and class indicators will be considered more deeply in chapter 6.

In addition to hinting at an important contextual factor that seems to account for the heterogeneity in patterns of class voting, this chapter has been able to offer three other contributions to the study of presidential support in Latin America. First, our analysis establishes the (limited) degree to which five different socioeconomic variables—three of them referring to a voter's location in the class structure and the other two tapping more directly the dimension of material comfort—influence vote intention across the whole Latin American region. This broad approach is particularly useful since most of the extant literature has tended to focus on a more restricted number of socioeconomic variables and to rely on case studies. Second, our results clearly show that material goods allow for a much better estimate than income of the impact of wealth on presidential support in Latin America, and that both measures of wealth have more of an influence than the indicators of class included in this analysis. Third, and finally, our brief examination of the role of clientelism indicates that, even if the phenomenon can be observed in the Latin American region, its actual impact on voters' decision making remains limited, and does not diminish the value of our more direct study of demographic or socioeconomic cleavages as determinants of the vote.

CHAPTER 4

# Anchor Variables and the Vote

In this chapter, we are interested in two variables that reinforce voter loyalty toward candidates of the same political party over time: party identification (ID) and ideological orientation. Since the publication of the classic *The American Voter* (Campbell et al. 1960), a number of works have shown that many voters tend to develop an attachment to a political party. For a substantial number of individuals, this party identification leads them to consistently support the same political party over time. Therefore, the behavior of these voters shows a large amount of party loyalty, with those switching to other parties being rare.

Work on party ID over the past few decades has mainly centered around three questions. The first has to do with whether this variable is still relevant in a context where partisan attachment is declining in many democracies. The second question, one over which much ink has been spilled, asks whether the very concept of party ID itself, created in the United States, can be used to explain electoral behavior in other countries. A third issue, raised in the wake of the third wave of democratization, asks whether party identification serves a similar purpose in emerging democracies (such as those in Latin America) as it does in more established democracies (Brader and Tucker 2001, 2008; Mainwaring 1999; Mainwaring and Torcal 2006; Mainwaring and Zoco 2007; Lupu 2012).

Overall, the responses to the two first questions have been reassuring. Recent work, notably done on the United States and Europe (Lewis-Beck et al. 2008; Nadeau, Lewis-Beck, and Bélanger 2013), has shown that party identification remains an important vote determinant in many countries. Clearly, partisan identification is still a strong determinant and predictor of voter behavior in long-established democracies.

With regard to the third question, the literature on party identification in emerging democracies is particularly pertinent to our study. Some authors have put forward the idea that voters in emerging democracies are not yet capable of developing a robust and durable attachment to political parties (Mainwaring 1999; Widner 1997). These authors have offered several reasons in support of this idea, notably: (a) the possibility that political leaders use mass media to directly target voters (Levitsky and Cameron 2003); (b) the inability of voters to identify with often ephemeral political parties (Roberts and Wibbels 1999); (c) a personalization of the political debate that has relegated parties to the background. The latter is a particularly significant phenomenon in Latin America, where many countries have adopted a presidential regime (Mainwaring and Torcal 2006). However, other authors have argued in favor of the opposite hypothesis, that both established and emerging democracies are similar with regard to the formation and effects of party identification (Van der Brug, Franklin, and Tóka 2008). In particular, Lupu and Stokes (2010) highlighted that political instability in Latin America did not prevent the reemergence of a large number of political parties after periods of dictatorship. Furthermore, voters still retained their strong party identification to these old parties.

The results of empirical studies on party identification in Latin America seem to tip the balance in favor of this second hypothesis. For example, Lupu (2012, 8, fig. 1) finds that approximately one-third of the voters in this region readily identify with a political party. What is more is that work on electoral behavior in Latin America generally concludes that party ID has a significant effect on voters' choices, even when measured with elaborate multivariate models (Nadeau, Bélanger, and Didier 2013; Nadeau et al. 2015a, 2015b). That being said, it seems plausible to think that contextual factors, and among them the fragmentation of partisan systems, may condition the link between partisanship and voters' behavior in Latin America (Huber, Kernell, and Leoni 2005; Lupu 2015).

However, findings related to the effect of ideological orientation on political preferences in Latin America are more mixed. First, it should be noted that the same arguments used to bolster the hypothesis of weak party identification in Latin America reappear with regard to individuals' ideological orientations. For some, the absence of political stability and the relative novelty of democracy in these countries do not create a context where citizens can develop the same ideological structure to understand political life as their counterparts in more established democracies (see Roberts and Wibbels 1999; Gonzalez and Queirolo 2009; Jou 2011; and Zeichmeister and Corral 2013).

According to this reasoning, the number of "ideologues" will be lower in Latin America than in more established democracies. Furthermore, the impact of voters' ideological orientations on vote choice will be smaller in these countries. However, what do empirical studies show? The first conclusion is that the majority of Latin American voters also use the concepts of "left" and "right" to interpret the political dynamics of their own country. For example, Zechmeister and Corral (2013; see also Zechmeister 2006) found that more than 80% of voters in this region were able to position themselves on a scale from extreme left to extreme right. Still, the percentage of people unable to position themselves on this scale is closer to that of the emerging democracies of eastern Europe, at 23%, than those of the more established democracies of western Europe, at 12% (see Mair 2010).

What about the effect of a voter's ideological orientation on their vote choice? Empirical work on this question tends to suggest that the structuring effect of ideology on political attitudes and vote choice is less pronounced and less systematic than for party identification. The overall conclusion is that the effect of ideology on political choices in Latin America varies greatly according to the degree of elite polarization and party system stability.

This brief literature review brings us to certain expectations regarding the relative impact of party identification and ideological orientation on an individual's vote choice in Latin America. First, it seems clear that the overall effect of party identification on vote choice will be greater than that of ideological orientation. Work on these two concepts, in Latin America and elsewhere, show that it is generally easier to develop an attachment to a concrete object such as a political party than to an abstract notion such as the left-right dichotomy in politics (Zeichmeister 2006; Zeichmeister and Corral 2013). In addition, some work in the United States has shown that party identification structures political attitudes (such as those having to do with the role of the state, equality, and moral conservatism), rather than the inverse (Goren 2005). The work of Box-Steffensmeier and De Boef (1996) found that the link between party identification and ideological orientation was much more well defined among politically sophisticated individuals. Thus, there seems to be a hierarchy of sorts between party identification and ideological orientation, with the former tending to develop before the latter. This suggestion allows us to propose two ideal-types that will be found among the Latin American cases: cases where party identification is the only vote determinant and cases where its impact coexists with that of ideological orientation. Thus, it would be very surprising, at least on first glance, to find cases where ideological orientation alone, independent from the impact of party identification, affects individuals' vote choice.

In this chapter, we will examine the effect of party identification and ideology in three different ways. First, we will look at the effect of these two variables on the explanatory power of our models. Next, we will consider the specific contribution of each of these variables. Finally, we will explore whether there is any trade-off between these variables, in order to see if a greater impact of party ID on vote choice for a particular country is accompanied by a smaller impact for ideology, and vice versa.

## Variables and Models

We now direct our attention to the results of the models that include individual party ID and ideological orientation variables. Conceptually, the model for this third block in our recursive causal system reads as follows:

$$\text{Vote} = f(\text{demographics, socioeconomics, anchors}) \qquad (4.1)$$

In terms of the variable labels used to this point, it can be expressed thusly,

$$\text{Vote} = f(\text{SDEM, SECN, PID, Ideology}) \qquad (4.2)$$

Hence, the quantitative models that will be examined in this chapter begin with both the demographic (SDEM) and socioeconomic (SECN) variables from the previous chapters. To these variables, we will add those for party identification (PID) and ideology. Coding of these variables has been done in the following way. The party ID variable took the value of 1 when a respondent identified with the party of the incumbent candidate or coalition, 0 if they identified with the opposition, and .5 if they did not identify with any party. A respondent's ideological orientation is measured with the help of a scale ranging from 1 to 10. The respondent is asked to position themselves on this scale, given that 1 corresponds to a very leftist position (extreme left) and 10 corresponds to a very rightist position (extreme right). The variable is then rescaled from 0 (extreme left) to 1 (extreme right).[1]

Before going on to the results of the multivariate models, it is both interesting and necessary to examine the distribution of both party ID and ideology variables for all countries together, and then by individual country. This information is presented in table 4.1. The first column of this table shows the percentage of respondents who identified with a political party (either in power or opposition) in all 18 countries in the study, along with the mean value for all countries. The second column shows the percentage of respondents in each country, as well as for the entire sample, who are able to place themselves on the left-right scale. Finally, the third column shows the average value of the responses obtained on this scale.[2]

TABLE 4.1. Percentage of Partisans, Ideologues, and Ideological Orientation in 18 Latin American Countries

|  | % of Partisans | % of Ideologues | Ideological Orientation |
|---|---|---|---|
| All countries | 31 | 80 | .51 |
| Dominican Republic | 61 | 82 | .60 |
| Uruguay | 55 | 91 | .43 |
| Paraguay | 45 | 72 | .54 |
| Nicaragua | 44 | 79 | .49 |
| Honduras | 41 | 82 | .56 |
| Venezuela | 35 | 86 | .50 |
| Costa Rica | 34 | 66 | .56 |
| El Salvador | 33 | 91 | .50 |
| Mexico | 30 | 86 | .53 |
| Colombia | 30 | 81 | .58 |
| Brazil | 28 | 78 | .52 |
| Panama | 27 | 85 | .54 |
| Bolivia | 23 | 77 | .47 |
| Argentina | 21 | 81 | .49 |
| Ecuador | 18 | 89 | .48 |
| Peru | 17 | 88 | .51 |
| Guatemala | 14 | 77 | .49 |
| Chile | 14 | 77 | .49 |

*Note:* Entries in column 1 display the percentages of party identifiers overall and in individual countries; entries in column 2 represent the percentage of respondents who classify themselves on a left-right scale (overall and for individual countries); entries in column 3 are the mean response of this left-right scale incumbent candidate or party.

Let us first examine the figures for party identification. The data show that a little more than 30% of respondents in the 18 Latin American countries studied showed some kind of attachment to a political party. However, this figure masks large variations from one country to another. In fact, we can make out three distinct groups of countries. The first includes the Dominican Republic, Uruguay, Paraguay, Nicaragua, and Honduras, where the number of partisans exceeds 40%. The percentage of partisans is particularly high in the Dominican Republic and Uruguay, where levels reach 61% and 55%, respectively. The second group is made up of 7 countries where the percentage of partisans approaches the mean of all the countries in the study (31%). In this group, we find 3 countries (Venezuela, Costa Rica, and El Salvador) where the proportion of partisans exceeds the overall mean by a few percentage points and 4 countries where it is slightly less than the overall mean (Mexico, Colombia, Brazil, and Panama). Finally, a third group of countries is characterized by the limited number of confirmed partisans. In some countries, political instability can explain the situation, as would be the case for Chile, Peru, or Colombia. The presence of Argentina in this group is surprising, especially given its experience with Peronism. In any case, the overall conclusion to be drawn is that there is great diversity to be found in each country's situation, ranging from relatively high levels of partisanship (in 5 countries), moderate levels (in 7 countries), and relatively low levels (in 6 countries).

Column 2 of table 4.1 shows the percentage of respondents being able to position themselves on a scale that measures their ideological orientation. This proportion is around 80%, which is similar to what was found by Zechmeister and Corral (2013). The variation between countries for ideology is smaller than that for partisanship. A first group contains 7 countries (Uruguay, El Salvador, Ecuador, Peru, Mexico, Venezuela, and Panama) and is characterized by a widespread awareness of left and right within the population. In this group, the percentage of respondents able to give their ideological orientation is between 85% and 91%. A second group is made up of 9 countries (Colombia, Honduras, the Dominican Republic, Argentina, Nicaragua, Brazil, Chile, and Guatemala) where the percentages fluctuate slightly (between 77% and 82%) around the overall mean (80%). Finally, 2 countries differentiate themselves from the other groups due to the relatively low number of citizens able to position themselves on a left-right scale. These countries are Paraguay

(72%) and Costa Rica, with barely 66% of individuals using the labels of "left" and "right." The case of Costa Rica is interesting, since it is often portrayed as a democracy where traditional polarization between left and right is particularly weak.

The last column in table 4.1 shows the mean values of the responses obtained on the left-right scale, but rescaled from 0 to 1. The overall mean is 0.51, which shows a remarkable balance within these countries as a whole between individuals identifying with the left or the right. The score for most countries is in the neighborhood of the median value of the distribution, which is 0.50. In fact, the score for 13 of the 18 countries lies between .46 and .54. However, 5 countries stand out. Colombia, Honduras, Costa Rica, and the Dominican Republic are slightly more to the right (with scores of .58, .56, .56, and .60 respectively), with Uruguay (.43) being more to the left.[3]

The results regarding party identification and ideology are both interesting and instructive. First, they allow us to say that approximately one in three Latin American respondents (31%) identifies with a political party, which is a lower level than what is observed in the more-established democracies of North America and Europe. However, this proportion masks large variation from one country to the next. Second, the results for ideology show that four out of five respondents (80%) are able to position themselves on a left-right scale. With some exceptions, these positions show a relative balance from one country to another between the percentage of left-wing and right-wing voters. Finally, the data show a positive relationship between the percentage of respondents identifying with a party and those positioning oneself on the left-right axis (the correlation is 0.23 and statistically significant at the 0.05 level). This moderate correlation gives us a first sign that there could be a relationship between party identification and vote choice in Latin America.

## Effect of Party ID and Ideology

We will now examine the effect of party ID and ideology on vote intentions in the eighteen countries included in our study. First, we will examine the bivariate relationships between these variables and vote choice. Then, we will analyze the results from the multivariate model presented in Equation 4.1.

*Party Identification, Ideology, and the Vote: Bivariate Relationships*

Table 4.2 presents a measure of the strength and direction of the association between party ID and vote choice (column 1), as well as ideological orientation and vote choice (column 2). This information is presented for all countries together as well as for each of them separately. A positive tau-b value for party ID means that the probability of voting for an incumbent candidate rises among those who identify with the candidate's party. A positive tau-b value for ideology means that right-wing voters will be more likely to support incumbents of the same political stripe (the reader is reminded that the dependent variable has been modified so that it takes a value of 1 when the incumbent is right-wing and 0 when the incumbent is left-wing), with the opposite being true for left-wing voters.

The data in table 4.2 should be interpreted with a certain degree of

TABLE 4.2. Party Identification, Ideology, and Voting Intentions in 18 Latin American Countries: Bivariate Relationships

|  | (1) Party ID Tau-b |  | (2) Ideology Tau-b |
| --- | --- | --- | --- |
| All countries | .48 | All countries | .21 |
| Dominican Republic | .76 | Uruguay | .53 |
| Uruguay | .72 | El Salvador | .46 |
| Nicaragua | .70 | Venezuela | .43 |
| Venezuela | .63 | Chile | .33 |
| El Salvador | .60 | Bolivia | .30 |
| Honduras | .60 | Nicaragua | .29 |
| Costa Rica | .54 | Dominican Republic | .19 |
| Bolivia | .52 | Mexico | .15 |
| Mexico | .50 | Colombia | .15 |
| Panama | .45 | Costa Rica | .14 |
| Guatemala | .41 | Honduras | .13 |
| Argentina | .39 | Ecuador | .10 |
| Ecuador | .36 | Paraguay | .08 |
| Peru | .34 | Brazil | −.05 |
| Paraguay | .32 | Peru | .04 |
| Chile | .18 | Guatemala | .02 |
| Colombia | .10 | Panama | .02 |
| Brazil | .09 | Argentina | −.01 |

*Note:* Entries are the tau-b for the relation between party identification, ideology and voting intentions overall and 18 Latin American countries.

prudence, since party ID and ideology are formed of a different number of categories. It should also be remembered that bivariate relationships cannot be directly interpreted as causal relations. Nevertheless, the information in this table is both interesting and useful in different ways. First, let us look at the measures for all the countries in the study together. The tau-b measuring the relationship between party ID and vote choice (.48) is about two and a half times larger than that between ideology and vote choice (.21). In addition, the tau-b for party ID is, in every case, statistically significant and of the expected sign (i.e., positive). The results are different for ideology. For this variable, many coefficients are weak: five are not significant and two are of the wrong sign. These first results suggest that the effect of party ID on vote choice in Latin America is larger and more systematic than that of ideology.

What about the relationships between the strength of the effects of party identification and ideological orientation for each country? At first glance, the measures of association seem to confirm that there are three rather well-defined groups of countries in Latin America: first, countries where party identification is still dominant but where ideological orientation also has a significant effect on vote choice (as in Uruguay, El Salvador, and Venezuela, for example); second, countries where only party identification has a large and expected impact on vote choice (as is the case of Guatemala, Panama, Honduras, Nicaragua, and Argentina, for example). Third, there are countries where party identification and ideological orientation follow neither of the foregoing patterns. Two cases stand out here: Brazil, where neither party identification nor ideological orientation have a significant influence on voters' electoral choice; Chile, which offers the only instance where the association between ideology and the vote ( at .33) exceeds that of party ID and the vote (at .18). These preliminary results, while interesting in many ways, still need to be confirmed with the help of a multivariate model, which we will examine in the next section.

### The Vote: A Multivariate Model

Detailed results from the regression analysis that includes demographic (SDEM) and socioeconomic (SECN) variables, along with party ID and ideology variables, are presented in table 4.3, as well as in appendix 2. We first consider the contribution of the latter two variables to the explanatory power of these models, which is quite large. For the whole set of countries in the study, the pseudo-$R^2$ goes from 0.11 to 0.43 when party ID and ideology are added to the model (see table A2.1, appendix 2). A key question is asking which variable plays a larger role in explaining the Latin American vote. The results clearly show that party ID has a much stronger impact than ideology does on voter choices. The most direct way to prove this is to include these variables one by one in the explanatory models. When the ideology variable is added to the 18-country model, the pseudo-$R^2$ increases by a relatively small amount, namely from 0.11 to 0.18. However, when the party ID variable is added to the same model, the pseudo-$R^2$ increases remarkably, namely from 0.11 to 0.41. We can therefore conclude that the improvement in the explanatory power of a vote model for all of Latin America is essentially due to including a party ID variable, rather than an ideology variable.

The stability of the effects observed for these two variables also underlines the dominance of party ID in the model. The changes in probabilities observed when these two variables are included are .65 for party ID and .19 for ideology (see table 4.3, column 4). When ideology is included in the model without party ID, the level of change in probabilities goes from

TABLE 4.3. Change in Probabilities for Voting Intentions in 18 Latin American Countries (LAPOP 2008, 2010, 2012)

|                     | (1)      | (2)      | (3)      | (4)      |
|---------------------|----------|----------|----------|----------|
| Months              | −.24**   | −.25**   | −.26**   | −.15**   |
| Age                 | —        | .03**    | .03**    | .03**    |
| Gender              | —        | .01**    | .02**    | .01      |
| Catholic            | —        | .04**    | .04**    | .01**    |
| Church attendance   | —        | .05**    | .06**    | .02**    |
| Region              | —        | .01      | −.01**   | −.01*    |
| Race                | —        | .08**    | .06**    | .03**    |
| Schooling           | —        | —        | −.00     | .01      |
| Income              | —        | —        | .04**    | .03**    |
| Unemployment        | —        | —        | −.03**   | −.03**   |
| Public sector       | —        | —        | −.01     | −.01     |
| Property            | —        | —        | .08**    | .05**    |
| Ideology            | —        | —        | —        | .19**    |
| Party identification| —        | —        | —        | .65**    |
| N                   | 52,489   | 51,394   | 45,332   | 38,363   |

**$p \leq .01$; *$p \leq .05$ (two-tailed tests). Entries represent change in probabilities. Country dummies are not shown (Mexico is the reference case). See appendix 4 for variable's specification.

.19 to .38. That is to say that adding party ID to the model considerably reduces the impact of ideology (which goes from .38 to .19). This is not the case for party ID. When this variable is included in the model without ideology, the change in probability is .70. This value barely changes when ideology is then added to the model (from .70 to .65).[4]

A simple examination of the changes in probabilities associated with the two variables also underlines the larger impact of partisan identification on the vote in Latin America (see fig. 4.1). The observed value of .65 for party ID, when using the data for all countries in the study, means that the probability of supporting an incumbent candidate increases 65 percentage points when a respondent goes from identifying with an opposition political party (value of 0) to identifying with the incumbent's party (value of 1). Likewise, the value of .19 for the ideology variable means that the probability that a respondent supports an incumbent candidate increases 19 percentage points when their ideological orientation goes from extreme left (originally a value of 1, but rescaled to 0) to extreme right (originally 10, but rescaled to 1).

The improvement in the performance of our voting model when partisan identification and ideology are included varies considerably from one country to the next. The biggest boosts are for the Dominican Republic (+.68) and Uruguay (+.63), with the effect being less striking for countries such as Peru (+.17), Guatemala (+.16), Paraguay (+.16), and Argentina (+.15). There is practically no improvement for Colombia (+.03), and Brazil (+.01).

The variation in the performance of these social-psychological variables raises the question about the respective impact of both variables in the 18 Latin American countries. We can ask ourselves if these differences are due to systematic patterns where both, one, or none of the variables play a significant role in explaining voting behavior in the different countries.

The data in table 4.4 show the impact of both variables for the 18 countries under study. The results show that the effect of party ID on vote choice is of the expected sign and statistically significant (at the .01 threshold) in all of the countries in the study. This effect is strong in almost every single country, with the exception of Chile, Colombia, and Brazil (see column 1 of table 4.4 and figure 4.1). The effect of the ideology variable is smaller and much less systematic (see column 2 of table 4.4 and figure 4.2). This variable is not of the expected sign (i.e., positive) in two countries (Brazil and Panama) and is not statistically significant (at the .01 level) in 7 out of 18 cases (Argentina, Brazil, Guatemala, Honduras, Panama, Peru, and Nicaragua). Once again, this highlights the less systematic character of the effect of ideology on vote choice in Latin America.

This category of cases where the effect of ideology is weak is useful. It allows us to create a typology of cases in Latin America with regard to the relative impact of ideology and party ID on vote choice. The first group is made up of four countries, where the significant effect of ideology "cohabitates" with the still dominant effect of party ID on vote choices. This category includes Bolivia (.87 vs. .30), El Salvador (.61 vs. .33), Uruguay (.46 vs. 25), and Venezuela (.70 vs. .29). In all of these cases, the impact of party ID is larger than that of ideology. But this dominance is not necessarily unconditional across countries. Rather, the relative effect of these two variables suggests that the two effects are significant, but party ID nonetheless reigns supreme.

But what about the other countries? Looking at the changes in prob-

TABLE 4.4. Changes in Probabilities for Party Identification and Ideology for Voting Intention for 18 Latin American Countries

|  | (1) Party ID | (2) Ideology |
|---|---|---|
| All countries | .65 | .19 |
| Guatemala | .94 | .03 |
| Bolivia | .87 | .30 |
| Ecuador | .79 | .14 |
| Mexico | .73 | .15 |
| Panama | .71 | −.02 |
| Venezuela | .70 | .29 |
| Argentina | .66 | .06 |
| Costa Rica | .68 | .13 |
| Nicaragua | .66 | .04 |
| Peru | .63 | .08 |
| El Salvador | .61 | .33 |
| Honduras | .60 | .04 |
| Dominican Republic | .51 | .08 |
| Uruguay | .46 | .25 |
| Paraguay | .40 | .13 |
| Chile | .24 | .63 |
| Colombia | .17 | .16 |
| Brazil | .09 | −.04 |

*Note:* Entries in the table are the changes in probability that the dependent variable takes the value 1 when the Party ID and Ideology variable varies from its minimum to its maximum value.

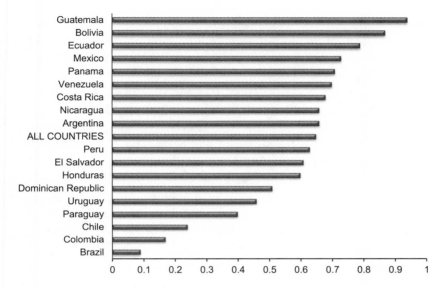

Fig. 4.1. Impact of Party Identification (PID) among Latin American countries

Note: Entries in the graph are the change in probabilities coefficients adjusted for other variables in the same model (LAPOP 2008, 2010 and 2012 data).

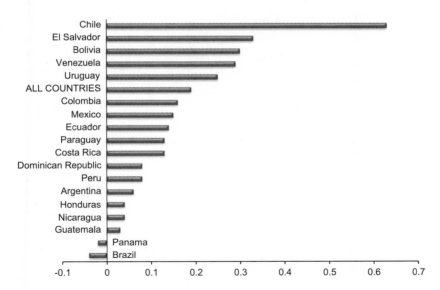

Fig. 4.2. Impact of Ideology among Latin American countries

Note: Entries in the graph are the change in probabilities coefficients adjusted for other variables in the same model (LAPOP 2008, 2010, and 2012 data).

abilities suggests that there are countries where party ID clearly wins out over ideology as an anchor variable explaining electoral behavior. This bloc of 11 countries is made up of Argentina (.66 vs. .06), Costa Rica (.68 vs. .13), the Dominican Republic (.51 vs. .08), Ecuador (.79 vs. .14), Guatemala (.94 vs. .03), Honduras (.60 vs. .04), Mexico (.73 vs. .15), Nicaragua (.66 vs. .04), Panama (.71 vs. –.02), Paraguay (.40 vs. .13), and Peru (.63 vs. .08). In this group of countries, the mean effect of party ID is .66 while that of ideology is .08. The domination of party ID over ideology in this group is unmistakable.

Three other countries still stand out. First are Brazil and Colombia, where the impact of both these social-psychological variables is weak. These countries do not mark themselves off from the other Latin American countries because of the relative weakness of the effect of ideology on the vote. As a matter of fact, the change in probability for Colombia (.16) is quite close to the average for the region (.19). What characterizes them is the very weak impact of party ID on voting decisions in these cases. This situation may be due to the extreme fractionalization of the party system in these countries, a point to which we will return in chapter 6. Second is Chile, the case that diverges the most radically from the common dominant patterns in Latin America. It is the only country where the impact of ideology on the vote (.63) greatly exceeds that of party identification (.24).

How can we explain the particular case of Chile? A first thing worth noticing is that deviant cases showing different voting patterns are not unusual. The impact of ideology, for instance, is clearly lower in Great Britain and Ireland than in the rest of western Europe. That being said, the domination of ideology in Chile may be due to two factors. One is the historical context. The dictatorship of Augusto Pinochet may well have crystallized opinion between the mainly leftist opponents and the mainly rightist supporters of this regime (Navia and Osorio 2016). Another, and perhaps more important factor, is the nature of electoral competition in this country. In Chile, presidential elections pit candidates heading clear right-wing coalitions (Coalition for Change, Alliance) against candidates heading clear left-wing coalitions (Concert of Parties for Democracy). The historical context and the priming of ideology in presidential contests could explain why this country is the only one in Latin America where ideology is clearly the key anchor variable explaining voting behavior.

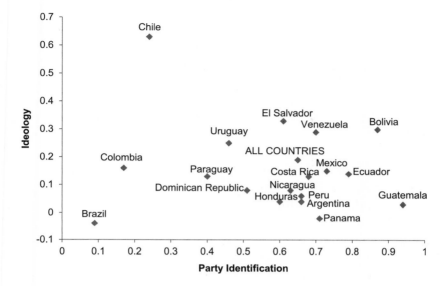

Fig. 4.3. Relationship between the effect of Party Identification and Ideology in 18 Latin American countries

This classification delineates three typical situations in Latin America concerning the impact of party identification. The most common pattern, observable in 11 countries, is the case where party ID absolutely dominates ideology as electorally determinant. A second pattern, visible in four countries, is still characterized by the domination of party ID, but its domination over ideology is less pronounced. The third pattern, including three countries, differs from the first two patterns. In Brazil and Colombia, the impact of both anchor variables is weak, whereas in Chile ideology clearly dominates the scene.

Figure 4.3, which shows the effect of party ID and ideology on vote choice in different countries, allows us to illustrate this classification of countries. The countries belonging to the group where the effect of both variables is significant and of the expected sign are mostly found in the upper-right quadrant, while countries where party ID unquestionably dominates are mostly found in the lower-right quadrant. In the upper right-quadrant are the four countries where the domination of party ID is less pronounced. Finally the three deviant cases are visible in the upper-left (Chile) and lower-left (Colombia and Brazil) quadrants.

## Conclusion

This chapter discusses the effect of two anchor variables on electoral be-havior: party ID and ideological orientation. These variables have a large impact on vote choice in the United States and Europe. Work that has been carried out on these variables in Latin America has also shown the importance of these variables, while pointing out a certain number of nu-ances. For example, some authors have stressed these countries' relatively recent and limited experience with democracy, and the accompanying instability in the party system, as potential reasons for why many Latin American voters have limited feelings of attachment to and identification with a political party. Others are more skeptical with regard to the effect of an individual's ideological positioning on his or her vote choice.

The goal of this chapter has been to systematically examine the effect of these variables, in one comprehensive multivariate model for 18 Latin American countries, using data collected from electoral studies carried out in 2008, 2010, and 2012. The results obtained are both clear and interest-ing. The first conclusion to be drawn is that social-psychological anchor variables, such as party ID or ideology, play an important role in explain-ing electoral behavior in Latin America. The inclusion of these variables considerably improves the explanatory power of these models. When these variables are included, the pseudo-$R^2$ for the model that includes all of the countries in the study increases from .11 to .43. Of course, the effect of these variables changes from country to country, but upon the addition of these two variables the pseudo-$R^2$ increases by at least .15 in 16 out of 18 countries.

The second conclusion relates to the very clear dominance of party ID over ideology in explaining electoral behavior in Latin America. The numbers are quite telling: including ideology in the general vote model increases the pseudo-$R^2$ from .11 to .18, but adding party ID causes it to jump to .41. While all of the coefficients linked to party ID are of the expected sign and statistically significant in all cases, 5 out of the 18 coefficients related to the ideology variable are either of the wrong sign or statistically insignificant. Finally, the effect of party ID is larger than that of ideology in all countries studied, with one notable exception, Chile.

The relationship between the relative strength of the effects of party ID and ideology offers an interesting final result from this chapter. The data show that Latin American countries can be regrouped into three groups.

The first group, the most common pattern, contains 11 countries such as Argentina, Guatemala, Honduras, and Panama. In this group, party ID completely dominates and the effect of ideology is comparatively weak. A smaller subset includes Bolivia, El Salvador, Uruguay, and Venezuela. Among them, party ID has a large impact on vote choice, but ideology also holds significant sway with voters. Finally, we find a residual subset, where neither party ID nor ideology plays a major role (Brazil and Colombia) or where only ideology plays a major role (Chile).

These results will be reexamined in chapter 6, to determine more precisely the profile of countries belonging to one group or the other. Based on the literature and the findings in this chapter and the preceding ones, two paths of explanation for cross-country differences seem promising. First, it seems logical to think that the fragmentation of the party system in a given country may affect the link between partisanship and voters' behavior in Latin America. More choices may mean voters know less about parties. Second, a priming effect may be at work for ideology. We may expect that the effect of ideology on the vote will be stronger when elite polarization is more intense and references to the left-right opposition more frequent.

CHAPTER 5

# Issues and the Vote

In democracies, voters respond to long-term and short-term forces, and Latin American electorates provide no exception. Social structure and psychological attachments, which we have considered in previous chapters, are prime examples of long-term forces shaping vote choice. These forces tend to be enduring, stable, and lasting—in a word, exogenous. With respect to the funnel of causality logic we have been following, they occur early on, at the wide-open mouth of the funnel. They serve to frame, or constrain, electoral choice, rendering it a "standing decision," in the words of V. O. Key (1966). However, short-term forces can move voters off their stand. They occur at the tip of the funnel, just before the act of voting itself. These forces, of which issues are a prime example, tend to be changing, unstable, and fickle—in a word, endogenous.

This variability does not mean that issues are unimportant for vote choice. On the contrary, this very fluctuation can give them heightened importance. Take as an illustration the issue of the economy. If public opinion holds that the government has been delivering good economic performance, then it will lean in the government's favor at the ballot box. But, if public opinion comes to see the economy as poor, then the government will lose votes, and maybe even lose office. Of course, other issues besides the economy can stimulate a voter to depart from his or her customary frame. Corruption can cause voters to break from their home party, tax policies can lead critics to abandon the government, violations of basic democratic principles can move electors to a protest vote.

No one would claim that issues are irrelevant to elections in Latin America. There are simply too many pressing problems in the region for that "head-in-the-sand" perspective. But it remains unclear how important issues are. Do they cumulate, moving together in a way that has clout, making governments accountable to the people? And if issues do matter, which ones are they? And for whom do they matter? These questions, aiming at the heart of how issues work their way through an electorate, have been asked for some time in established democracies. We have learned that, even in these ongoing systems, where democracy has become routine, issues do not easily catch the ear of the political leadership. Getting the attention of ruling elites might be more difficult in the more fragile democracies that characterize Latin America. After all, the region may remember its dictators, and clientelism and ethnic cleavages could still abide, not to mention the pockets of grinding poverty, or the brooding oversight from its giant neighbor to the north.

Below, we first define issues that have relevance in the electoral space. Next we consider the conditions, sometimes difficult, under which an issue can enter into the voter's candidate calculation. Then, we look at what issues appear to be more important for the Latin American public. After that, we sort the issues into different types, considering how these types may have a variable impact on the vote. Regarding those issues, we see the contours of opinion in the region. Then, we see how opinion differs, across the region and across issues. After discussing how these issues are measured, we embed them in well-specified voting models, containing several long-term forces, as well as multiple issues. To conclude, we assess the role of different issues in influencing support for or against ruling parties. As we shall see, issues are important, and economic issues particularly so.

## Conditions for Issue Voting

Every day we human beings face things to deal with, things that may be called "issues." For example, should I wear my winter coat, need I pay the gas bill today, ought I put my course online, is the mayor taking bribes from private building contractors? While all these may be issues in some sense, they are not in the public domain, except perhaps the last. In the public domain, where politics takes place, there are many issues, questions to be decided one way or another. But some of these issues will be latent, rather than manifest, because they are on no relevant actor's radar. Thus, we must ask what the conditions are whereby an issue enters the arena of political debate. There are basically three: (1) the voter has to see the issue; (2) the voter has to have a preference on the issue; (3) the voter must believe the parties or candidates differ on the issue. These criteria, first laid down in *The American Voter*, are not readily met (Campbell et al. 1960, chap. 8; see also Lewis-Beck et al. 2008, chap. 8).

Take the example of air pollution in rural farm communities caused, some say, by hog-feeder lots. For that to become an election issue, a voter must detect the altered air, believe it is bad, and decide that local candidate preferences differ on what to do about it. Finally, suppose all three of the criteria are met, e.g., voter X smells the hogs, thinks it's bad, and recognizes that candidate X, unlike candidate Y, wants to change the situation. Still, a particular voter X might not think the air pollution issue in itself important, at least compared to others, like taxes or roads or police. Thus, in our study, we would like to identify issues that, because they are important, can be expected to generate attention, and differences of opinion, on the part of voters and candidates.

## Important Political Issues

For democracies around the world, a host of issues may resonate loudly within the political discourse of the day. What do comparative data show on issue attention in a variety of free electoral systems? Carrying out a wide-ranging investigation of 39 democracies, with the help of the Comparative Study of Electoral Systems data, Singer (2011, 292) found that citizens offered 11 "issue categories" as "most important" for their country. In order, these issues ranked as follows: the economy, social policy, foreign policy, corruption, crime, immigration, environment, taxes, agriculture, social values, and ethnicity.

Fortunately for our purposes, Singer's investigation (2011, 294, table 2) includes four Latin American nations. Here are the top five issue categories for these countries (along with the respective percentages who said they were important):

1. **Brazil** — economic performance and management (70.38), crime (15.41), social policy (5.69), corruption and competence (3.51), foreign policy and terrorism (.56);
2. **Chile** — economic performance and management (48.30),

crime (35.37), social policy (10.03), corruption and competence (2.55), foreign policy and terrorism (.34);

3. **Mexico** — economic performance and management (48.85), crime (20.89), corruption and competence (13.95), foreign policy and terrorism (2.90), social policy (2.60);

4. **Peru** — economic performance and management (45.28), foreign policy and terrorism (16.24), corruption and competence (14.38), crime (5.96), social policy (4.55).

What we observe is that the top five issues are the same, across these four Latin American nations. Moreover, we observe that economic performance and management, by far, are of the most importance, thereby helping to justify considerable attention to that realm.

Using the AmericasBarometer data at hand (2008–12) allows us to measure much the same five issue categories, although packaged in a slightly different way. Overall, we sort issues into two kinds, valence vs. positional, a classification scheme established by the classic paper of Stokes (1963). Valence issues distinguish themselves by achieving a consensus of public opinion, i.e., everyone agrees on the outcome. For example, virtually all voters favor a prosperous economy, safe streets, and a corruption-free bureaucracy. Positional issues, in contrast, show considerable discord in public opinion, i.e., there exists wide disagreement over policy. For example, voters favor different levels of tax progressivity, neighborhood policing, or bureaucratic oversight. In sum, valence issues stress the evaluation of performance, while positional issues stress the evaluation of policy. Leading treatments of these issue types in the literature discuss whether valence issues dominate positional ones, or vice-versa (Fiorina 1981; Clarke et al. 2004).

This question of the importance of valence versus positional issues shall be examined here, as constrained by the data available. Measuring across all 18 nations, we are able to assemble data on four valence issues and two positional issues. With regard to the former, we examine the state of the economy, corruption, crime, and democracy. With regard to the latter, we examine the state's intervention in the economics of the private sector and in limiting free speech. Let us consider the valence issues, starting with the economy, which we feature. This economics measure bases itself on the respondent's sociotropic retrospective evaluation (labeled SRE) of the performance of the national economy (Fiorina 1981; Key 1966; Kinder and Kiewiet 1981; Lewis-Beck 1988). Our corruption measure (labeled Corruption) comes from respondent assessment of the extent to which the current administration combats corruption, on a seven-point scale (from "not at all" to "a lot"). The level of crime measure (labeled Safety) derives from a similar measure, which asks about what is being done to improve citizen safety. Finally, we measure how well democratic procedures and principles are being fostered by the government in power. This item, which also has a seven-point scale, we label Democracy. In sum, we analyze the impact of these four issues: National Economy, Corruption, Safety, and Democracy. (For details on the measurement of these and the other issue measures, see appendix 4.)

Turning to the positional issues, we look first at state intervention (labeled State). This distinction, which offers a second economic dimension, conforms with our ongoing desire to test valence economic evaluations versus positional economic evaluations (Lewis-Beck and Nadeau 2011). The State variable is built from three scales tapping the degree to which the respondent favors greater government intervention in the private sector. Our second issue variable here, which measures government constraints on freedom of speech, allows a further test of the valence versus positional dimensions—namely, democratic rights versus authoritarianism. This Authoritarianism variable (labeled AUTH) is built from a seven-point scale, asking respondents their agreement with government checks on the "voice and vote of opposition parties." The role of authoritarianism seems especially important to explore, given the emergence of national leaders who have used, and perhaps have had used against them, unconstitutional tactics, e.g., Chavez, Correa, Kirchner, Morales, and Zelaya (see the relevant discussion in Weyland, de la Torres, and Kornblith 2013).

These six issues, some valence and some positional, would appear to resonate for broad sectors of the Latin American publics. Further, they are "easy" issues, i.e., they have evocative meaning and are not technical, having been part of the national political discussion for a considerable period. (On "easy" versus "hard" issues, see Carmines and Stimson [1980].) Certainly, they are important issues, and tend toward the top of issue lists for this region. We would expect them to affect vote choice, independent of other forces. It is that expectation we now explore.

## The Multivariate Model for the Eighteen Nations

In words, our multivariate model for block four, the last in our block recursive causal system, reads as follows:

Vote = $f$(demographics, socioeconomics, political anchors, issues)   (5.1)

The variables of demographics (SDEM), socioeconomics (SECN), and anchors (PID and ideology) are as measured in the previous chapters. To these variables are now added six issues (ISSUES). Specifically, we add four valence issues (national economy, corruption, crime, democratic rights), and two positional issues (state economic intervention and government limits on speech). We begin with analysis for the entire (18 nation) region, then look selectively at individual nations. Below, we discuss the effects of these six issues in turn. We begin with valence issues, giving pride of place to the economy, the most studied of these issues.

### Valence Issues: Economic Voting

Research on classic economic voting has made the greatest advances in the high-income democracies. (For reviews, see Duch 2007; Hellwig 2010; Lewis-Beck and Stegmaier 2000, 2007; Stegmaier and Lewis-Beck 2013.) This body of work consistently reports statistically, and usually substantively, significant effects, whereby voters punish the government for bad economic performance, and reward it for good. Research on the lower-income democracies remains less plentiful. However, a recent review essay, in looking at these regions (including Latin America), shows that virtually every study undertaken demonstrates the standard result: significant economic voting (Lewis-Beck and Stegmaier 2008). Further, in his global study of classical economic voting, which includes nations from all the major lower-income regions, Gélineau (2013) finds a clear pattern of statistical significance in the expected direction.

Economic voting work on Latin American democracies per se does exist, and it consistently suggests the economy has an electoral tie (see the helpful review by Remmer and Gélineau 2003). Scattered individual-nation studies generally show a significant economic effect. Here is a sampling of post-2000 country studies of economic voting: Argentina (Remmer and Gélineau 2003); Mexico (Moreno 2009); Nicaragua (Anderson, Lewis-Beck, and Stegmaier 2003); Peru (Arce and Carrion 2010); and Venezuela (Weyland 2003; Nadeau, Bélanger, and Didier 2013). Valuable as these studies are, they explore different dependent political measures (e.g., vote versus popularity) and different independent economic measures (e.g., subjective versus objective). Further, the assessment of effects tends to differ in terms of source (pocketbook or nation) and timeline (retrospective or prospective). On top of these inconsistencies, they focus on just one country, one case.

Fortunately, there have been some pooled studies, looking at subsets of Latin American nations (Benton 2005; Echegaray 2005; Gélineau 2007; Johnson and Schwindt-Bayer 2009; Remmer 1991). Pooled analyses have tended to confirm the classic economic voting idea of reward for good performance and punishment for bad performance. For example, in the first of these studies, Remmer (1991, 311), looking at 21 Latin American presidential elections (1982–90), concludes that her "results provide some support for the view that incumbents pay the price for short-term economic setbacks." Benton (2005), following up, examines 39 presidential elections (1980–2003) from 13 Latin American nations. She finds sharp economic effects, with a 1.0 percentage point drop in GDP per capita generating a 1.7 percentage point drop in the incumbent party vote (Benton 2005, 430).

The pooled results provide encouraging evidence for the economic voter hypothesis. However, there are disagreements. First, what macroeconomic indicators count? Second, are the economic effects contingent? With respect to the first, Remmer (1991) finds inflation to be the important macroeconomic variable, as do Johnson and Schwindt-Bayer (2009). In contrast, Benton (2005) finds it is economic growth that counts. Taking another direction, Johnson and Ryu (2010) argue that growth and inflation both matter. In a current attempt at resolution, Singer (2013) addresses both of these questions. Using a comprehensive aggregate dataset (18 countries and 79 elections, 1982–2010), he finds an economic vote driven by both inflation and GDP growth (Singer 2013, 177). However, these effects are contingent, with inflation only significant for the 1982–89 and 1990–99 periods, and GDP growth only significant for the 2000–2010 period. He concludes that "this analysis provides further evidence that the economy's impact is context contingent" (Singer 2013, 181).

Since, after all, voting decisions are taken by individual citizens, it seems the above questions regarding the "if, how, and when" of the economic vote should ultimately be answered via microanalysis of national survey data. However, such survey investigations for the region are scare, especially those that have a pooled design and are cross-national and cross-time (and so parallel the above aggregate studies). Lewis-Beck and Ratto (2013) did carry out such an exercise, examining a pool of national Latinobarometer surveys from 12 Latin American democracies (1996–2004). They conclude that "the finding is of highly significant, even strong, sociotropic retrospective economic effects on the incumbent vote" (Lewis-Beck and Ratto 2013, abstract).

This Lewis-Beck and Ratto (2013) result has value, suggesting that, across the Latin American region, individual voters do indeed react to economic conditions when making their electoral choices. Such a finding offers a useful counter to the serious argument that the aggregate results reported above are mere products of the ecological fallacy, reflecting only spurious macroconnections (Robinson 1950). However, it does not speak to problems raised by the foregoing Singer (2013) study, i.e., which economic conditions are important, and when? More pointedly, the Lewis-Beck and Ratto study rests on an earlier time period (1996–2004), a period for which Singer reports the dominance of inflation. It barely touches the latter period that Singer identifies, when growth dominates (2000–2010). Furthermore, there are some troubling methodological aspects of the Lewis-Beck and Ratto (2013) study. For one, the national samples for certain surveys are quite small (sometimes just 300). For another, the voting model appears too sparse in its specification (e.g., issues other than the economy are not included). For yet another, the central control variable of party identification has an idiosyncratic measure (based on "trust in the president" for 2000 and 2004).

In sum, the foregoing pooled efforts have worth. However, these aggregate and survey studies, while showing steady improvements in design, still exhibit fundamental shortcomings when the object is to generalize across the region about the effects of the economy on elections. By way of contrast, the work of Gélineau and Singer (2015) overcomes many of these obstacles, analyzing multiple recent LatinoBarometer and AmericasBarometer surveys, with analysis techniques different from ours (i.e., two-stage hierarchical modeling). In their comprehensive chapter in *The Latin American Voter*, they conclude that "[t]he economy has a large effect because voters consider the economy an important political issue and believe politicians are responsible for economic outcomes" (Gélineau and Singer 2015, 282). We expect a similar result, showing that contemporary Latin American voters reliably sanction their governments when they fail to deliver on the economy. In pursuit of these aims, we carried out logistic regression analyses on this large pool of Latin American national voting surveys, which we discuss further below.

## Valence Results: Economic Voting

The independent economic variable, sociotropic retrospective evaluations of the national economy, takes the label SRE. We are encouraged to examine these multivariate results because of the initial strength of the simple association between economic perception and incumbent vote (where tau-b = .26). The percentage differences tell a vivid story. Region-wide, when respondents saw the economy as "worse," only 37% expressed support for the government. In contrast, when they saw the economy as "better," fully 75% expressed support for the government.

The question at hand, then, is whether this strong economic–elections connection continues in the face of heavy multivariate controls, such as those imposed in table 5.1, column 5. The overall performance of this model shows promise. Explained variance reaches a pseudo-$R^2$ = 0.51, with 79.2% of the cases correctly predicted, and all issues variables displaying statistically significant coefficients in the expected sign. SRE, our economic issue variable of prime concern for now, continues strongly linked to incumbent support, with a logistic regression coefficient of .88, easily achieving significance at the 0.01 level. This secure economic voting effect is found despite the inclusion of an extensive set of controls. (Interestingly, this SRE coefficient is not far from the value recently found in a pooled analysis of 10 European countries [Nadeau, Lewis-Beck, and Bélanger 2013, table 1, column 6].) These findings thus provide a firm basis for the claim that economic voting can be observed in Latin America, operating as in most established democracies.

Perhaps the SRE coefficient itself is not stable, varying across countries. For instance, maybe the apparent overall economic voting effect derives from only a few of the countries in the pool. However, when we test for this possibility by estimating the SRE parameter in each separate country, we see that it is always in the expected direction, and statistically significant (at .01 and beyond) in all but two (Costa Rica and Honduras). The median coefficient value, across these 18 nations, equals .84. Of course, variation exists around that central tendency (see column 5, in the relevant tables A2.3–A2.37, in appendix 2). In addition to the low values for Brazil

TABLE 5.1. Logistic Regression Models for Voting Intentions in 18 Latin American Countries (LAPOP 2008, 2010, 2012)

| | (1) | (2) | (3) | (4) | (5) |
|---|---|---|---|---|---|
| Months | -1.03** | -1.11** | -1.14** | -.94** | -.65** |
| | (.04) | (.04) | (.05) | (.06) | (.07) |
| Age | — | .13** | .15** | .19** | .03 |
| | | (.04) | (.05) | (.07) | (.08) |
| Gender | — | .06** | .07** | .05 | .01 |
| | | (.02) | (.02) | (.03) | (.03) |
| Catholic | — | .17** | 18** | .08** | .08* |
| | | (.02) | (.02) | (.03) | (.03) |
| Church attendance | — | .22** | .25** | .14** | .13** |
| | | (.03) | (.03) | (.04) | (.04) |
| Region | — | .04 | -.06** | -.05 | -.06* |
| | | (.02) | (.02) | (.03) | (.03) |
| Race | — | .37** | .27** | .19** | .15** |
| | | (.03) | (.03) | (.04) | (.05) |
| Schooling | — | | -.00 | .07 | .01 |
| | | | (.03) | (.04) | (.04) |
| Income | — | — | .17** | .16** | .11* |
| | | | (.04) | (.05) | (.05) |
| Unemployment | — | — | -.12** | -.19** | -.09* |
| | | | (.03) | (.04) | (.04) |
| Public sector | — | — | -.04 | -.04 | .05 |
| | | | (.03) | (.04) | (.05) |
| Property | — | — | .35** | .32** | .23** |
| | | | (.06) | (.08) | (.08) |
| Ideology | — | — | — | 1.18** | .91** |
| | | | | (.05) | (.05) |
| Party identification | — | — | — | 4.00** | 3.70** |
| | | | | (.05) | (.05) |
| State | — | — | — | — | .32** |
| | | | | | (.06) |
| AUTH | — | — | — | — | -.23** |
| | | | | | (.04) |
| Safety | — | — | — | — | .68** |
| | | | | | (.07) |
| Corruption | — | — | — | — | .94** |
| | | | | | (.07) |
| Democracy | — | — | — | — | 1.05** |
| | | | | | (.07) |
| SRE | — | — | — | — | 0.88** |
| | | | | | (.04) |
| Constant | .28** | -.22* | -.28** | -2.73** | -4.25** |
| | (.05) | (.06) | (.07) | (.10) | (.12) |
| Nagelkerke pseudo-$R^2$ | .097 | .105 | .11 | .43 | .51 |
| % correctly predicted | 61.5% | 63.0% | 63.4% | 75.7% | 79.2% |
| $N$ | 52,489 | 51,394 | 45,332 | 38,363 | 35,820 |

**p ≤ .01; *p ≤ .05 (two-tailed tests). Mexico is the reference case for country dummies. (Dummy coefficients not shown). Entries are unstandardized logistic regression coefficients, with standard errors in parentheses. See appendix 4 for variable's specification.

(equal to .44), Costa Rica (equal to .31), and Honduras (equal to .05), we see some values that well exceed 1.00. At the extreme high end are the Dominican Republic and Uruguay (equal to 1.34), and Venezuela (equal to 2.27). It may well be that these (and perhaps other countries with high values on this sociotropic variable) are subject to especially strong economic pressures. This idea, which leads to the testing for possible interaction effects, is explored further in chapter 6.

A final concern, with regard to the SRE estimate, is the endogeneity problem. Some have argued that individual perceptions about the state of the national economy can be endogenous to vote choice (e.g., Evans and Andersen 2006). That is, an individual who supports the incumbent candidate may hold a more optimistic view of recent national economic conditions, compared to an individual who supports the opposition candidate. As a precaution, therefore, we imposed an extensive set of controls, including past voting and ideology and party identification; further, we applied an instrumental variables analysis (Nadeau et al. 2015b). These controls amount to various "exogeneity tests," which the SRE estimate survives. As a final, general point, we would also note that our work on this endogeneity problem for democratic elections in other regions of the world, namely North America and western Europe, shows that, if anything, the sociotropic measure, in its routine standard use, actually underestimates the effects of economic voting (see, respectively, Lewis-Beck, Nadeau, and Elias 2008; and Nadeau, Bélanger, and Lewis-Beck 2013).

## Economic Voting and Government Accountability

The question of economic voting in Latin America has value for normative, as well as scientific, reasons. If, in the lower-income democracies such as those of Latin America, governments escape sanction for economic downturns, then prospects for serious improvement of everyday living conditions are dim. But, if governments are punished at the ballot box for bad economic performance, then they have an incentive to improve the material well-being of the citizenry. What do our results show? First, the governments under study generally face vote loss when the public perceives poor economic performance. This finding appears unambiguously, according to the statistical significance tests. However, in itself it may not be enough of an incentive to alter policy. As we know, a finding may be statistically significant but substantively trivial.

What, then, do our findings show substantively? Granting that an economic voting effect exists, is its magnitude great enough to seriously threaten governments with defeat? Fortunately, we can estimate the usual magnitude of that effect. According to our simulation (see table 5.2, column 5), which assumes all other variables stay at their mean value, the probability of supporting an incumbent increases by 13 percentage points when the voter's economic evaluation goes from negative to positive (i.e., from "gotten worse" to "gotten better"). Hence, given the rather volatile state of national economies in Latin American countries, the economic perceptions of voters can certainly affect the reelection prospects of presidents in this less well-off region of the world.

What are the limits of this substantively important electoral effect of economic voting in Latin America? Is it general, or does it depend on particular conditions? We can explore the question of dependency in

TABLE 5.2. Change in Probabilities for Voting Intentions in 18 Latin American Countries (LAPOP 2008, 2010, 2012)

| | (1) | (2) | (3) | (4) | (5) |
|---|---|---|---|---|---|
| Months | −.24** | −.25** | −.26** | −.15** | −.10** |
| Age | — | .03** | .03** | .03** | .01 |
| Gender | — | .01** | .02** | .01 | .00 |
| Catholic | — | .04** | .04** | .01** | .01** |
| Church attendance | — | .05** | .06** | .02** | .02** |
| Region | — | .01 | −.01** | −.01* | −.01* |
| Race | — | .08** | .06** | .03** | .02** |
| Schooling | — | — | −.00 | .01 | .00 |
| Income | — | — | .04** | .03** | .01* |
| Unemployment | — | — | −.03** | −.03** | −.01* |
| Public sector | — | — | −.01 | −.01 | .01 |
| Property | — | — | .08** | .05** | .04** |
| Ideology | — | — | — | .19** | .13** |
| Party identification | — | — | — | .65** | .54** |
| State | — | — | — | — | .05** |
| AUTH | — | — | — | — | −.03** |
| Safety | — | — | — | — | .10** |
| Corruption | — | — | — | — | .14** |
| Democracy | — | — | — | — | .15** |
| SRE | — | — | — | — | .13** |
| N | 52,489 | 51,394 | 45,332 | 38,363 | 35,820 |

**p ≤ .01; *p ≤ .05 (two-tailed tests). Mexico is the reference case for country dummies. (Dummy coefficients not shown.) Entries represent change in probabilities. See appendix 4 for variable's specification.

two ways: time dependency and country dependency. With respect to time, the study at hand looks at a period (2008–12) that is contemporary, but narrow. Recall that the pooled survey study of Lewis-Beck and Ratto (2013) looks at an earlier period (1996–2004). If they find clearly different effects from ours, it would suggest a time dependency. But they do not. In a simulation comparable to ours, they find the probability of an incumbent vote increases by as much as 21 percentage points, a result not that far from what we get. In other words, at least across these two time periods, an economic assessment of "worse" has a nontrivial effect. Of course, the macrocomponents dominating that assessment of "worse," e.g., inflation vs. growth, may be different from period to period, as Singer (2013) makes clear. This suggests that voters, after all, weigh multiple macrocomponents in arriving at an overall, comprehensive judgment about the state of the economy.

## Valence Issues: Noneconomic Ones

It may seem lopsided to group the valence issues into the economic and the noneconomic. But the noneconomic generally have less reach, country to country. Nevertheless, in the entire pool each of these other valence issues—corruption, democracy, safety—handily achieves a high level of statistical significance. Further, region-wide, they achieve moderate associations (tau-b) with the vote choice, i.e., respectively, .33, .33, and .31. These results assure us as to their general importance. Furthermore, they are conceptually united, in that they are all valence issues. Latin American voters appear to want these issues effectively dealt with by their governments, and they tend to punish them with an opposition vote if the goods are not delivered.

At the national level, as opposed to the regional, the pattern appears a bit less consistent, suggesting the need to examine these noneconomic valence issues one at a time. Let us begin with the issue of safety, or crime, a matter of some moment in the minds of Latin American voters (Pérez 2003). First, it should be recognized that there are not many relevant studies. Some national investigations have looked at the link between political violence and government popularity, e.g., on Peru and Colombia (see, respectively, Arce 2003; Holmes and Amin Gutiérrez de Piñeres 2003). More directly, there are a few studies examining the effects that crime has on electoral choice, but they are not at the regional level. Finally, it is known that Latin American citizens generally fear crime, and that may be unsurprising (Quann and Hung 2002).

But fear of being a crime victim does not necessarily translate into an electoral response, whereby governments are punished. National studies that have tried to explicitly tie crime victimization to a vote yield mostly negative results (Bateson 2012; Carreras 2013). Thus, personal assault, as bad as it is, does not seem to reach the ballot box unless there is a public policy link. For instance, I might see that the crime in my neighborhood could be reduced by more frequent police patrols. In that case, I would more likely vote for a party that promised safer streets. That is to say, my response becomes "sociotropic," seeking public collective action to solve the issue of rising crime (Kiewiet and Lewis-Beck 2012). That response lies at the bottom of our generally positive results, which indicate that voters want governments that make the streets safer, and will tend to vote for them.

Still, that response—a vote in favor of administrations providing more safety—was not statistically significant in 9 of the region's countries (Argentina, Brazil, Chile, Costa Rica, Ecuador, Honduras, Nicaragua, Panama, and Paraguay). (See column 5 in the relevant tables A2.3–A2.37, in appendix 2.) What do these results mean? First, it implies that, for at least some of these countries, crime is less salient. Four of these 9 nations— Argentina, Chile, Costa Rica, Paraguay—do have relatively low homicide rates (per 100,000), as reported in the data of the United Nations (Office of Drugs and Crime 2012): each has a homicide rate under 10.0, whereas the median for the entire 18 equals 14.4. Overall, however, the homicide rate, a supposedly objective measure, correlates only weakly with our subjective measure, the perception of government performance. For example, looking at the top 10 countries in terms of the homicide rate, five have above the overall average perception of safety performance (Ecuador, Colombia, the Dominican Republic, Mexico, Nicaragua), but the other five are below average in perception of safety performance (Honduras, Venezuela, Guatemala, Brazil, Peru).

The empirical disconnect between these two measures invites further consideration of the wording of the question, which assesses "the extent the current administration improves citizen safety." Perhaps in these particular nine countries where the safety question fails to be significantly related to vote intention, the voters overall tend not to believe that their current administration has effective policies for improving public safety. The survey data do support such an argument. For this nine-country subset, the mean performance value = .44, on a 0–1 scale. On average, then, these citizens are in fact slightly negative in their performance evaluation. Recall, in our list of conditions for an issue to influence party choice, that the voter must perceive that the parties can make a difference. In this subset of nations, it would appear that most voters believe that government crime-fighting efforts, regardless of the political stripe of the party, have been less than effective. Or, relatedly, the difference it may make lacks strength, and thus gets crowded out by other issues where they see more movement.

Those other issues might include the other two noneconomic concerns we examine: democratic performance and control of corruption. These two issues both deal with the effective and fair functioning of the traditional state apparatus, and they clearly have more traction than the safety question. Both usually manage statistical significance, and in the expected direction (14 out of 18 countries on the democracy issue, 13 out of 18 on the corruption issue). (See column 5 in the relevant tables A2.3–A2.37, in appendix 2.) Voters value "good government" and "democratic rights," and are more likely to reward government candidates who deliver these goods. Let us first look at corruption. A sociotropic effect similar to that found for the safety issue shows up, with more perceived corruption encouraging a vote against the government. Whether this effect varies, depending on other factors, has been explored via examination of different interactions, especially with variables related to the economy. A provocative finding from this work concerns the role of corruption in more open economies. Apparently, when compared to more closed economies, these more open nations exhibit a greater likelihood of voting for the incumbent despite corruption. This suggests that voters there may be more forgiving, because they see that the government, under the condition of a more porous economy, can do less about the corruption they observe. (See the investigations, respectively, of Manzetti and Wilson 2006 and Zechmeister and Zizumbo-Colunga 2013.)

While these potential interactions with corruption should not be ignored, our concern here rests on diagnosing its main effect on incumbent support. We see that it carries a positive coefficient in every nation but one. However, there exist big variations from country to country. For example, the effect in Bolivia (1.63) is about twice the effect in Brazil (at .82). (See, respectively, table A2.5 and A2.7 in appendix 2.) Still, corruption effects are pervasive, and in brute terms, across the region, its probability of change estimate exceeds slightly that of the economy, .14 versus .13, respectively (see column 5 in table 5.2). Indeed, it appears as a valence issue par excellence, but in the realm of public morality rather than public economics.

The noneconomic issue we have not yet really talked about concerns the protection of democratic rights, a topic of lively concern in these mostly new democracies. Such protections are related to the performance on other issues, such as those of crime and corruption, which we have just examined. Indeed, across the region, the three performance dimensions of corruption, democracy, and safety are highly correlated, with an average r = .67. Thus, to the extent a Latin American government performs well on one of these dimensions, it tends to do so on the others. In a general way, then, they are joined together, in the regional representation crisis that at least some have observed (Mainwaring et al. 2006). Different researchers have also demonstrated that increased insecurity poses a threat to democratic values (Beirne 1997; Howard, Newman, and Pridemore 2000; Pérez 2011; Prillaman 2003). Further, the breakdown of law and order, and the inability of the courts to administer justice, helps undermine aspiring democratic Latin American governments (Wilkinson 1986). Of course, some come to attach such values to the proper working of democracy itself. In the results here we do observe that, in the region as a whole, when incumbents are perceived to foster more democratic protections, they experience a significant gain in votes. Moreover, the magnitude of this coefficient carries a positive sign in every country under study.

## Positional Issues: State Intervention and Free Speech

Given the dominant place of the national economy on the Latin American issue agenda, it seemed appropriate to begin our discussion of valence issues there. Now, we turn to economics as a positional issue (i.e., opinion arrayed along a dimension) rather than as a valence issue (i.e., opinion concentrated at a single value along a dimension). While valence economic voting has been the subject of something like 500 books and papers, positional economic voting has only seen a handful of publications (Lewis-Beck and Nadeau 2011; Stegmaier and Lewis-Beck 2013). Furthermore, given its Downsian flavor, some might argue that it is not really independent of voting along a left-right dimension. For example, a link between an increasing preference for progressive taxation and left party voting may merely reflect the voter's general identification with the ideological left.

However, in fact, for the few studies carried out, attitudes toward progressive taxation (and attitudes on other economic policy issues, such as government regulation) have been found to exert an influence separate from general left-right ideology (Lewis-Beck and Nadeau 2009; Foucault, Lewis-Beck, and Nadeau 2011). These Anglo-Saxon findings repeat themselves for Spain, which is culturally closer to Latin America (Fraile and Lewis-Beck 2010). Thus, we are encouraged to examine the impact of our State variable (measuring preference for government intervention in the market) on vote choice (for or against the government).

In table 5.1, column 5, as noted, we have our model of Equation 5.1 estimated for the entire region. We observe that the logistic regression coefficient for the State variable = .32, positive and highly significant ($p >$ .01). This suggests that, quite apart from voters' general left-right ideological identification (which is controlled), when they are more prostate, i.e., in favor of government intervention in the economy, they are more likely to vote for a leftist government.

Of course, results vary by country, as tables A2.3–A2.37 reveal (see column 5, appendix 2). Nevertheless, the support for the State hypothesis appears quite weak once a country-by-country analysis becomes the focus. While 13 of the 18 countries carry coefficients with the expected sign (plus), 5 do not. Moreover, only two of these correctly signed coefficients are statistically significant, i.e., for Chile and El Salvador. Among those with an unexpected (negative) sign, only one reaches significance (perhaps a random result given $N = 18$ countries). On balance, it appears that, while positional economic voting clearly exists in a few of these nations, for the other nations the pattern appears faint at best. At least as measured here, the concept of state economic intervention would seem to be absorbed into the more general left-right dimension, which operates as an important force in most of these countries.

However, this is not the last word. Baker and Greene (2011) have argued that Latin American voters, in general, vote their policy preferences. They go on to look specifically at positional economic preferences, with these same 18 countries, and employing AmericasBarometer data as well. In contrast to our results, they find that 14 of the 18 countries show significant positional economic effects (Baker and Greene 2015). We find these results heartening, and attribute their greater strength to methodological differences between our two studies. For example, they looked at partial correlations between respondent self-placement on a state dimension and placement of their party preference on a left-right dimension. We, in contrast, employ a left-right self-placement measure directly in our regression equation, as a control variable. These differences offer an opportunity for further exploration of this promising avenue for future economic voting research.

Let us look now at the impact of our second positional issue, that of attitudes toward government limiting freedoms of voice and vote for the opposition. We see (in table 5.1, column 5) that this Authoritarianism variable carries a negative coefficient (–.23), meaning that those favoring more restrictions on freedom of speech are more likely to support left-wing incumbents, such as Chavez, Morales, or Correa. This coefficient, while easily statistically significant for the region as a whole, has a fascinating pattern of variability, when the country-by-country results are examined (see column 5 in the relevant tables A2.3–A2.37, in appendix 2). One-half of the coefficients carry positive signs, and the other half carry negative signs. This suggests, interestingly, that attitudes toward government suppression of free speech can push voters either direction, to a left incumbent or a right incumbent. When we look at the pattern of statistical significance, we see a bit of evidence for this. There are five statistically significant coefficients, with four in the direction of favoring a left incumbent (Argentina, Bolivia, Ecuador, Uruguay) but another favoring a right incumbent (Colombia). An implication is that authoritarianism, viewed as an electoral force, acts as a special trigger for left-wing populism. (Most recently, Weyland, de la Torres, and Kornblith [2013] has made such an argument. We pursue this perspective more fully in the next chapter.)

The inclusion of the authoritarianism variable, relatively new in such analyses, carries with it several benefits. First, it taps an unheralded dimension in voting behavior studies in Latin America. Second, it adds a second positional dimension to the model, one on the democratic value of free speech. It must be said that these dimensions—government economic intervention and limitations on free speech—cover a lot of debated political ground in Latin America. Third, it adds another positional versus valence test to stand beside the economic one.

## Valence and Positional Issues: Their Comparative Impact on Vote Choice

How does the electoral impact of positional issues compare to valence issues? We can begin to answer this question because we have multiple measures. Unfortunately, we do not have as many positional measures as we would like. Still, we have two important positional measures: state intervention and authoritarianism. Let us compare their effects to those of our four valence issues: economy, safety, corruption, and democracy. First, we examine the pattern of statistical significance (.05 or greater, two-tail) on a country-by-country basis. The two positional issues achieve that level of significance only 3 of 18 times (for the State variable), and 5 of 18 times (for the AUTH variable). By way of contrast, the four valence issues achieve that level of significance 9 of 18 times (for the Safety variable), 13 of 18 times (for the Corruption variable), 14 of 18 times (for the Democracy variable), and 16 of 18 times (for the SRE variable). (To confirm these counts, see column 5, in the relevant tables A2.3–A2.37, in Appendix 2.)

In sum, when we look at the individual country results, the positional issues are mostly not significant, while the valence issues mostly are. This result, although lopsided, does help explain the reported neglect of behavioral studies of voting examining the impact of positional issues, as compared to valence ones (Clarke et al. 2004: Kiewiet 1983; Lewis-Beck and Nadeau 2011). The relatively greater strength of the valence issues persists when we look at the change in vote probabilities these variables can induce in Latin America as a whole (see column 5, table 5.2). In the entire region, the positional variables of State and AUTH do manage statistically significant probability changes (at .01). However, these probability changes are small, with values of .05 and .03, respectively. Moreover, these effects appear dwarfed when compared to the statistically significant, and substantively greater, probability shifts from the four valence issues: Safety (at .10), Corruption (at .14), Democracy (at .15), and SRE (at .13).

Another way of comparing the impact of positional versus valence issues comes from a visual assessment of the estimated probability changes in a country-by-country analysis (see figs. 5.1–5.6). As a guide, take as a substantive cutoff a probability change estimated value of .05 or greater. The State variable passes this threshold only eight times in the expected (positive) direction (fig. 5.1). The Authoritarianism variable makes this cutoff 10 times, but their signs are roughly split in half, with 4 positive

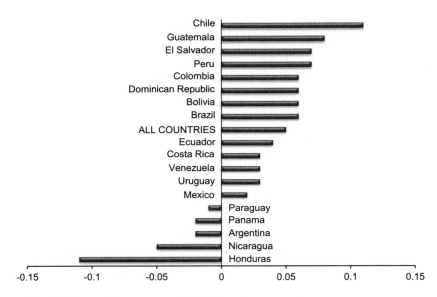

Fig. 5.1. Impact of State among 18 Latin American countries
*Note:* Entries in the graph are the change in probabilities coefficients adjusted for other variables in the same model (LAPOP 2008, 2010, and 2012 data).

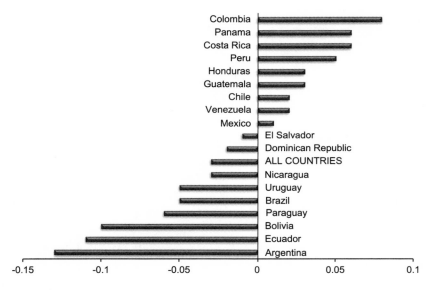

Fig. 5.2. Impact of Authoritarianism among 18 Latin American countries
*Note:* Entries in the graph are the change in probabilities coefficients adjusted for other variables in the same model (LAPOP 2008, 2010, and 2012 data).

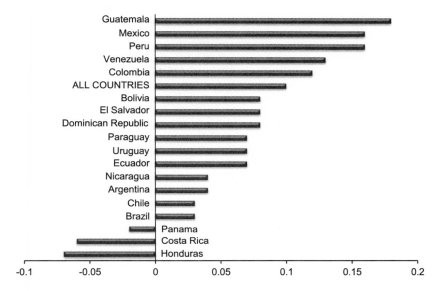

Fig. 5.3. Impact of Safety among 18 Latin American countries

*Note:* Entries in the graph are the change in probabilities coefficients adjusted for other variables in the same model (LAPOP 2008, 2010, and 2012 data).

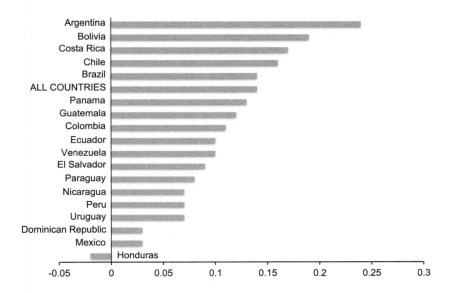

Fig. 5.4. Impact of Corruption among 18 Latin American countries

*Note:* Entries in the graph are the change in probabilities coefficients adjusted for other variables in the same model (LAPOP 2008, 2010, and 2012 data).

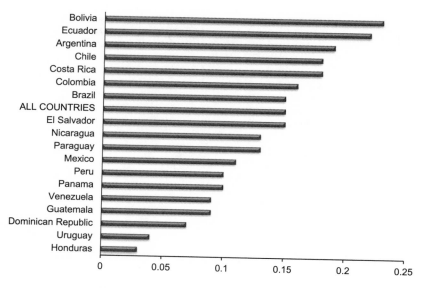

Fig. 5.5. Impact of Democracy among 18 Latin American countries
*Note:* Entries in the graph are the change in probabilities coefficients adjusted for other variables in the same model (LAPOP 2008, 2010, and 2012 data).

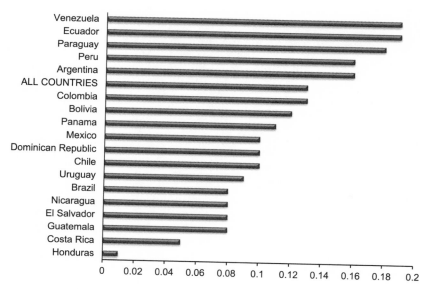

Fig. 5.6. Impact of SRE among 18 Latin American countries
*Note:* Entries in the graph are the change in probabilities coefficients adjusted for other variables in the same model (LAPOP 2008, 2010, and 2012 data).

and 6 negative (fig. 5.2). Turning to the valence issue of safety, it attains this benchmark 11 times in the expected (positive) direction (fig. 5.3). Moreover, the remaining valence issues—corruption, democracy, and the economy—almost invariably exercise an important probability shift in favor of the incumbent, irrespective of the nation under consideration: corruption meets the cutoff 15 times, democracy 16 times, the economy 17 times, each time in the expected direction (fig. 5.4–5.6). Clearly, valence issues dominate position issues in shaping the Latin American vote, at least as they are measured here.

## Issues: Their Cumulative Impact on Vote Choice in Latin America

Now let us ask a more general question: What does the consideration of all our issues, valence or positional, add to our understanding of how the Latin American voter decides? One answer comes from examination of the increment to explained variance they provide, when added into the final vote choice model. In the entire 18-nation pool, we observe that the pseudo-$R^2$ rises, substantially, from .43 to .51, when our six issues are added to the model (see table 5.1, columns 4 and 5). Moreover, while this added increment changes from country to country, it generally manages to provide an important increment (see the relevant tables A2.3–A2.37, columns 4 and 5, in appendix 2). For Argentina and Ecuador, at one extreme, it actually adds an increment of .14. (This addition for Argentina seems especially noteworthy, given that the model lacks an explicit measure of Peronism. Still, the final Argentinian model manages a fit of .49 [see table A2.3 in appendix 2]. For more on these data and the Argentinian case, see Nadeau et al. 2015a.) For Honduras, at the other extreme, virtually nothing appears to be added, with an increment that rounds to .00. (Interestingly, the single relevant issue there may be the state intervention variable, for it shows statistical significance in the final model, which registers a respectable explained variance of .57; see table A2.23 in appendix 2). The typical contribution to the variance explained, country by country, can be measured by median increment at .055. This substantively meaningful increase confirms the notion that issues are important for vote choice in Latin America nations.

## Conclusion

While economic voting has been vigorously studied, the work has been confined mostly to high-income democracies in North America and western Europe. With respect to lower-income democracies, economic voting research remains scattered, although somewhat more concentrated in Latin America. These efforts suggest an economics and elections connection in that region, although the research designs employed have been less advanced, consisting mostly of single-country studies, more often than not based on aggregate data. There are a few pooled investigations, based on samples (or subsamples) of Latin American nations. The leading studies of this kind pool data, almost always at the aggregate level, from a dozen or more countries. Overwhelmingly, they demonstrate that changing macroeconomic conditions relate to changing electoral outcomes for incumbent parties or candidates.

These aggregate pooled results offer support for the classic economic voting hypothesis of reward and punishment, at least insofar as they can. However, they pose difficulties when the individual vote choice itself receives consideration. What economic variables attract voter attention? Over what time horizon? How strong are the effects? Are these effects conditional? Unstable? Such questions may receive firmer answers from analysis of data that pools individuals, as well as nations. Pooled election surveys, across several nations, are quite rare for Latin America. Lewis-Beck and Ratto (2013) employ Latinobarometer surveys from 12 nations (1996–2004). The book chapter on the economy in *The Latin American Voter*, by Gélineau and Singer (2015), pools Latinobarometer and Americas Barometer data. Finally, the chapter at hand employs AmericasBarometer surveys from 18 nations and covers the period 2008–2012.

Applying a richly specified model of voting behavior to these LAPOP data, the economic vote signal comes through loud and clear. Sociotropic retrospective economic evaluations have a statistically and substantively significant impact on vote choice in the democracies of this region. Voters appear to evaluate different economic indicators, weigh them, and arrive at an overall assessment of how the economy has been doing. When they assess last year's national economy as "better," rather than "worse," their probability of an incumbent vote increases 13 percentage points on average. That effect, which survives a rigorous battery of tests, is far from trivial, and can topple governments. It operates first as a general additive influence, persisting across nations and across time, with a substantial and more or less regular intensity. Besides this steady influence of the economic vote, it may be even more intense under certain extreme economic conditions. This is a valuable scientific conclusion, indicating that economic voting works in the lower-income democracies of Latin America pretty much as it does in the high-income democracies elsewhere. Furthermore, it is a valuable political conclusion, suggesting that governments in resource-constrained democracies such as these cannot escape punishment for bad economic policy. In the end, the people will have their say, in pushing their leaders to provide for better material conditions for themselves and their families.

Besides classical economic voting, we also found evidence of positional voting, where voters punish or reward government performance according to their policy preferences with regard to state intervention regulating the private economy or free speech. Still, this evidence is not as easily sorted out. Apparently, while these preferences do exist, they are subsumed, in part, by the voters' general ideological identification left or right. But, also, another part may be due to measurement differences from the work of other researchers on positional economic voting in Latin America. In terms of the second positional issue, that of preferences for government limits on free speech for the opposition, the pattern appears complex, with left-wing populism sometimes generating significant curbs on freedom for the opposition. This, a topic for further research, is taken up in the next chapter.

While the valence issue of the national economy stands out in importance, it is by no means the whole story. Valenced, noneconomic issues push Latin American voters hard in the direction of voting against the government when valued public goods are not delivered. What are these public goods? Those we have addressed here include safe streets, fair rule, and democratic rights. The last, democratic protections and procedures, seem especially valued. This comes as no surprise, given that democracy represents new growth in most of Latin America. Also, without a healthy democracy, it becomes difficult to fight crime and corruption. These issues significantly influence the fate of governing parties in the region, independent of the potent vibrations emanating from the economy itself. Overall, issues, whether economic or noneconomic, matter substantially for vote choice in the nations of this region. Any explanatory models that ignore them will poorly serve the budding theories of political behavior being applied to Latin American democracies.

CHAPTER 6

# A Comparative Perspective

In previous chapters, we looked at how four blocks of variables influence vote choice in Latin America. We were inspired by the Michigan model and chose the variables for our study based on this model, which stipulates that an individual's vote choice depends on both long-term and short-term factors. Long-term factors include individual demographic characteristics (such as age, gender, region, education, and religion), their socioeconomic characteristics (such as employment status, employment sector, income, and material possessions), ideological orientation, and party identification. The short-term factors refer to various issues at the center of political debates in Latin America (such as corruption, violence, and the economic situation).

Up until this point, we have focused our attention on the overall effect of these variables in all 18 countries in our study. Now, we will more carefully consider how these factors vary across countries. First, we will examine the overall performance of our vote models from one country to another. Then, we will turn our attention to key variables to see whether voters in Latin America base their vote choice on similar factors. These analyses will allow us to see if the Michigan model can account for electoral behavior in most of the countries in our study. We will see that it seems to be the case, despite some inevitable differences from one country to another.

## Overall Performance of the Model

There are various ways in which we can measure the performance of a model with a dichotomous dependent variable (as in the current study). In this chapter, we will continue to use the same measure used since the beginning of this study: the Nagelkerke pseudo-$R^2$. We have seen that the value of this measure is 0.51 when all countries are grouped together and all variables are included in the model. This value is lower than what is generally observed for established democracies, such as in western Europe or the United States (Bengtsonn et al. 2013; Clarke et al. 2012; Lewis-Beck and Nadeau 2012; Nadeau, Lewis-Beck, and Bélanger 2013). However, the difference is similar to the gap between the established democracies of western Europe and the emerging democracies of eastern Europe (Schmitt and Scheuer 2013). These differences can be explained by the less pronounced development of individual ideological orientations and party identification in less established democracies. Schmitt and Scheuer (2013, 19), after exploring the determinants of vote choice in both groups of countries, concluded that "a quarter of a century after regime change, vote choices in post-communist eastern Europe still seem to be based more on circumstantial than on structural factors."

Transposing this conclusion to Latin America may seem paradoxical, since previous analyses have emphasized the importance of party identification in these countries as a structural factor explaining vote choice (see chapter 4). Partisanship does indeed play a key role in explaining vote choice in Latin America, but the impact of this variable remains lower in Latin America than in most established democracies. As for ideology, this conclusion is even clearer (with the notable exception of Chile). In short, the impact of social-psychological variables such as party identification and ideology on vote choice is significantly lower in Latin America than in Canada, the United States, or Europe, which explains why the Michigan model does not perform as well there as it does in established democracies. That doesn't mean that the Michigan model is underperforming when traveling south. The issue is not geography but history. Democracy is still emerging in Latin America. With the passage of time one might expect that Latin American voters will develop stronger partisan affiliations and a deeper familiarity with the left-right distinction. If this conjecture is right, the performance of the Michigan model in Latin America, measured in terms of explained variance, will eventually parallel that observed in established democracies.

Table 6.1 presents information about how the vote model performs in individual countries. The mean value for this table is 0.49, which corresponds to the average pseudo-$R^2$ values for the 18 countries studied. What is interesting is the distribution of these values. From these values, we can make out five groups of countries. A first group of four countries (the Dominican Republic, Uruguay, Venezuela, and Nicaragua) is characterized by a high pseudo-$R^2$ (.78, .78, .76, and .72, respectively). At the other end of the distribution, there is another group of three countries characterized by rather low pseudo-$R^2$ values: Paraguay (.28), Colombia (.27), and Brazil (.15). The remaining 11 countries lie somewhere between these two extremes. We can divide those countries into cases for which the model's performance is close to the mean, as is the case for Argentina (.49), Guatemala (.48), and Costa Rica (.47); slightly higher than the mean, as in El Salvador (.64), Bolivia (.63), and Honduras (.57); and slightly lower than the mean, as in Mexico (.41), Panama (.40), Peru (.39), Chile (.37), and Ecuador (.37).

Such discrepancies within a given group of countries are not unusual. In a study of 10 European countries, Nadeau, Lewis-Beck, and Bélanger (2013) noticed a distribution similar to the one shown in table 6.1, with some countries where the vote model has high explanatory power (e.g., France) and others where its performance is lower (e.g., Ireland). Differences between countries are often the result of differences in social-psychological variables such as party identification and ideology. The vote model performance is generally lower in established democracies where electoral choices are not structured by this type of variable (such as Ireland; see Foucault and Nadeau 2014), as well as in emerging democracies in which such attitudes are less developed (such as the former Communist countries of eastern Europe; see Schmitt and Scheuer 2013).

The results for Latin America seem to conform to this pattern. We noted in chapter 4 that party identification, rather than ideology, was the main social-psychological variable that explains vote choice in Latin America. We can therefore hypothesize that countries where the effect of this

TABLE 6.1. Nagelkerke Pseudo-$R^2$ Values for Voting Model

| Very high | | High | | Average | | Low | | Very low | |
|---|---|---|---|---|---|---|---|---|---|
| Uruguay | 0.78 | El Salvador | 0.64 | All countries | 0.49 | Mexico | 0.41 | Paraguay | 0.28 |
| Dominican | 0.78 | Bolivia | 0.63 | Argentina | 0.49 | Panama | 0.40 | Colombia | 0.27 |
| Republic | | Honduras | 0.57 | Guatemala | 0.48 | Peru | 0.39 | Brazil | 0.15 |
| Venezuela | 0.76 | | | Costa Rica | 0.47 | Chile | 0.37 | | |
| Nicaragua | 0.72 | | | | | Ecuador | 0.37 | | |

variable is the most pronounced will also be those where the vote model performs the best. This relationship is clearly confirmed in figure 6.1. This graph shows the relationship between the value of the logistic regression coefficient for the party identification variable and the pseudo-$R^2$ value for each of the 18 countries studied.[1] Both the direction and strength of this relationship are clear (the simple correlation between these two variables is 0.83). The figure also highlights the contrast between the large effect of party identification on vote choice in the four countries for which the explanatory performance of vote models is high (the Dominican Republic, Uruguay, Venezuela, and Nicaragua; in these countries, the average value of the logistic regression coefficient for party identification is 6.1) and the much weaker link between these two variables in countries in which the performance is clearly lower (Paraguay, Colombia, and Brazil; in these countries, the average value of the logistic regression coefficient for partisan identification is 1.2). Even in between these extremes, we see that there is a close relationship between strength of party identification on vote choice and the vote model's overall explanatory performance. The average value for the regression coefficient is 5.0 for the three countries (El Salvador, Bolivia, and Honduras) showing a slightly above-average performance. It is 4.5 for three countries (Argentina, Guatemala, and Costa Rica), which indicates a performance either equal to or very close to the average, and 3.6 in five other countries (Mexico, Panama, Peru, Chile, and Ecuador), showing a performance slightly below the average.

There are three main implications that can be derived from the data on the performance of our Michigan-inspired voting models in Latin America. First, the results confirm that the performance of these models is generally lower than those used in established democracies, notably in western Europe (Nadeau, Lewis-Beck, and Bélanger 2013; Foucault and Nadeau 2014). Second, we observe that the performance gaps between Latin American countries are similar to those observed in other regional blocks of countries. Finally, the driving variable behind these variations is a social-psychological one: that of partisan identification (again, with the exception of Chile). This result is consistent with, but also different from, what has been observed in western Europe. In western Europe, the key variable explaining vote choice is ideological orientation, and the performance of vote models in these countries depends on the strength of this variable (Kritzinger et al. 2013; Nadeau et al. 2012; Nadeau, Lewis-Beck, and Bélanger 2013; Bengtsonn et al. 2013). However, Great Britain is

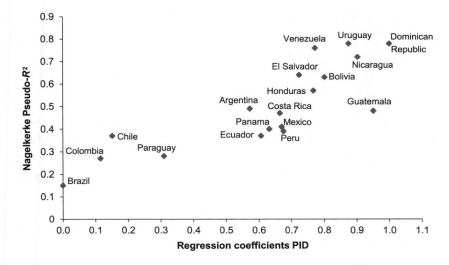

Fig. 6.1. Relationship between the Party Identification variable and pseudo-$R^2$ values in Latin American vote models

an exception (Clarke et al. 2012), since the key variable there in determining vote choice is party identification. This is in line with findings for most English-speaking countries, such as the United States (Lewis-Beck et al. 2008), Canada (Blais et al. 2002), Australia (Vowles 2005), and New Zealand (Jackman 2003). In this vein, vote model performance in Latin America is also more driven by the impact of party identification (Nadeau, Bélanger, and Didier 2013; Nadeau et al. 2014; Nadeau et al. 2015a, 2015b).

These preliminary analyses have allowed us to take a first look at the overall performance of the Michigan model in each of the 18 countries studied. We will now see how the individual components of this model (i.e., various types of short- and long-term variables) help explain vote choices in Latin America.

## Components of the Michigan Model

We now focus on the various elements of the Michigan model to see how they can explain voter behavior in Latin America. The individual parts of the model are presented below:

$$\text{Vote} = f(\text{SDEM, SECN, Anchors, Issues}) \qquad (6.1)$$

The components of Equation 6.1 correspond with the blocks of variables used in previous chapters to predict vote choice. With the help of a model that combined all of the countries in the study, we found that the main determinants of vote choice for each of these categories were race and religion for demographic variables, material wealth for socioeconomic variables, partisan identification for social-psychological variables, and issues of corruption, democratic rights, and the economy for short-term factors. We will now see how the effect of these key variables changes in different Latin American countries.

### Demographic Variables

The first block, demographic variables (see chapter 2), is composed of six variables: age, gender, religious affiliation, church attendance, race, and region. The effect of gender is relatively weak and varies significantly from one country to another. The impact of the regional variable also varies greatly from one country to another and is not significant overall (the effect of this variable is positive and significant in five cases, negative and significant in four instances, and not significant in nine countries). The impact of age is stronger but uncovers a large amount of variation between countries. This is not necessarily surprising. Voters in some Latin American countries have experienced major political upheavals, which often involved periods of dictatorship. Life-cycle effects that would lead an individual to vote for a conservative party simultaneously clash with cohort effects that would push them to vote for a more leftist party. This conflict might explain the fact that the impact of age varies in Latin American countries (the effect of this variable is positive in nine countries and negative in nine others; this effect is not significant in 10 cases, positive and significant in five cases, and negative and significant in three cases). That being said, the overall impact remains positive and one may conjecture that, with the passage of time, age will be more tightly connected to vote choice, with younger voters being more on the left of the spectrum, and older voters more inclined to support the right.

The three variables that seem to best capture the effect of demographics on vote choice in Latin America are religious affiliation (Catholics vs.

others), church attendance, and race (indigenous, mestizo, or white). Table 6.2 presents the effect of these variables for each country. In line with previous chapters, this table presents changes in probabilities. Furthermore, we only report measures that are statistically significant. To highlight the most stable results, we keep only those that are statistically significant when socioeconomic variables are also included in the models.

The results for the race variable are presented in the first column of table 6.2. This variable is statistically significant and points in the expected direction (i.e., positive) in six cases when demographic and socioeconomic variables are included in the model: Argentina, Bolivia, Brazil, Colombia, the Dominican Republic, and Guatemala (there is no case for which it is statistically significant and wrongly signed when the socioeconomic variables are included in the models). This implies that while white voters are more likely to support the right, nonwhites are more likely to vote for the left. The magnitude of the effects observed in some countries indicates that race is the most important demographic determinant in the full model containing all the countries studied. Moreover, countries in which we observe the strongest effects are those that we would expect. For example,

TABLE 6.2. Changes in Probabilities for Long-Term Variables in Latin American Voting Models

| Country | Race | Catholic | Church attendance | Property | PID | Ideology |
|---|---|---|---|---|---|---|
| Argentina | .08 | — | — | .44 | .66 | — |
| Bolivia | .22 | .07 | .15 | .22 | .87 | .30 |
| Brazil | .15 | — | — | .25 | .09 | — |
| Chile | — | — | — | — | .24 | .63 |
| Colombia | .12 | .05 | .07 | — | .17 | .16 |
| Costa Rica | — | — | .11 | — | .68 | .13 |
| Dominican Republic | .07 | — | — | — | .51 | .08 |
| Ecuador | — | — | — | .11 | .79 | .14 |
| El Salvador | — | .10 | — | — | .61 | .33 |
| Guatemala | .15 | — | — | .18 | .94 | — |
| Honduras | — | — | — | — | .60 | — |
| Mexico | — | — | .08 | — | .73 | .15 |
| Nicaragua | — | .09 | .08 | — | .66 | .04 |
| Panama | — | .08 | .11 | — | .71 | — |
| Paraguay | — | — | — | .22 | .40 | .13 |
| Peru | — | .07 | — | — | .63 | .08 |
| Uruguay | — | .14 | .14 | — | .46 | .25 |
| Venezuela | — | .07 | — | .33 | .70 | .29 |

*Note:* Only statistically significant coefficients are reported (95% or better; two-tailed tests).

the largest effect is seen in Bolivia where Evo Morales, a leftist nonwhite president, was voted into power (see next section).

The other variables for which the effect is more systematic measure the impact of religion on the vote (table 6.2, columns 2 and 3). The data show that the effect of religious affiliation (i.e., being Catholic or not) is statistically significant and has the expected sign (positive) in eight countries. Thus, there seems to be a link between Catholicism and support for the right in Bolivia, Colombia, Peru, Uruguay, Venezuela, Honduras, Nicaragua, and Panama. The negative relationship between Catholicism and support for the right in El Salvador might be explained by the presence of a movement of "progressive Catholicism" in this country that sought to make an impact and a protest against political violence (Peterson 1996). An episode among others illustrating this tradition is the tragic assassination of the Archbishop of San Salvador, Oscar Romero in 1980. Furthermore, recent work has shown that the Catholics in El Salvador vote significantly to the left of the growing group of Protestant followers in this country (Boss and Smith 2015, fig. 4.2).[2] The date also show that church attendance is significant and has the expected sign (positive) in seven countries, namely Bolivia, Colombia, Costa Rica, Mexico, Nicaragua, Panama, and Uruguay. Overall, the impact of religion is visible in 10 countries. For 5 countries (Bolivia, Colombia, Nicaragua, Panama, and Uruguay), both religious affiliation and attendance matters; in 3 countries (El Salvador, Peru, and Venezuela) only affiliation matters, whereas churchgoing (but not religious affiliation) exerts an impact on the vote in Costa Rica and Mexico. Finally, for both religious affiliation and church attendance, no coefficient appears wrongly signed and significant when socioeconomic variables are included in the models.

The combined effect of race and religion is illuminating. The effect of race and religion (either affiliation or attendance) works together in two countries: Bolivia and Colombia. Race is significant but not religion in Argentina, Brazil, the Dominican Republic, and Guatemala. The reverse is true for Costa Rica, El Salvador, Mexico, Nicaragua, Panama, Peru, Uruguay, and Venezuela. This shows that in 14 out of the 18 Latin American countries, race or religion, or both, significantly influence vote choice in one way or another. Other sociodemographic variables also have an influence, but their effect is much less systematic.

The conclusion is clear. In Latin America, an individual's demographic profile weighs upon his or her vote choice, with religion and race having

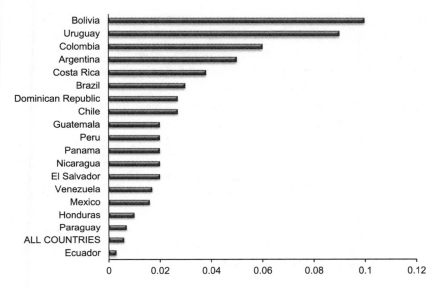

Fig. 6.2. Changes in pseudo-$R^2$ values upon inclusion of demographic variables in voting models for 18 Latin American countries

the most influence within this category of long-term factors. This inter-pretation is supported by figure 6.2. This graph shows the increase in the pseudo-$R^2$ after including demographic variables in the model. The three cases in which the increase is the highest (Bolivia, Uruguay, and Colom-bia) are the countries in which race and religion were statistically signifi-cant either separately or together. On the other hand, the three countries in which this increase is the lowest (Ecuador, Honduras, and Paraguay) are cases where neither one nor the other of these variables was significant.

### The Effect of Socioeconomic Variables

The socioeconomic variables, included in the second block (see chapter 3), are the following five: education, income, employment status (unem-ployed), employment sector, and wealth (measured by a scale itemizing various material possessions). The two variables that exert the most system-atic effect on vote choice are income and wealth. The income variable has the expected sign (i.e., positive) in 13 out of 18 cases and is statistically significant in 8 countries. For this variable, two results are striking. The first is that two of the eight statistically significant coefficients are not of the expected sign: the income coefficient is negative and significant in Honduras and Uruguay, while it is positive and significant in Bolivia, Chile, Costa Rica, the Dominican Republic, Peru, and Venezuela. The impact of income on the vote is also rather limited. The mean value for the change in probability in the eight countries where this variable is significant is .07.

The socioeconomic variable that displays the largest and most systematic effect is wealth, as measured by an individual's material possessions. This variable is of the expected sign and statistically significant in 7 out of 18 countries (it is also significant using a one-tailed test for Mexico and Nicaragua). Furthermore, there is no case in which this variable is both of the opposite sign and statistically significant. The effect of that variable is large, as it varies between 11 and 44 percentage points in countries where it is significant (the average is .25). Moreover, in most of these cases this effect remained significant for these seven countries even when social-psychological variables and issues were added to the models. Furthermore, this variable retained 85% of its impact when anchor variables are included. In contrast, four of the eight coefficients for income lost their statistical significance. By far, material wealth is the most important and systematic socioeconomic determinant of voting behavior in Latin America. This finding is supported by figure 6.3, which shows the contribution of socioeconomic variables to explaining vote choice. The results speak for themselves. Whereas the increase in the level of explained variance is close to .05 on average for the seven countries where material wealth is statistically significant (Argentina, Bolivia, Brazil, Ecuador, Guatemala, Paraguay, and Venezuela), it is only .02 for the remaining 11 countries where it is not the case.

### Social-Psychological Variables: The Anchors

In chapter 4, which treats the political anchor variables (the third block of our causal system), we see that party identification is the most important social-psychological variable guiding Latin American voters. This result is confirmed once again in table 6.2, which shows that the effect of party identification is statistically significant in all 18 countries. Moreover, party identification has a stronger effect than ideology in all cases but one, the

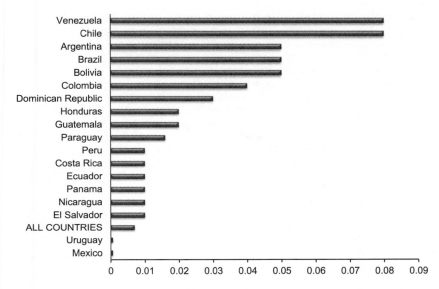

Fig. 6.3. Changes in pseudo-$R^2$ values upon inclusion of Socioeconomic Variables in voting models for 18 Latin American countries

exception being Chile. Party identification has a rather sizeable impact on vote choice in 15 countries; its impact is noticeably lower for Chile (.24), Colombia (.17), and Brazil (.09). There are less systematic effects for ideology. This variable is not statistically significant in five cases (Argentina, Brazil, Guatemala, Honduras, and Panama) and has a relatively low impact in eight countries: Nicaragua (.04), Peru (.08), Costa Rica (.13), Paraguay (.13), Ecuador (.14), Mexico (.15), Colombia (.16), and the Dominican Republic (.08). The impact of ideology is more important in four countries, namely Uruguay (.25), Venezuela (.29), Bolivia (.30), and El Salvador (.33). Finally, Chile clearly stands out from the pack. Due to its peculiar historical and political context (see chapter 4), Chile is the only country in Latin America where the impact of ideology on the vote is strong (.63) and greatly exceeds that of party identification (.24).

The preceding remarks should not hide the fact that party identification remains the most important vote determinant in most Latin American countries. The most common pattern in this region is the clear domination of party ID over ideology in the explanation of the vote. This pattern is particularly visible in 11 countries, namely Argentina, Costa Rica, the Do-

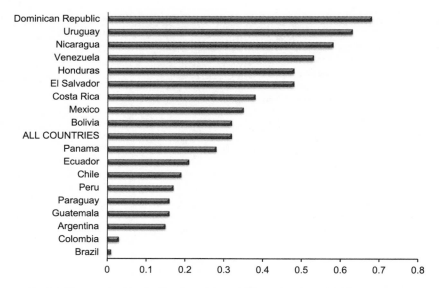

Fig. 6.4. Changes in pseudo-$R^2$ values upon addition of anchor variables to demographic and Socioeconomic variables in voting models for 18 Latin American countries

minican Republic, Ecuador, Guatemala, Honduras, Mexico, Nicaragua, Panama, Paraguay, and Peru. In this group, the average impact of partisan identification and ideology is .66 and .08, respectively. In a group of four other countries—El Salvador, Uruguay, Bolivia and Venezuela—the effect of partisanship in explaining the vote is clearly dominant but the impact of ideology remains important (the average impact for party ID and ideology in this group is .66 and .29, respectively). The cases of Brazil and Colombia are different since they are the only two countries in Latin America where the impact of both anchor variables is relatively weak. Finally, Chile is the only country where the relative impact of these variables reminds us of the domination of ideology over party ID, a pattern that holds in most European countries.

Figure 6.4 confirms that including social-psychological variables, and above all party identification, substantially improves the performance of the models (the pseudo-$R^2$ for the 18 countries in the study goes from .11 to .43 when these variables are added to the model). This confirms once again that partisanship is the key determinant of voting behavior in Latin America.

*Issues*

Our theoretical expectation was that short-term factors like issues are likely to play an important role in the emerging democracies of Latin America (see chapter 5). Among them, valence issues are expected to exert a stronger effect on the vote, since dealing with them does not require much effort from voters, besides being aware of the incumbent's recent performance on specific questions (e.g., the state of the economy, the level of crime). Positional issues, on the other hand, require more information and sophistication. Judging the performance of the incumbent is easier than taking sides on complex debates about the role of the state or the importance of the opposition in the democratic process. This might be especially true in emergent democracies. For these reasons, we expect the impact of positional issues on the vote to be significantly lower than for valence issues. As a matter of fact, our results strongly confirm this expectation. The change in probability for the two positional issues, the role of the State and authoritarianism, register .05 and –.03, respectively, whereas the impact of the four valence issues ranges from .07 to .13. The impact of short-term factors on the vote in Latin America, then, appears largely due to valence issues.

The data in table 6.3 confirm this expectation. The valence issues included in our model (crime, corruption, democratic rights, and economics) have a large and systematic effect in most of the 18 countries studied. Only in Honduras are none of these issues statistically significant. Costa Rica, Panama, and Paraguay, in which just two out of four issues are significant, are also notable exceptions. Other than that, we see that there is a block of 10 countries where three of these four issues have a significant influence on vote choice. Finally, we notice a group of four countries where all four issues are clearly linked to vote choice (Bolivia, Colombia, El Salvador, and Venezuela).

We saw earlier that the issue of fighting crime had the smallest and least systematic impact among the issues studied. The change in probability associated with this variable across all Latin America countries is 7 percentage points, whereas this change is 13, 11, and 10 percentage points for democratic rights, the economy, and corruption, respectively. The issue of violence plays a significant role in 9 of 18 countries, which is a relatively small number of countries when compared to corruption (13/18), democratic rights (14/18), and the economy (16/18).

Figure 6.5 shows how the role of issues in explaining vote choice differs across the countries in our study. A look at the nine countries where the impact of issues is higher shows the consistent and strong impact of the economy and the protection of democratic rights. The coefficients for these issues are significant in 17 out of 18 cases and their effect on voting choices is large (.15 in both cases). Not surprisingly, the impact is considerably lower for another, smaller group, where issues play a lesser role in explaining vote decisions (Honduras, Panama, Costa Rica, Uruguay, the Dominican Republic, and Nicaragua).

## Making Sense of Country Differences

The previous section allowed us to paint an overall picture of the results obtained using the Michigan model to explain voting behavior in Latin America. Overall, the results show that this model can be successfully used to explain the behavior of voters in this area of the world. That conclusion bases itself on the overall performance of the model, which is very similar

TABLE 6.3. Changes in Probabilities for Issues in Latin American Voting Models

| Country | Safety | Corruption | Rights | Economy |
|---|---|---|---|---|
| Argentina | — | .24 | .19 | .16 |
| Bolivia | .08 | .19 | .23 | .12 |
| Brazil | — | .14 | .15 | .08 |
| Chile | — | .16 | .18 | .10 |
| Colombia | .12 | .11 | .16 | .13 |
| Costa Rica | — | .17 | .18 | — |
| Dominican Republic | .08 | — | .07 | .10 |
| Ecuador | — | .10 | .22 | .19 |
| El Salvador | .08 | .09 | .15 | .08 |
| Guatemala | .18 | .12 | — | .08 |
| Honduras | — | — | — | — |
| Mexico | .16 | — | .11 | .10 |
| Nicaragua | — | .07 | .13 | .08 |
| Panama | — | .13 | — | .11 |
| Paraguay | — | — | .13 | .18 |
| Peru | .15 | — | .10 | .16 |
| Uruguay | .07 | .07 | — | .09 |
| Venezuela | .13 | .10 | .09 | .19 |

*Note:* Only statistically significant coefficients are reported (95% or better; two-tailed tests).

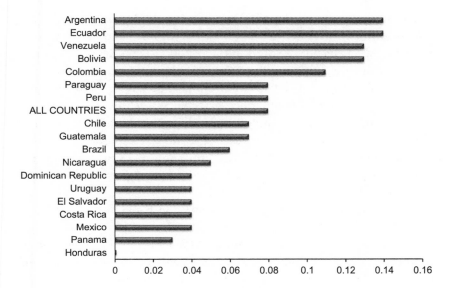

Fig. 6.5. Changes in pseudo-$R^2$ values upon addition of issue variables to anchor, demographic, and Socioeconomic variables in voting models for 18 Latin American countries

to what has been observed in other emerging democracies, such as those in eastern Europe.

Our interest in the Michigan model also lies in its flexibility. In the Latin American context, it allows us to identify what voters in this region have in common with others, at the same time bringing out unique aspects of Latin American voting behavior. The effect of the race variable, the persistence of the impact of religion, and the particular configuration of issues at the center of the political debate (including questions of security, respect for democratic rights, and corruption) characterize voting behavior in Latin America. The dominance of party identification over ideology as a key social-psychological factor in determining vote choice also distinguishes Latin America from Europe. Interestingly, even exceptional cases manifest themselves differently between the two regions. Ideology is the dominant factor in Europe, except in the United Kingdom, where party identification plays a more important role. Party identification dominates in Latin America, except in Chile, where ideology is a key determinant of voter behavior.

Thus, we can say that our interest in using the Michigan model systematically in Latin America is twofold. On the one hand, it allows us to show that the behavior of voters in the region rests on the same foundations identified elsewhere in the world. At the same time it also allows us to draw out the differences in electoral motivations between Latin Americans and citizens of other democracies. While this is important, it is not entirely new. For example, the Michigan model has been used to highlight notable differences in voter behavior in established and emergent democracies, as well as in the comparison of Europe (dominated by ideology) and the Anglo-Saxon countries (where party identification plays a dominant role).

The preceding section highlights the tension between political scientists' desire to draw general conclusions about voter behavior while pointing out the existence of often significant differences in the voter motivations of each country. These differences are neither particularly surprising nor particularly marked among the Latin American countries. That said, explanations can be provided in an attempt to account for certain of these differences. Of course, none of them are entirely satisfactory. However, a brief discussion of them might suggest avenues for future research, in order to better understand the differences between countries that the Michigan model has brought to light. In doing so, we will focus on eight variables belonging to the different blocks, namely race (demographic), property, schooling and income (socioeconomic), party identification and ideology (anchor), and attitudes toward authoritarianism and national economic perceptions (issues).

### Demographic Variables: Race

The impact of race varies greatly from one country to another. For example, the likelihood of voting for a right-leaning candidate increases by 22 percentage points in Bolivia when the voter is white, even when socioeconomic variables are included in the model. In fact, the impact of this variable seems particularly pronounced in four countries: Bolivia (.22), Brazil (.15), Guatemala (.15), and Colombia (.12).

Why is the effect of race more pronounced within this group of countries? One possible explanation comes from work on the United States that has shown a link between the proportion of African Americans in a region and the importance of the racial question on political attitudes (Giles and Buckner 1993; Giles and Hertz 1994). Transposed to Latin America, this hypothesis would state that the race variable should play more of a role when indigenous and black citizens make up a large proportion of the population. This hypothesis can be tested by comparing the percentage of respondents who define themselves as indigenous or black with the effect of the race variable in a given country.

This relationship is examined in table 6.4 (see appendix 3 for complete regression results). To do so, we have created a dichotomous variable that takes the value of 1 for the six countries where the self-reported percentages of blacks and indigenous are the highest (Guatemala, Panama, Bolivia, the Dominican Republic, Brazil, and Colombia) and 0 otherwise. This variable, DRACE6, is included in the model in two ways, first as a main effect, and second as an interactive term with the race variable used so far. As discussed below, we expect a positive sign for this multiplicative variable.[3]

The result displayed in column 2 shows that this is indeed the case. The impact of race is much stronger in countries with higher levels of nonwhite populations. Whereas the probability of supporting a right-wing party increases 4 percentage points for white respondents in general, it jumps another 11 percentage points in the six countries where the proportion of nonwhites is the highest. Clearly race matters in Latin America; but it matters more in some countries than others.

### Socioeconomic Variables: Property, Income, and Schooling

The variable measuring respondents' material possessions is the socioeconomic indicator that exerts the greatest and most systematic impact on vote choice in Latin America. It is then interesting to ask whether the effect of this property variable is greater in some countries than others. A first hypothesis is that its impact would be higher where inequalities are more pronounced. But this is apparently not the case. Another interesting conjecture is that property matters more in countries where more sustained redistributive policies have been implemented. This hypothesis can be examined using the information in column 3 of table 6.4. The variable DGINI6 is a dichotomous variable that takes the value of 1 for the six countries with Gini coefficients having the largest decreases for the five-year period before

TABLE 6.4. Change in Probabilities for Voting Intentions in 18 Latin American Countries with Interactive Variables (LAPOP 2008, 2010, 2012)

| | (1) | (2) | (3) | (4) | (5) |
|---|---|---|---|---|---|
| Months | -.24** | -.25** | -.26** | -.16** | -.10** |
| Age | — | .03* | .03* | .03** | .01 |
| Gender | — | .01** | .02** | .01 | .00 |
| Catholic | — | .04** | .04** | .01** | .01** |
| Church attendance | — | .05** | .05** | .02** | .02** |
| Region | — | .01 | -.02** | -.01* | -.01* |
| Race | — | .04** | .02* | .01 | .00 |
| Drace06 | — | -.05** | -.05** | -.07** | -.06** |
| Drace06*Race | — | .11** | .11** | .06** | .05** |
| Schooling | — | — | -.02* | -.01 | -.01 |
| DLR06 | — | — | .07** | -.18** | -.07** |
| DLR06*schooling | — | — | .04** | .05** | .04** |
| Income | — | — | .01 | .00 | -.00 |
| DLR06*income | — | — | .07** | .06** | .04** |
| Unemployment | — | — | -.02** | -.03** | -.01 |
| Public sector | — | — | -.01 | -.00 | .01 |
| Property | — | — | -.01 | -.00 | -.01 |
| Dgini06 | — | — | -.37** | -.14** | -.06** |
| Dgini06*Property | — | — | .28** | .18** | .14** |
| Ideology | — | — | — | .08** | .04** |
| DLR06*ideology | — | — | — | .27** | .24** |
| Party identification | — | — | — | .73** | .60** |
| Dfrac06 | — | — | — | .05** | -.01 |
| Dfrac06*Party ID | — | — | — | -.33** | -.26** |
| State | — | — | — | — | .04** |
| AUTH | — | — | — | — | -.00 |
| DAUTH6 | — | — | — | — | .19** |
| DAUTH6*AUTH | — | — | — | — | -.10** |
| Safety | — | — | — | — | .10** |
| Corruption | — | — | — | — | .13** |
| Democracy | — | — | — | — | .15** |
| SRE | — | — | — | — | .11** |
| ECN06 | — | — | — | — | -.17** |
| ECN06*SRE | — | — | — | — | .05** |
| N | 52,489 | 51,394 | 45,332 | 38,363 | 35,820 |

**p ≤ .01; *p ≤ .05 (two-tailed tests). Entries represent change in probabilities. Country dummies not shown. See appendix 4 for variable's specification.

the LAPOP surveys (2003–2005–2007 vs. 2008–2010–2012; these countries include Argentina, Bolivia, Chile, Ecuador, Peru, and Venezuela; see Gindling and Trejos 2013 and Gasparini, Cruces, and Tornarolli 2011).[4]

This variable is included in the model as a main effect and in interaction with property (DGINI6 x Property). The results in column 3 neatly show that the impact of material possessions on the vote is stronger where significant redistributive policies have taken place. It appears, as a matter of fact, that the impact of patrimony is mainly located in this group of countries: the interactive term is significant and strong (.28) whereas the variable measuring its impact in the rest of Latin America is not. Property matters but mainly in countries where intense redistributive policies were implemented.

The fact that the impact of schooling is not significant, and that the effect of income seems relatively low, may appear perplexing at first glance.[5] This raises the possibility that these class-based indicators may have a stronger effect on vote choice in certain circumstances. Previous work suggests that the impact of class-based politics and ideology in Latin America may depend on the "radicalism" of sitting presidents, as measured on the general left-right dimension (Ellner 2013, 2014; Remmer 2012; Wiesehomeier and Benoit 2009; Wiesehomeier 2010). Based on the former indicators, the six countries where ideological polarization is more pronounced are Bolivia, Chile, Ecuador, El Salvador, Uruguay, and Venezuela.[6]

The data in table 6.4 (column 3) allow us to examine these possibilities. The variable DLR6 takes the value of 1 for the six countries characterized by the highest degree of class-based polarization. Multiplicative terms including this variable, schooling, and income are included (DLR6 × Schooling; DLR6 × Income) to see if the impact of these variables increases in this block of countries. The results show that it is indeed the case. The probability that better-educated respondents (compared to lesser-educated ones) support right-wing incumbents increases by 4 points in polarized countries while being weakly negative elsewhere. The impact for income is stronger: the probability that a wealthier respondent supports a right-wing incumbent jumps from 1 to 7 points in the group of countries including Bolivia, Chile, Ecuador, El Salvador, Uruguay, and Venezuela. These effects, while significant, appear weaker than for the other interactions (race and property) examined so far. In the next section, we will examine if left-wing radicalism seems more able to propel an ideologically based vote, as opposed to a class-based vote per se.

*Anchor Variables: Party Identification and Ideology*

We can confidently say that party identification is the most important determinant of voting behavior in Latin America. But its effect varies from one country to another. How can we explain the fact that this variable plays a lesser role in some countries (such as Chile, Brazil, and Colombia)? In the first case, the explanation seems simple enough. For historical reasons and because of the political context in Chile, ideology has emerged as the anchor variable of choice in this country. But how to explain, for instance, the situations of Brazil and Colombia? A possible explanation is based on work that shows that identifying with political parties is more likely to occur in stable democracies, where parties have already been competing against each other and contesting elections for quite some time. A stable democracy, where political competition is structured around a limited number of parties that have withstood the test of time, allows for the development and transmission of a lasting attachment to a particular party. In short, the limited lifespan and increasing number of political parties in emerging democracies could be seen as obstacles to developing a stable party identification, which would reduce the impact of this variable on vote choice (see chapter 4).

Something frequently observed in "younger" democracies is a greater fractionalization of partisan groups. This greater degree of fractionalization is not without consequence. In a thorough and convincing study, Huber, Kernell, and Leoni (2005, 365) conclude that "fewer parties in government increase partisanship." More generally, party system fractionalization seems to reduce voters' ability to develop attachment to parties, either via socialization (Campbell et al. 1960) or based on running tallies about which parties best serve their interests (see Fiorina 1981; Powell and Whiten 1993; Powell 2000; Achen 2002; Nadeau, Niemi, and Yoshinka 2002). Thus, it is plausible to think that party fractionalization could not only reduce the number of partisans but also dampen the effect of party identification on vote choice.

The data in table 6.4 (column 4) allow us to examine this possibility. The variable DFRAC6 takes the value of 1 for the six countries characterized by the highest degree of partisan fractionalization.[7] A multiplicative term including this variable and party identification is included (DFRAC6 × Party ID) to see if the impact of this anchor variable diminishes in the block of countries with the highest level of partisan fragmentation. The results show that the impact of partisanship indeed decreases substantially in this group of countries. The probability that a respondent identifying with the incumbent party will vote for its candidate decreases from 73 to 40 percentage points when party fragmentation is high. Thus, party ID matters a lot in Latin America, but its impact is less pronounced in countries characterized by a fragmented political scene.

Ideology is also an important anchor variable, at least in some countries. This raises the question: Why is ideology a more decisive factor in some countries than others? As previously seen, left-wing radicalism may be the factor propelling ideologically oriented voting. But there is more than that. Previous work suggests that the impact ideology has in Latin America also depends on leadership rhetoric and attitudes (Alcántara 2015; Alcántara and Rivas 2006; Rosas and Zechmeister 2000; Saiegh 2009; Zechmeister 2006; Zoco 2006), as well as parties' polarization along ideological lines (Rosas 2005; Sulmont 2014). These conditions appear to be met in the six countries previously identified as more extreme on the left-right scale, namely Bolivia, Chile, Ecuador, El Salvador, Uruguay, and Venezuela.[8] Rhetoric and radicalism seem to work hand in hand to prime ideology in Latin America.

The data in table 6.4 (column 4) allow us to examine this possibility. The variable DLR6 takes the value of 1 for the six countries characterized by the highest degree of ideological polarization. A multiplicative term including this variable and ideology is included (DLR6 x Ideology), in order to see if the impact of this variable increases in this block of countries. The results are clear-cut. The probability that a right-wing respondent supports an incumbent from the same orientation jumps from 8 to 35 points in the group of countries including Bolivia, Chile, Ecuador, El Salvador, Uruguay, and Venezuela.

### Issues: Authoritarianism and the Economy

We finally examine cross-country differences in the impact of issues. Two categories of questions are examined. First, a positional issue: authoritarianism, namely respondents' opinion about the idea of limiting the voice of the opposition. Second, a valence issue: the state of the economy, the topic most systematically related to vote choice in Latin America (see chapter 5).

Various studies have shown that there is a widespread preference for democracy on the part of both elites and citizens in Latin America (Corral 2011). Still, a certain number of countries in this region have recently experienced an "authoritarian drift" (Weyland, de la Torres, and Kornblith 2013). This evolution happened more frequently, though not exclusively, in countries headed by left-wing leaders following the path of Hugo Chávez.[9] According to Kurt Weyland and his colleagues: "The Chávez phenomenon has had strong demonstration and contagion effects beyond Venezuela. . . . Presidents Evo Morales of Bolivia (2006– ) and Rafael Correa of Ecuador (2007– ) have emulated Chávez's script. Similarly, strong informal pressures and disrespect for constitutional principles have enabled Daniel Ortega (2007– ) to establish his hegemony in Nicaragua (2007– ). President Manuel Zelaya of Honduras (2006–2009) also sought to follow in the footsteps of Chávez, Morales and Correa. . . . Even President Christina Fernández de Kirchner of Argentina (2007– ), whose fervent supporters take inspiration from Chávez, is eyeing constitutional changes and renewed reelection" (18–19).

We use the list of cases established by Weyland and his collaborators to see if their recent evolution has contributed to "prime" attitudes toward authoritarianism in these countries. The dominant pattern uncovered in chapter 5 is that sharing authoritarian values (i.e., agreeing that silencing the voice of the opposition might be necessary for the progress of society) is negatively linked to support for right-wing parties. Our expectation is that this pattern would be more pronounced in countries experiencing an authoritarian drift. The data in table 6.4 (column 5) allow us to examine this possibility. The variable DAUTH6 takes the value of 1 for the six countries having recently experienced this dynamic. A multiplicative term including this variable and attitudes toward authoritarianism is included (DAUTH6 × AUTH) to see if the impact of this variable increases in this block of countries. The results show that the impact of authoritarianism indeed increases in a significant fashion in this group of countries. The probability that a respondent sharing authoritarian values supports a right-wing party decreases by 10 percentage points in the countries identified by Weyland and his colleagues, while being insignificant elsewhere in Latin America. This finding carries two implications. It shows that the impact of authoritarianism is now relatively limited in Latin America. But it also demonstrates that its saliency has recently increased in a certain number of countries experiencing an authoritarian drift.

The valence issue of the economy has the most systematic effect of all, and attains statistical significance in all cases save two (Honduras and Costa Rica). The effect of this variable also varies the least from country to country, seeming to confirm its endurance across time and through space (Lewis-Beck 1988; Vavreck 2009; Lewis-Beck and Stegmaier 2013; Nadeau, Lewis-Beck, and Bélanger 2013). Nevertheless, it may be that the effect of the economy on the vote will be stronger in countries undergoing severe economic problems. Given the particular context of Latin America, the best indicator measuring economic difficulties is the misery index, which sums the unemployment and the inflation rates in a given country.[10] The six countries displaying the highest scores on this index are Venezuela, Argentina, Colombia, the Dominican Republic, Uruguay, and Nicaragua (ECN6). Is the impact of the economy stronger in this block of countries? The results in table 6.4 (column 5) show that this is the case. Moving from a negative to a positive perception of the economy increases the probability of voting for the incumbent by 11 points in Latin America in general. But this impact jumps to 16 points in the six countries facing more severe economic problems.

## Conclusion

In this chapter, we discussed the results for our voting models in comparative perspective. We did so by first demonstrating the general utility of the Michigan model for explaining Latin American voting behavior. Then, we explored whether these 18 countries could be profitably grouped according to the factors that exert the most influence on vote choice. We can now draw three main conclusions. First, it seems that the explanatory power of the Michigan model for Latin American countries is similar to that observed in the emerging democracies of eastern Europe, and different from what has been observed in the established democracies of western Europe. Second, the dispersion in performance levels of the model, across these Latin American countries, resembles results from other groups of countries simultaneously studied with the same model, such as western Europe. Third, the gap between the overall performance of the Michigan model in Latin America, as compared to the more established western European democracies, comes from the weaker effect of social-psychological variables, namely party identification and ideology. This conclusion is not surprising, given that these anchoring attitudes show more development over time in a relatively stable environment (Converse and Pierce 1992; Green, Palmquist, and Schickler 2002; Huber, Kernell, and Leoni 2005; Lupu 2015). Therefore, we anticipate that the explanatory power of these voting models in Latin America will eventually converge, falling in line with more established democracies. We can affirm that, given its observed performance, the Michigan model offers, at minimum, an adequate explanatory framework for understanding electoral preferences in Latin America.

The Michigan model bases itself on a combination of long- and short-term factors. These factors, while identified, can vary in strength from one country, or one continent, to another. We see that, within this theoretical framework, voter behavior in Latin America has its own strengths, including the importance of race and religion on vote choice,[11] the clear dominance of party identification over ideology, and the salience of issues such as corruption and respect for democratic rights. Moreover, both economic and material considerations play an important role in vote choice in Latin America, as elsewhere. Overall, these similarities and differences give electoral behavior in Latin America its particular color.

By lumping Latin American countries into a single group, we can easily characterize voter behavior in this region. However, grouping countries together like this, as has also been done for the more established democracies of western Europe, tends to overlook significant differences across countries. For example, in France the main variable structuring vote choice is ideology; but in the United Kingdom this variable has a rather weak effect, while party identification has the main structuring factor. Yet neither or these factors play a large role in Ireland. For reasons such as these, it is obviously difficult (if not impossible) to draw blanket generalizations that apply to all European countries.

The results of our analyses also underlined some interesting variations in voting behavior among the Latin American countries. These differences between countries can be accounted for, at least in part. The effect of race is more pronounced in countries where more people identify themselves as black or indigenous. The link between material wealth and support for the right is stronger in countries that have implemented intense policies to mitigate inequalities. The effect of party identification is weaker where the party system is strongly fractionalized. The effect of income, schooling, and, above all, ideology, is stronger in countries where more radical leftist leaders use a clear left-right rhetoric. Opinions about the role of the opposition in the democratic process matter more in countries having experienced an authoritarian shift. Finally, the impact of the economy is higher in countries experiencing more severe economic problems.

These several conclusions, which point to the existence of noteworthy interaction effects operating beneath the general political surface, are certainly worth watching, as we attempt to understand the flux and flow of politics in the mass publics of Latin America. Nevertheless, it is important to emphasize that all the trends described in this chapter (whether based on main or conditional effects) are precisely that: trends. They do testify to the fact that the behavior of Latin American voters roots itself in motivations similar to that of voters in most democracies. However, these motivations also express themselves in a particular way in the Latin American context (and sometimes according to country-specific contexts). Our interest in using the Michigan model is due precisely to its ability to bring out overall trends, while paying attention to dynamics unique to each country.

# Conclusion

Latin America has had to overcome a number of important roadblocks before becoming a democratic region of the world. The establishment of civilian governments, elected by the population after competitive election campaigns, has been a key step on its path to democratic consolidation over the past half century. In this context, how do Latin American voters orient themselves when it comes to democratically selecting their political leaders? Does the voting behavior of Latin Americans respond to the same set of "laws" as in more established electoral democracies? Does it also take on some particular colors that are specific to the region's social and economic context?

We began our study of how Latin America votes by asking whether a theory of Latin American presidential vote choice was possible. As a useful start, we decided to make use of the funnel-of-causality model of individual vote choice first developed in the United States by the Michigan school. The model combines long- and short-term factors that may influence the decision to vote for a particular candidate in a given election. As such, it enables one to identify the structure that underlies the individual-level mechanism of vote choice. For the first time in the study of the Latin American presidential vote, we have applied this model systematically to all 18 countries of the region, using a contemporary set of identical survey data. The obvious first question to ask in this concluding chapter is: How well does the Michigan model of voting behavior work in the context of Latin American presidential elections?

## Michigan Goes South?

Explanations of individual vote choice that rely on the funnel of causality usually give greater weight to long-term variables, which include the demographic and socioeconomic characteristics of individuals, as well as their partisan and ideological attachment to the actors of the competitive party system. Based on the analyses presented in this book, which look at presidential vote intentions over a period of four years (2008–12), what can be concluded regarding the relative weight of long- and short-term determinants of voting behavior in Latin America?

Considering the Latin American region as a whole, we find that demographic and socioeconomic cleavages (the first and second blocks of independent variables included in our model) account for only a small portion of the variance in presidential vote intention during this relatively recent time period. When it comes to long-term determinants of the vote, the social-psychological anchors of partisan and ideological identification (our third block of independent variables) account for much more of the variation in individual-level vote choice. The first three blocks of variables account for 84% of the explained variance (i.e., the adjusted pseudo-$R^2$ value of 0.43 divided by the value of 0.51, the pseudo-$R^2$ for the complete version of the model that includes short-term explanatory factors). However, that estimate needs to be interpreted in light of the fact that we only have one block of short-term variables included in our model, that of issues. In short, while it might be believed that Latin American voters are particularly sensitive to issues like crime, corruption, or economics, it turns out that their voting behavior is nonetheless very much anchored in social cleavages and, especially, party identification and political ideology.

If we look at the individual countries, we find that there are 9 out of the 18 countries for which we can say that presidential voting intention is very much anchored by social-psychological factors and where social cleavages only weakly explain voting behavior.[1] There are 4 other countries that also display a strong impact of long-term variables, but where social cleavages exert an influence almost as substantial as social-psychological anchors.[2] The remaining 5 countries show greater balance across the blocks of variables in terms of their influence on vote choice, due to a greater-than-average impact of issues (the fourth block).[3]

Within the block of demographic determinants, we have found that the main variables that explain Latin American presidential vote intention are race and religion. White voters and Catholic ones, as well as those voters attending church, are more supportive of right-leaning incumbent candidates. Among socioeconomic variables, material wealth is clearly a driving force: the more material goods an individual owns, the more likely he or she is to support a right-wing incumbent candidate. Taken together, the impact of these various long-term determinants of presidential voting intention suggests a substantial role for class polarization in Latin American electoral politics. In terms of the social-psychological anchor variables, on balance party identification has a greater influence on the vote than ideological identification across most, although not all, Latin American countries. As for the block of issue variables, we have found that the fight against corruption, the respect for democratic rights, and perceptions about the state of national economic conditions are the short-term determinants that exert the most important influence on presidential incumbent support in the Latin American region.

To sum up, we have demonstrated that the funnel of causality model does a good job explaining individual-level vote intention in Latin America, behaving as one would expect, with long-term variables (especially partisan identification) outweighing short-term ones in a majority of the countries. Hence, it is possible to employ a general theory of voting behavior to explain Latin American presidential elections.

How does our "general theory" compare to parallel theoretical conclusions that might be drawn from the seminal work of Carlin, Singer, and Zechmeister (2015)? There are certainly similarities, for both works take inspiration from the Michigan model of Campbell, Converse, Miller, and Stokes (1960). Nevertheless, our two works do not tell an identical story. For one, our investigation gives a larger role to race and ethnicity in vote choice. For another, we find that Latin American voters respond to concerns about democracy and authoritarianism—dimensions that Carlin et al. (2015) do not explore quantitatively. However, they do find that economic policy has more importance than we give it. For us, in contrast, the key economic weight comes from valence economics, rather than policy economics. Also, squarely in *The American Voter* tradition (Campbell, Converse, Miller, and Stokes 1960), we give party identification a larger role than they do. A last difference we should mention involves our attention to certain contextual factors that Carlin, Singer, and Zechmeister (2015) do not pursue, specifically, the impact of national racial composition and income inequality on presidential voting behavior. Overall, while these differences between the two studies may be considered "at the margin," they are still important markers pointing to valuable avenues for further research on Latin American elections.

While the theoretical framework that we have applied to the Latin American region seems useful for explaining presidential support, voters in Latin America do not necessarily respond to this set of laws in a manner similar to what has been observed in more established electoral democracies. Comparisons across regions drawing on a Michigan-type explanatory model of vote choice are of more limited value if the survey data used are not the same across countries and regions, or the modeling itself is dissimilar. That is to say, when applying a funnel-of-causality type of model, researchers do not always include the same measures, nor do they have an identical number of blocks of variables in their estimation. However, the spirit remains the same: the researchers' intent is to capture what they believe to be the most salient social cleavages, anchor variables, and short-term factors that may affect the vote in their country (or region) of study. While any comparison of models remains imperfect for the reasons just mentioned, it is nonetheless useful to ask how the findings obtained from our application of a Michigan-type model to Latin America compare with those in other democracies.

As the discussion in chapter 6 made clear, the model used in this book explains a bit less of the variance in voting behavior when compared to studies from the more mature democracies. In fact, the Michigan model's performance is more akin to that found in the emerging democracies of eastern Europe. How can we account for this phenomenon? There are at least three possibilities. First, like voters in eastern European countries, Latin American citizens seem to rely less on their social-psychological attachments (to a party or to an ideological pole) when making up their minds than voters in more mature democracies. This is due to political parties in their region not always having deep roots, and to the content of political ideologies not necessarily being as well defined or as strongly consistent as in western European or North American societies. The gap in model performance is thus due, in large part, to the fact that anchor variables do not (yet) have as much of an influence on voting behavior in these consolidating democracies. That is to say, even though these variables may already explain a good portion of vote choice in these countries, their influence is still not as significant as in more consolidated democracies.

Second, the difference may be due to some omitted variables. For example, we were able to include only one block of short-term determinants of the vote—economic and noneconomic issues—in our explanatory model. One could think of candidate or party leader personalities, and of strategic considerations, as being additional short-term influences on vote choice that could be added to the model for Latin America, if/when appropriate data are available. These aspects were not included in the AmericasBarometer opinion surveys employed in this book, nor were the measures typically used to account for positional issue voting, such as the measurement of the distance (proximity) between a voter's issue preferences and the candidates' position on those same issues. Strategic considerations seem particularly important to take into account for explaining Latin American presidential elections because of the two-round electoral system that is in use in the region. Indeed, strategic voting is likely to play a role during the first round, where more than two presidential candidates compete in order to make it to the second round (Blais et al. 2011). The dual ballot structure, and the strategic possibilities that it affords, certainly represent one key area where a Michigan-type model of Latin American vote choice could be extended, like it has been done for the case of France (Converse and Pierce 1986; Nadeau et al. 2012).

Third, the model performance gap may be due to the voting behavior of Latin Americans being less predictable, from a Michigan-type perspective, than in more established democracies, perhaps owing to the influence of clientelism—although we have shown in chapter 3 that clientelism does not seem to be reflected much in the opinion data that we used. Whatever the case may be, there is certainly room for future analyses of presidential voting behavior in Latin America, in order to explore additional factors that might motivate individual voter decisions in that region.

### One Region, One Voter?

The application of an overarching theory of vote choice to the study of presidential elections across Latin America has proven useful, allowing us to identify the similarities and differences between voting behavior in the region as a whole, and compared to other regions of the world. Put differently, this approach has helped to define the general characteristics of the Latin American voter. Treating Latin America as a single unit of analysis has brought to light some of the specificities of the vote in this region, but also the fact that voting behavior in Latin America shares important structural aspects with other democracies around the globe—particularly consolidating ones.

Nevertheless, it would be foolish to argue that voters in all 18 Latin American countries behave in the same way and respond similarly to the same vote determinants when selecting their president. Each country's politics has its particular color, just like each electoral campaign has its own specific dynamics. Uncovering the intraregional variations in the respective influence of different vote determinants has been another one of this book's research goals. We have been able to achieve this goal thanks to our application of a single, sustained explanatory model to all Latin American countries. Indeed, the use of an overarching theory of the vote has proven to be the necessary condition for studying cross-country similarities and differences within the Latin American region in a systematic manner.

Unsurprisingly, chapter 6 found important intraregional differences in the impact of our explanatory variables. In some of the Latin American countries, social cleavages matter more than in others. Party identification has a much stronger influence on presidential voting intention in some countries than in others. Likewise, some issues matter more to the vote in some Latin American countries than in others. What has constituted a more interesting and telling finding of chapter 6, however, is that these intraregional discrepancies in the relative effect of our explanatory factors are linked to a large extent to the sociopolitical context of each country. For example, the influence of race on presidential vote choice is stronger in countries where more people identify themselves as nonwhite. The impact of property on incumbent vote intention is more pronounced in countries where inequalities are more important, and where radical left presidents have pushed for policies that address those inequalities. Class-based or ideology-based voting, or both, is more prominent in places where leaders clearly associated with the left have been in power. Party identification matters less to the vote in countries where the party system is more fractionalized. In countries where authoritarianism is more present, authoritarian attitudes are more salient to the presidential vote decision. Finally, in countries having recently experienced bad economic conditions, evaluations of the state of the national economy weigh more heavily on the voter's mind.

While it remains an abstraction to speak of one Latin American voter, it is striking to see that the intraregional variations observed in the influence of vote determinants tend to align with the specific sociopolitical conditions of individual countries within the region. Party system fractionalization, economic inequalities, racial diversity, poor national economic conditions, and the presence of strong leaders from the political left perhaps displaying a more authoritarian approach to politics—these are factors linked to the relative strength of the explanatory variables we have identified in our accounting of presidential incumbent support. There might be many Latin American "voters" but overall their vote decision is motivated by a similar set of considerations, even when the salience of these considerations may vary, depending on the contexts of the country. The only way to meaningfully assess the magnitude and scope of these intraregional variations is via a general theory of the Latin American vote, as we have done in this book.

## Studying the Vote Decision Process in Latin America

There are a number of questions that our findings about individual-level presidential vote choice in Latin America raise, and that we think would be worthy of being studied in more depth in future electoral research in this region of the world.

A first question has to do with the impact that electoral campaigns can have on the vote. During campaigns, presidential candidates aim at influencing the vote of citizens by making some issues more salient than others, and by appealing to the values of what they consider to be their core constituency. In the process, candidates end up mobilizing those voters who identify with their partisan formation, or are responding positively to their social class discourse. Challengers also attack incumbent candidates on their performance record, or can raise allegations of corruption involving the party in power. In other words, most of the relationships between vote choice and a host of independent variables that we have uncovered in this book's analyses are the end product of mobilization efforts on the part of presidential candidates. Electoral campaigns constitute a crucial part of this process, because their intensity allows the candidates to obtain the attention of the population, triggering both long-term attachments or short-term considerations in voters' minds. The findings reported here are limited in this respect, since they relate to voting behavior outside the campaign context—a limitation that comes with our choice of dataset. A few recent studies of Latin America have started to examine more directly the link between vote choice and the candidates' campaign strategies and discourse (e.g., Ames 1994; Rottinghaus and Alberro 2005; Langston and

Morgenstern 2009; Boas 2015, 2016), as well as the impact of social networks and the media's coverage of campaigns (e.g., Boas 2005; Lawson and McCann 2005; Baker, Ames, and Renno 2006; Porto 2007; Boas and Hidalgo 2011). More studies of this kind are needed in order to really unpack the role and effect of campaigns in Latin American presidential elections.

Another question, which relates to the previous one, involves the fact that the dependent variable in our study has been vote intention in favor of the incumbent president. While in an ideal world one would prefer to use actual (reported) vote choice as the variable to be explained, that measure was not valid for our purposes, since in many of our cases the presidential election that the reported vote variable referred to was held more than three years prior to the data collection. As they stand, our current results are based more on a hypothetical (or theoretical) presidential contest—without a known challenger—than on a real competition between actual candidates running for office. Of course, this is another limitation associated with the choice of dataset, one that forced us to dichotomize an electoral decision that might, in several of these countries, include multiple opposing parties or coalition partners of the incumbent. One consequence of this incumbent-centric focus may be to tilt the results in the direction of performance criteria over other short-term factors. The robustness of our main findings certainly ought to be checked against actual vote choice—that is, within the more realistic context of an actual presidential election campaign with multiple known opponents. However, we do not believe that our results, based on what is in fact a measure of the current incumbent's popularity, would be drastically different if our model were to be applied to an explanation of actual vote choice. One key reason why our conclusions are likely to hold is that we have been more concerned with modeling the decisional (or cognitive) process than its outcome. The only real difference to be found is probably that our current findings underestimate the impact of some of these decisional factors because, as stated above, they have not been activated by an actual electoral campaign.

In any case, the kind of survey data that would be needed to study actual vote choice in Latin America may remain unavailable for quite some time. Three important conditions would need to be met for such opinion data to materialize: (1) that academic research teams in each of the 18 Latin American countries use a more or less standardized survey questionnaire designed to study vote choice; (2) that these opinion surveys be administered at the time of each individual presidential election in these countries;

and (3) that they be administered on national samples of the highest quality possible. These conditions are not jointly met at the moment due to a shortage of scientific, financial, or other means. Ideally, a model similar to the Comparative Study of Electoral Systems should be implemented within the Latin American region—or perhaps the CSES itself will eventually be able to include data from all Latin American countries.[4] Scholars interested in the study of Latin American voting behavior certainly do not lack the interest or the willingness; they just need more time and resources to produce the kind of public opinion data that North American or European voting behavior researchers have had access to so far.

Future studies, ones that rely on more sophisticated data or estimation techniques, or both, will no doubt be able to provide additional evidence in support of the notion that vote choice in Latin America responds to a set of social-psychological and contextual forces that are similar to those found in most electoral democracies across the world—and perhaps, within a generation or two, they will come to show some level of convergence between the Latin American region and established Western democracies in terms of their voting behavior. Until then, our study has been able to show that it is possible to apply an overarching theory of voting behavior to all 18 countries of Latin America by making the most out of the best microsociological empirical data currently available. In doing so, it has also helped to refine our understanding of the ways in which the Latin American region is similar, and yet different.

# Appendix 1: Descriptive Table and Alternative Methods of Estimation

TABLE A1.1. Mean Values of Demographic and Socioeconomic Characteristics for Total and Valid Vote Intention Samples

| Characteristics | Total sample | Vote intention sample | Difference (Vote intention sample—total sample) |
|---|---|---|---|
| Age | .285 | .292* | .007* |
| Gender | .502 | .505 | .003 |
| Catholic | .473 | .478 | .005 |
| Church attendance | .518 | .526 | −.008* |
| Region | .461 | .456 | −.005 |
| White/Asian | .319 | .315 | −.004 |
| Mestizos/mulattos | .571 | .575 | .004 |
| Blacks/indigenous | .110 | .109 | −.001 |
| Schooling | .486 | .483 | −.003 |
| Income | .525 | .524 | −.001 |
| Unemployment | .433 | .425 | −.008* |
| Public sector | .442 | .433 | −.009* |
| Property | .501 | .496 | −.005* |

*Note:* Entries in table are mean values.
* indicates statistically significant differences at $p < .01$ (two-tailed).

## Model with the Same Number of Cases (n = 35,820)

TABLE A1.2. Logistic Regression Models for Voting Intentions in 18 Latin American Countries (LAPOP 2008, 2010, 2012)

|  | (1) | (2) | (3) | (4) | (5) |
|---|---|---|---|---|---|
| Months | −1.09** | −1.14** | −1.13** | −.95** | −.65** |
|  | (.05) | (.05) | (.05) | (.06) | (.07) |
| Age | — | .18** | .13* | .19** | .03 |
|  |  | (.05) | (.06) | (.07) | (.08) |
| Gender | — | .05* | .06** | .05 | .01 |
|  |  | (.02) | (.02) | (.03) | (.03) |
| Catholic | — | .21** | 21** | .08** | .08* |
|  |  | (.02) | (.02) | (.03) | (.03) |
| Church attendance | — | .24** | .27** | .16** | .13** |
|  |  | (.03) | (.03) | (.04) | (.04) |
| Region | — | .01 | −.06* | −.05 | −.06* |
|  |  | (.02) | (.02) | (.03) | (.03) |
| Race | — | .34** | .29** | .19** | .15** |
|  |  | (.04) | (.04) | (.04) | (.05) |
| Schooling | — | — | −.03 | .05 | .01 |
|  |  |  | (.03) | (.04) | (.04) |
| Income | — | — | .16** | .17** | .11* |
|  |  |  | (.04) | (.05) | (.05) |
| Unemployment | — | — | −.15** | −.21** | −.09* |
|  |  |  | (.03) | (.04) | (.04) |
| Public sector | — | — | −.02 | −.04 | .05 |
|  |  |  | (.04) | (.04) | (.05) |
| Property | — | — | .35** | .34** | .23** |
|  |  |  | (.07) | (.08) | (.08) |
| Ideology | — | — | — | 1.18** | .91** |
|  |  |  |  | (.05) | (.05) |
| Party identification | — | — | — | 4.00** | 3.70** |
|  |  |  |  | (.05) | (.05) |
| State | — | — | — | — | .32** |
|  |  |  |  |  | (.06) |
| AUTH | — | — | — | — | −.23** |
|  |  |  |  |  | (.04) |
| Safety | — | — | — | — | .68** |
|  |  |  |  |  | (.07) |
| Corruption | — | — | — | — | .94** |
|  |  |  |  |  | (.07) |
| Democracy | — | — | — | — | 1.05** |
|  |  |  |  |  | (.07) |
| SRE | — | — | — | — | 0.88** |
|  |  |  |  |  | (.04) |
| Constant | .32** | −.22** | −.28** | −2.73** | −4.25** |
|  | (.05) | (.07) | (.08) | (.10) | (.12) |
| Nagelkerke pseudo-$R^2$ | .10 | .11 | .11 | .43 | .52 |
| % correctly predicted | 61.9% | 63.0% | 63.3% | 75.6% | 79.2% |
| N | 35,820 | 35,820 | 35,820 | 35,820 | 35,820 |

**$p ≤ .01$; *$p ≤ .05$ (two-tailed tests). Country dummies are not shown (Mexico is the reference case). Entries are unstandardized logistic regression coefficients, with standard errors in parentheses. See appendix 4 for variable's specification.

## Model with Imputed Values for Missing Cases (INCOME and IDEOLOGY)

TABLE A1.3. Logistic Regression Models for Voting Intentions in 18 Latin American Countries (LAPOP 2008, 2010, 2012)

| | (1) | (2) | (3) | (4) | (5) |
|---|---|---|---|---|---|
| Months | −1.03** | −1.11** | −1.11** | −.93** | −.69** |
| | (.04) | (.04) | (.04) | (.05) | (.06) |
| Age | — | .13** | .14** | .21** | .05 |
| | | (.04) | (.05) | (.06) | (.06) |
| Gender | — | .06** | .08** | .06** | .02 |
| | | (.02) | (.02) | (.02) | (.02) |
| Catholic | — | .17** | .17** | .06* | .06* |
| | | (.02) | (.02) | (.02) | (.03) |
| Church attendance | — | .22** | .24** | .13** | .11** |
| | | (.03) | (.03) | (.03) | (.04) |
| Region | — | .04 | −.05* | −.06* | −.08** |
| | | (.02) | (.02) | (.02) | (.03) |
| Race | — | .37** | .30** | .21** | .18** |
| | | (.03) | (.03) | (.04) | (.04) |
| Schooling | — | — | .01 | .09* | .02 |
| | | | (.03) | (.03) | (.04) |
| Income | — | — | .16** | .16** | .09 |
| | | | (.04) | (.04) | (.05) |
| Unemployment | — | — | −.10** | −.16** | −.06 |
| | | | (.03) | (.03) | (.04) |
| Public sector | — | — | −.02 | −.03 | .08 |
| | | | (.03) | (.04) | (.04) |
| Property | — | — | .40** | .41** | .33** |
| | | | (.06) | (.06) | (.07) |
| Ideology | — | — | — | 1.18** | .90** |
| | | | | (.04) | (.05) |
| Party identification | — | — | — | 4.00** | 3.71** |
| | | | | (.04) | (.05) |
| State | — | — | — | — | .34** |
| | | | | | (.05) |
| AUTH | — | — | — | — | −.25** |
| | | | | | (.04) |
| Safety | — | — | — | — | .63** |
| | | | | | (.06) |
| Corruption | — | — | — | — | 1.04** |
| | | | | | (.06) |
| Democracy | — | — | — | — | 1.03** |
| | | | | | (.06) |
| SRE | — | — | — | — | 0.87** |
| | | | | | (.04) |
| Constant | .28** | −.22** | −.36** | −2.81** | −4.32** |
| | (.05) | (.06) | (.07) | (.09) | (.11) |
| Nagelkerke pseudo-$R^2$ | .10 | .10 | .11 | .42 | .50 |
| % correctly predicted | 61.5% | 63.0% | 63.3% | 75.0% | 78.7% |
| N | 52,489 | 51,394 | 51,217 | 50,973 | 46,081 |

**p ≤ .01; *p ≤ .05 (two-tailed tests). Country dummies are not shown (Mexico is the reference case). Entries are unstandardized logistic regression coefficients, with standard errors in parentheses. See appendix 4 for variable's specification. Missing values for ideology are coded at 0.5. Imputed values for income correspond to the predicted values generated by the following model: Income = $f$ (age, gender, Catholic, region, race, schooling, income, unemployment, public sector, and property).

## Model with Weighted Results

TABLE A1.4. Logistic Regression Models for Voting Intentions in 18 Latin American Countries (LAPOP 2008, 2010, 2012)

|  | (1) | (2) | (3) | (4) | (5) |
|---|---|---|---|---|---|
| Months | −1.04** | −1.11** | −1.13** | −.96** | −.65** |
|  | (.04) | (.04) | (.05) | (.06) | (.07) |
| Age | — | .17** | .15** | .19** | .03 |
|  |  | (.04) | (.05) | (.07) | (.08) |
| Gender | — | .07** | .08** | .06* | .02 |
|  |  | (.02) | (.02) | (.03) | (.03) |
| Catholic | — | .18** | .19** | .08* | .09** |
|  |  | (.02) | (.02) | (.02) | (.03) |
| Church attendance | — | .21** | .23** | .11** | .10* |
|  |  | (.03) | (.03) | (.04) | (.05) |
| Region | — | −.00 | −.09** | −.08* | −.09** |
|  |  | (.02) | (.02) | (.03) | (.03) |
| Race | — | .33** | .24** | .16** | .12* |
|  |  | (.03) | (.03) | (.04) | (.05) |
| Schooling | — | — | −.05 | .03 | −.03 |
|  |  |  | (.03) | (.04) | (.05) |
| Income | — | — | .15** | .13** | .11* |
|  |  |  | (.04) | (.05) | (.05) |
| Unemployment | — | — | −.10** | −.18** | −.08 |
|  |  |  | (.03) | (.04) | (.05) |
| Public sector | — | — | −.07 | −.07 | .04 |
|  |  |  | (.03) | (.04) | (.05) |
| Property | — | — | .32** | .28** | .19* |
|  |  |  | (.06) | (.08) | (.09) |
| Ideology | — | — | — | 1.16** | .89** |
|  |  |  |  | (.05) | (.06) |
| Party identification | — | — | — | 4.07** | 3.78** |
|  |  |  |  | (.05) | (.06) |
| State | — | — | — | — | .34** |
|  |  |  |  |  | (.07) |
| AUTH | — | — | — | — | −.19** |
|  |  |  |  |  | (.05) |
| Safety | — | — | — | — | .70** |
|  |  |  |  |  | (.07) |
| Corruption | — | — | — | — | .95** |
|  |  |  |  |  | (.07) |
| Democracy | — | — | — | — | .98** |
|  |  |  |  |  | (.07) |
| SRE | — | — | — | — | .91** |
|  |  |  |  |  | (.04) |
| Constant | .28** | −.20** | −.21** | −2.63** | −4.21** |
|  | (.05) | (.06) | (.08) | (.10) | (.13) |
| Nagelkerke pseudo-$R^2$ | .09 | .10 | .11 | .43 | .51 |
| % correctly predicted | 61.5% | 62.9% | 63.3% | 75.5% | 79.1% |
| $N$ | 52,489 | 51,393 | 45,332 | 38,363 | 35,820 |

**$p \leq .01$; *$p \leq .05$ (two-tailed tests). Country dummies are not shown (Mexico is the reference case). Entries are unstandardized logistic regression coefficients, with standard errors in parentheses. See appendix 4 for variable's specification. LAPOP weights are used so that each country in the study has an identical weight in the pooled sample (LAPOP weights each country dataset so that each country has an $N$ of 1,500).

# Appendix 2: Regressions and Changes in Probabilities Tables

TABLE A2.1. Logistic Regression Models for Voting Intentions in 18 Latin American Countries (LAPOP 2008, 2010, 2012)

|                    | (1)      | (2)      | (3)      | (4)      | (5)      |
|--------------------|----------|----------|----------|----------|----------|
| Months             | −1.03**  | −1.11**  | −1.14**  | −.94**   | −.65**   |
|                    | (.04)    | (.04)    | (.05)    | (.06)    | (.07)    |
| Age                | —        | .13**    | .15**    | .19**    | .03      |
|                    |          | (.04)    | (.05)    | (.07)    | (.08)    |
| Gender             | —        | .06**    | .07**    | .05      | .01      |
|                    |          | (.02)    | (.02)    | (.03)    | (.03)    |
| Catholic           | —        | .17**    | 18**     | .08**    | .08*     |
|                    |          | (.02)    | (.02)    | (.03)    | (.03)    |
| Church attendance  | —        | .22**    | .25**    | .14**    | .13**    |
|                    |          | (.03)    | (.03)    | (.04)    | (.04)    |
| Region             | —        | .04      | −.06**   | −.05     | −.06*    |
|                    |          | (.02)    | (.02)    | (.03)    | (.03)    |
| Race               | —        | .37**    | .27**    | .19**    | .15**    |
|                    |          | (.03)    | (.03)    | (.04)    | (.05)    |
| Schooling          | —        | —        | −.00     | .07      | .01      |
|                    |          |          | (.03)    | (.04)    | (.04)    |
| Income             | —        | —        | .17**    | .16**    | .11*     |
|                    |          |          | (.04)    | (.05)    | (.05)    |
| Unemployment       | —        | —        | −.12**   | −.19**   | −.09*    |
|                    |          |          | (.03)    | (.04)    | (.04)    |
| Public sector      | —        | —        | −.04     | −.04     | .05      |
|                    |          |          | (.03)    | (.04)    | (.05)    |
| Property           | —        | —        | .35**    | .32**    | .23**    |
|                    |          |          | (.06)    | (.08)    | (.08)    |
| Ideology           | —        | —        | —        | 1.18**   | .91**    |
|                    |          |          |          | (.05)    | (.05)    |
| Party identification | —      | —        | —        | 4.00**   | 3.70**   |
|                    |          |          |          | (.05)    | (.05)    |

| | (1) | (2) | (3) | (4) | (5) |
|---|---|---|---|---|---|
| State | — | — | — | — | .32** |
| | | | | | (.06) |
| AUTH | — | — | — | — | −.23** |
| | | | | | (.04) |
| Safety | — | — | — | — | .68** |
| | | | | | (.07) |
| Corruption | — | — | — | — | .94** |
| | | | | | (.07) |
| Democracy | — | — | — | — | 1.05** |
| | | | | | (.07) |
| SRE | — | — | — | — | 0.88** |
| | | | | | (.04) |
| Argentina | −.25** | −.12 | −.18* | −.55** | −.10 |
| | (.06) | (.06) | (.08) | (.09) | (.10) |
| Bolivia | .23** | .26** | .17** | −.31** | −.16 |
| | (.05) | (.06) | (.06) | (.08) | (.09) |
| Brazil | 1.12** | 1.22** | 1.14** | 1.48** | 1.51** |
| | (.06) | (.06) | (.07) | (.09) | (.10) |
| Chile | −.60** | −.54** | −.62** | −.63** | −.84** |
| | (.06) | (.06) | (.07) | (.08) | (.09) |
| Colombia | 1.11** | 1.10** | 1.14** | 1.68** | 1.42** |
| | (.06) | (.06) | (.07) | (.08) | (.09) |
| Costa Rica | .44** | .38** | .42** | .09 | .03 |
| | (.06) | (.06) | (.06) | (.09) | (.09) |
| Dominican Republic | .73** | .77** | .78** | .33** | .48** |
| | (.05) | (.05) | (.06) | (.08) | (.08) |
| Ecuador | .65** | .72** | .63** | .43** | .48** |
| | (.05) | (.06) | (.07) | (.08) | (.09) |
| El Salvador | .17** | .21** | .16* | .04 | .14 |
| | (.05) | (.06) | (.06) | (.08) | (.09) |
| Guatemala | −.39** | −.39** | −.46** | −.54** | −.25** |
| | (.06) | (.06) | (.07) | (.08) | (.09) |
| Honduras | −.07 | −.09 | −.04 | −.30** | .02 |
| | (.06) | (.06) | (.07) | (.09) | (.09) |
| Nicaragua | .25** | .28** | .10 | −.39** | −.09 |
| | (.06) | (.06) | (.07) | (.09) | (.10) |
| Panama | .05 | .04 | .06 | −.19* | −.21** |
| | (.06) | (.06) | (.06) | (.08) | (.08) |
| Paraguay | −.29** | −.21** | −.25** | −.31** | .12 |
| | (.06) | (.06) | (.07) | (.09) | (.10) |
| Peru | −1.01** | −1.00** | −1.00** | −1.11** | −.87** |
| | (.06) | (.06) | (.07) | (.08) | (.09) |
| Uruguay | .60** | .66** | .55** | .14 | −.19 |
| | (.05) | (.06) | (.07) | (.09) | (.10) |
| Venezuela | .63** | .77** | .68** | .20** | .56** |
| | (.06) | (.06) | (.07) | (.09) | (.11) |
| Constant | .28** | −.22* | −.28** | −2.73** | −4.25** |
| | (.05) | (.06) | (.07) | (.10) | (.12) |
| Nagelkerke pseudo-$R^2$ | .097 | .105 | .11 | .43 | .51 |
| % correctly predicted | 61.5% | 63.0% | 63.4% | 75.7% | 79.2% |
| N | 52,489 | 51,394 | 45,332 | 38,363 | 35,820 |

**\*\***$p \leq .01$; **\***$p \leq .05$ (two-tailed tests). Mexico is the reference case for country dummies. Entries are unstandardized logistic regression coefficients, with standard errors in parentheses. See appendix 4 for variable's specification.

TABLE A2.2. Change in Probabilities for Voting Intentions in 18 Latin American Countries (LAPOP 2008, 2010, 2012)

| | (1) | (2) | (3) | (4) | (5) |
|---|---|---|---|---|---|
| Months | −.24** | −.25** | −.26** | −.15** | −.10** |
| Age | — | .03** | .03** | .03** | .01 |
| Gender | — | .01** | .02** | .01 | .00 |
| Catholic | — | .04** | .04** | .01** | .01** |
| Church attendance | — | .05** | .06** | .02** | .02** |
| Region | — | .01 | −.01** | −.01* | −.01* |
| Race | — | .08** | .06** | .03** | .02** |
| Schooling | — | — | −.00 | .01 | .00 |
| Income | — | — | .04** | .03** | .01* |
| Unemployment | — | — | −.03** | −.03** | −.01* |
| Public sector | — | — | −.01 | −.01 | .01 |
| Property | — | — | .08** | .05** | .04** |
| Ideology | — | — | — | .19** | .13** |
| Party identification | — | — | — | .65** | .54** |
| State | — | — | — | — | .05** |
| AUTH | — | — | — | — | −.03** |
| Safety | — | — | — | — | .10** |
| Corruption | — | — | — | — | .14** |
| Democracy | — | — | — | — | .15** |
| SRE | — | — | — | — | .13** |
| Argentina | −.06** | −.03 | −.04* | −.09** | −.01 |
| Bolivia | .05** | .06** | .04** | −.05** | −.02 |
| Brazil | .26** | .28** | .26** | .24** | .22** |
| Chile | −.14** | −.13** | −.14** | −.10** | −.12** |
| Colombia | .26** | .25** | .26** | .28** | .21** |
| Costa Rica | .10** | .09** | .10** | .02 | .01 |
| Dominican Republic | .17** | .18** | .18** | .05** | .07** |
| Ecuador | .15** | .17** | .14** | .07** | .07** |
| El Salvador | .04** | .05** | .04* | .01 | .02 |
| Guatemala | −.09** | −.09** | −.11** | −.09** | −.04** |
| Honduras | −.02 | −.02 | −.01 | −.05** | −.00 |
| Nicaragua | .06** | .06** | .02 | −.06** | −.01 |
| Panama | .01 | .01 | .01 | −.03* | −.03** |
| Paraguay | −.07** | −.05** | −.06** | −.05** | .02 |
| Peru | −.23** | −.23** | −.23** | −.18** | −.13** |
| Uruguay | .14** | .15** | .13** | .02 | −.03 |
| Venezuela | .15** | .18** | .16** | .03* | .08** |
| N | 52,489 | 51,394 | 45,332 | 38,363 | 35,820 |

**p ≤ .01; *p ≤ .05 (two-tailed tests). Mexico is the reference case for country dummies. Entries represent change in probabilities. See appendix 4 for variable's specification.

TABLE A2.3. Logistic Regression Models for Voting Intentions in Argentina (2008, 2010, 2012)

| | (1) | (2) | (3) | (4) | (5) |
|---|---|---|---|---|---|
| Months | −3.11** | −2.83** | −3.10** | −2.63** | −2.32** |
| | (.24) | (.26) | (.31) | (.36) | (.42) |
| Age | — | −.96** | −.91** | −.70* | −.74 |
| | | (.23) | (.29) | (.35) | (.40) |
| Gender | — | .13 | .11 | .14 | .02 |
| | | (.09) | (.10) | (.12) | (.14) |
| Catholic | — | .11 | .02 | −.02 | −.05 |
| | | (.11) | (.13) | (.15) | (.17) |
| Church attendance | — | −.10 | −.01 | −.02 | .36 |
| | | (.14) | (.16) | (.19) | (.22) |
| Region | — | .49** | .45** | .55** | .37* |
| | | (.10) | (.12) | (.14) | (.16) |
| Race | — | .72** | .38** | .37 | −.03 |
| | | (.15) | (.17) | (.20) | (.23) |
| Schooling | — | — | .43** | .15 | −.02 |
| | | | (.16) | (.19) | (.22) |
| Income | — | — | .22 | .24 | .23 |
| | | | (.18) | (.21) | (.24) |
| Unemployment | — | — | .04 | −.05 | .02 |
| | | | (.21) | (.25) | (.28) |
| Public sector | — | — | .25 | .09 | .07 |
| | | | (.15) | (.17) | (.19) |
| Property | — | — | 2.06** | 2.05** | 2.25** |
| | | | (.36) | (.42) | (.48) |
| Ideology | — | — | — | .34 | .42 |
| | | | | (.30) | (.35) |
| Party identification | — | — | — | 3.65** | 3.54** |
| | | | | (.27) | (.30) |
| State | — | — | — | — | −.12 |
| | | | | | (.34) |
| AUTH | — | — | — | — | −.84** |
| | | | | | (.23) |
| Safety | — | — | — | — | .26 |
| | | | | | (.40) |
| Corruption | — | — | — | — | 1.57** |
| | | | | | (.40) |
| Democracy | — | — | — | — | 1.24** |
| | | | | | (.34) |
| SRE | — | — | — | — | 1.05** |
| | | | | | (.20) |
| Constant | .37** | .71** | −.10 | −2.47** | −3.51** |
| | (.06) | (.20) | (.27) | (.39) | (.54) |
| Nagelkerke pseudo-$R^2$ | .10 | .15 | .20 | .35 | .49 |
| % correctly predicted | 61.3% | 64.9% | 67.5% | 73.8% | 79.4% |
| N | 2,473 | 2,294 | 1,797 | 1,555 | 1,434 |

**$p \leq .01$; *$p \leq .05$ (two-tailed tests). Entries are unstandardized logistic regression coefficients, with standard errors in parentheses.

TABLE A2.4. Change in Probabilities for Voting Intentions in Argentina (2008, 2010, 2012)

| | (1) | (2) | (3) | (4) | (5) |
|---|---|---|---|---|---|
| Months | −.72** | −.63** | −.66** | −.48** | −.35** |
| Age | — | −.21** | −.19** | −.13* | −.11* |
| Gender | — | .03 | .02 | .03 | .00 |
| Catholic | — | .03 | .01 | −.00 | −.01 |
| Church attendance | — | −.02 | −.00 | −.00 | .05 |
| Region | — | .11** | .10** | .10** | .06* |
| Race | — | .16** | .08* | .07 | −.01 |
| Schooling | — | — | .09** | .03 | −.00 |
| Income | — | — | .05 | .04 | .04 |
| Unemployment | — | — | .01 | −.01 | .00 |
| Public sector | — | — | .05 | .02 | .01 |
| Property | — | — | .44** | .37** | .34** |
| Ideology | — | — | — | .06 | .06 |
| Party identification | — | — | — | .66** | .53** |
| State | — | — | — | — | −.02 |
| AUTH | — | — | — | — | −.13** |
| Safety | — | — | — | — | .04 |
| Corruption | — | — | — | — | .24** |
| Democracy | — | — | — | — | .19** |
| SRE | — | — | — | — | .16** |
| N | 2,573 | 2,294 | 1,797 | 1,555 | 1,434 |

**p ≤ .01; *p ≤ .05 (two-tailed tests). Entries represent change in probabilities.

TABLE A2.5. Logistic Regression Models for Voting Intentions in Bolivia (2008, 2010, 2012)

| | (1) | (2) | (3) | (4) | (5) |
|---|---|---|---|---|---|
| Months | −1.47** | −1.68** | −1.77** | −1.75** | −1.46** |
| | (.15) | (.16) | (.17) | (.23) | (.27) |
| Age | — | −.92** | −.66** | −.26 | −.65* |
| | | (.16) | (.20) | (.26) | (.31) |
| Gender | — | .11 | .20** | .15 | .04 |
| | | (.06) | (.07) | (.09) | (.10) |
| Catholic | — | .28** | .33** | .27* | .12 |
| | | (.07) | (.08) | (.11) | (.13) |
| Church attendance | — | .67** | .69** | .49** | .59** |
| | | (.11) | (.12) | (.15) | (.18) |
| Region | — | .69** | .29** | .22* | .16 |
| | | (.06) | (.07) | (.10) | (.11) |
| Race | — | 1.46** | 1.04** | .62** | .12 |
| | | (.12) | (.14) | (.19) | (.23) |
| Schooling | — | — | .24** | .22 | .13 |
| | | | (.10) | (.13) | (.15) |
| Income | — | — | 1.04** | .71** | .42* |
| | | | (.12) | (.16) | (.18) |
| Unemployment | — | — | −.26 | −.46* | −.51* |
| | | | (.15) | (.20) | (.24) |
| Public sector | — | — | .39** | .33* | .29 |
| | | | (.12) | (.15) | (.18) |
| Property | — | — | 1.01** | 1.15** | 1.05** |
| | | | (.20) | (.26) | (.31) |
| Ideology | — | — | — | 1.97** | 1.35** |
| | | | | (.19) | (.23) |
| Party identification | — | — | — | 5.74** | 4.81** |
| | | | | (.28) | (.29) |
| State | — | — | — | — | .47 |
| | | | | | (.27) |
| AUTH | — | — | — | — | −.80** |
| | | | | | (.19) |
| Safety | — | — | — | — | .71** |
| | | | | | (.27) |
| Corruption | — | — | — | — | 1.63** |
| | | | | | (.27) |
| Democracy | — | — | — | — | 1.90** |
| | | | | | (.28) |
| SRE | — | — | — | — | 1.02** |
| | | | | | (.15) |
| Constant | .64** | −.19 | −1.10** | −5.17** | −6.06** |
| | (.05) | (.16) | (.20) | (.32) | (.43) |
| Nagelkerke pseudo-$R^2$ | .03 | .13 | .18 | .50 | .63 |
| % correctly predicted | 62.3% | 63.9% | 66.5% | 77.5% | 83.7% |
| N | 5,139 | 5,084 | 4,465 | 3,658 | 3,433 |

**$p \leq .01$; * $p \leq .05$ (two-tailed tests). Entries are unstandardized logistic regression coefficients, with standard errors in parentheses.

TABLE A2.6. Change in Probabilities for Voting Intentions in Bolivia (2008, 2010, 2012)

| | (1) | (2) | (3) | (4) | (5) |
|---|---|---|---|---|---|
| Months | −.36** | −.37** | −.38** | .27** | −.17** |
| Age | — | −.20** | −.14** | −.04 | −.08* |
| Gender | — | .02 | .04** | .02 | .01 |
| Catholic | — | .06** | .07** | .04* | .01 |
| Church attendance | — | .15** | .15** | .07** | .07** |
| Region | — | .15** | .06** | .03* | .02 |
| Race | — | .33** | .22** | .09** | .01 |
| Schooling | — | — | .05* | .03 | .02 |
| Income | — | — | .22** | .11** | .05* |
| Unemployment | — | — | −.06 | −.07* | −.06* |
| Public sector | — | — | .08** | .05* | .03 |
| Property | — | — | .22** | .18** | .13** |
| Ideology | — | — | — | .30** | .16** |
| Party identification | — | — | — | .87** | .57** |
| State | — | — | — | — | .06 |
| AUTH | — | — | — | — | −.10** |
| Safety | — | — | — | — | .08** |
| Corruption | — | — | — | — | .19** |
| Democracy | — | — | — | — | .23** |
| SRE | — | — | — | — | .12** |
| N | 5,139 | 5,084 | 4,465 | 3,658 | 3,433 |

**$p \leq .01$; *$p \leq .05$ (two-tailed tests). Entries represent change in probabilities.

TABLE A2.7. Logistic Regression Models for Voting Intentions in Brazil (2008, 2010, 2012)

| | (1) | (2) | (3) | (4) | (5) |
|---|---|---|---|---|---|
| Months | −.08 | −.07 | −.16 | .16 | −.45 |
| | (.20) | (.21) | (.25) | (.31) | (.34) |
| Age | — | .11 | .66** | .53 | .75* |
| | | (.21) | (.25) | (.29) | (.32) |
| Gender | — | −.12 | −.12 | −.07 | −.15 |
| | | (.08) | (.09) | (.10) | (.11) |
| Catholic | — | −.10 | −.07 | −.04 | −.02 |
| | | (.08) | (.09) | (.11) | (.11) |
| Church attendance | — | .04 | .12 | .10 | .17 |
| | | (.12) | (.13) | (.15) | (.16) |
| Region | — | .19* | −.02 | −.09 | −.17 |
| | | (.09) | (.10) | (.11) | (.12) |
| Race | — | .96** | .81** | .72** | .70** |
| | | (.12) | (.13) | (.15) | (.16) |
| Schooling | — | — | .74** | .83** | .87** |
| | | | (.17) | (.19) | (.20) |
| Income | — | — | .01 | .03 | .17 |
| | | | (.15) | (.18) | (.19) |
| Unemployment | — | — | .01 | .03 | −.05 |
| | | | (.13) | (.15) | (.16) |
| Public sector | — | — | .08 | .07 | .00 |
| | | | (.17) | (.19) | (.20) |
| Property | — | — | 1.32** | 1.35** | .93** |
| | | | (.27) | (.31) | (.34) |
| Ideology | — | — | — | −.23 | −.14 |
| | | | | (.18) | (.20) |
| Party identification | — | — | — | .48** | .36 |
| | | | | (.17) | (.18) |
| State | — | — | — | — | .33 |
| | | | | | (.23) |
| AUTH | — | — | — | — | −.26 |
| | | | | | (.17) |
| Safety | — | — | — | — | .16 |
| | | | | | (.27) |
| Corruption | — | — | — | — | .82** |
| | | | | | (.25) |
| Democracy | — | — | — | — | .88** |
| | | | | | (.25) |
| SRE | — | — | — | — | .44** |
| | | | | | (.15) |
| Constant | .99** | .56** | −.67** | −.78** | −1.73** |
| | (.09) | (.20) | (.27) | (.34) | (.43) |
| Nagelkerke pseudo-$R^2$ | .0001 | .03 | .08 | .09 | .15 |
| % correctly predicted | 72.2% | 72.1% | 73.1% | 74.7% | 75.7% |
| $N$ | 3,415 | 3,298 | 2,868 | 2,299 | 2,041 |

**$p \leq .01$; *$p \leq .05$ (two-tailed tests). Entries are unstandardized logistic regression coefficients, with standard errors in parentheses.

TABLE A2.8. Change in Probabilities for Voting Intentions in Brazil (2008, 2010, 2012)

| | (1) | (2) | (3) | (4) | (5) |
|---|---|---|---|---|---|
| Months | −.02 | −.02 | −.03 | .03 | −.08 |
| Age | — | .02 | .12** | .10 | .13* |
| Gender | — | −.02 | −.02 | −.01 | −.03 |
| Catholic | — | −.02 | −.01 | −.01 | −.00 |
| Church attendance | — | .01 | −.02 | .02 | .03 |
| Region | — | .04* | −.01 | −.02 | −.03 |
| Race | — | .19** | .15** | .13** | .12** |
| Schooling | — | — | .14** | .15** | .15** |
| Income | — | — | .00 | .01 | .03 |
| Unemployment | — | — | .00 | .01 | −.01 |
| Public sector | — | — | .02 | .01 | .00 |
| Property | — | — | .25** | .24** | .16** |
| Ideology | — | — | — | −.04 | −.02 |
| Party identification | — | — | — | .09** | .06 |
| State | — | — | — | — | .06 |
| AUTH | — | — | — | — | −.05 |
| Safety | — | — | — | — | .03 |
| Corruption | — | — | — | — | .14** |
| Democracy | — | — | — | — | .15** |
| SRE | — | — | — | — | .08** |
| N | 3,415 | 3,298 | 2,868 | 2,299 | 2,041 |

**$p \leq .01$; *$p \leq .05$ (two-tailed tests). Entries represent change in probabilities.

TABLE A2.9. Logistic Regression Models for Voting Intentions in Chile (2008, 2010, 2012)

| | (1) | (2) | (3) | (4) | (5) |
|---|---|---|---|---|---|
| Months | .19 | 1.07** | 2.04** | 2.49** | 4.04** |
| | (.24) | (.29) | (.34) | (.40) | (.48) |
| Age | — | .29 | .58* | .45 | .44 |
| | | (.22) | (.28) | (.34) | (.36) |
| Gender | — | -.22* | -.02 | -.17 | -.20 |
| | | (.09) | (.10) | (.12) | (.13) |
| Catholic | — | -.28** | -.15 | -.25* | -.22 |
| | | (.09) | (.11) | (.12) | (.13) |
| Church attendance | — | .32* | .18 | -.03 | -.11 |
| | | (.14) | (.15) | (.18) | (.19) |
| Region | — | -.18 | -.25* | -.20 | -.16 |
| | | (.10) | (.12) | (.14) | (.15) |
| Race | — | -.25 | -.03 | -.03 | .08 |
| | | (.13) | (.16) | (.19) | (.20) |
| Schooling | — | — | .44** | .55** | .53** |
| | | | (.15) | (.18) | (.20) |
| Income | — | — | .87** | .87** | .90** |
| | | | (.17) | (.20) | (.22) |
| Unemployment | — | — | -.71** | -.55** | -.35 |
| | | | (.18) | (.21) | (.24) |
| Public sector | — | — | -.25 | -.34 | -.34 |
| | | | (.18) | (.22) | (.25) |
| Property | — | — | -.67 | -.80 | -.93* |
| | | | (.37) | (.43) | (.47) |
| Ideology | — | — | — | 3.52** | 3.31** |
| | | | | (.25) | (.27) |
| Party identification | — | — | — | 1.36** | 1.20** |
| | | | | (.24) | (.26) |
| State | — | — | — | — | .64* |
| | | | | | (.31) |
| AUTH | — | — | — | — | .10 |
| | | | | | (.20) |
| Safety | — | — | — | — | .21 |
| | | | | | (.35) |
| Corruption | — | — | — | — | .94** |
| | | | | | (.36) |
| Democracy | — | — | — | — | 1.11** |
| | | | | | (.38) |
| SRE | — | — | — | — | .58** |
| | | | | | (.19) |
| Constant | -.61** | -.76** | -1.37** | -3.62** | -5.93** |
| | (.07) | (.16) | (.23) | (.33) | (.50) |
| Nagelkerke pseudo-$R^2$ | .0003 | .03 | .11 | .30 | .37 |
| % correctly predicted | 63.8% | 64.5% | 67.4% | 73.4% | 75.4% |
| N | 2,389 | 2,367 | 2,068 | 1,764 | 1,647 |

**$p \leq .01$; *$p \leq .05$ (two-tailed tests). Entries are unstandardized logistic regression coefficients, with standard errors in parentheses.

TABLE A2.10. Change in Probabilities for Voting Intentions in Chile (2008, 2010, 2012)

| | (1) | (2) | (3) | (4) | (5) |
|---|---|---|---|---|---|
| Months | −.04 | −.24** | −.43** | −.46** | −.67** |
| Age | — | .07 | .12* | .08 | .07 |
| Gender | — | −.05* | −.01 | −.03 | −.03 |
| Catholic | — | −.06** | −.03 | −.05* | −.04 |
| Church attendance | — | .07* | .04 | −.01 | −.02 |
| Region | — | −.04 | −.05* | −.04 | −.03 |
| Race | — | −.06 | −.01 | −.01 | .01 |
| Schooling | — | — | .09** | .10** | .09** |
| Income | — | — | .19** | .16** | .15** |
| Unemployment | — | — | −.15** | −.10** | −.06 |
| Public sector | — | — | −.05 | −.06 | −.06 |
| Property | — | — | −.14 | −.14 | −.15* |
| Ideology | — | — | — | .63** | .55** |
| Party identification | — | — | — | .24** | .20** |
| State | — | — | — | — | .11* |
| AUTH | — | — | — | — | .02 |
| Safety | — | — | — | — | .03 |
| Corruption | — | — | — | — | .16** |
| Democracy | — | — | — | — | .18** |
| SRE | — | — | — | — | .10** |
| N | 2,389 | 2,367 | 2,068 | 1,764 | 1,647 |

**p ≤ .01; *p ≤ .05 (two-tailed tests). Entries represent change in probabilities.

TABLE A2.11. Logistic Regression Models for Voting Intentions in Colombia (2008, 2010, 2012)

| | (1) | (2) | (3) | (4) | (5) |
|---|---|---|---|---|---|
| Months | 1.73** | 1.41** | 1.87** | 1.94** | 2.14** |
| | (.26) | (.27) | (.30) | (.33) | (.37) |
| Age | — | .57* | .12 | .02 | .42 |
| | | (.27) | (.33) | (.37) | (.41) |
| Gender | — | .27** | .23* | .19 | .25 |
| | | (.10) | (.11) | (.12) | (.13) |
| Catholic | — | .28* | .28* | .28* | .18 |
| | | (.11) | (.12) | (.14) | (.15) |
| Church attendance | — | .30 | .37* | .25 | .17 |
| | | (.15) | (.17) | (.19) | (.20) |
| Region | — | -.79** | -.55** | -.57** | -.54** |
| | | (.10) | (.12) | (.13) | (.14) |
| Race | — | .56** | .66** | .63** | .62** |
| | | (.14) | (.16) | (.18) | (.19) |
| Schooling | — | — | -.54** | -.35 | -.21 |
| | | | (.18) | (.19) | (.21) |
| Income | — | — | -.31 | -.27 | -.40 |
| | | | (.22) | (.24) | (.26) |
| Unemployment | — | — | .23 | .24 | .38 |
| | | | (.18) | (.19) | (.21) |
| Public sector | — | — | .80** | .83** | .91** |
| | | | (.21) | (.22) | (.24) |
| Property | — | — | -.51 | -.64 | -.40 |
| | | | (.35) | (.39) | (.42) |
| Ideology | — | — | — | .89** | .44 |
| | | | | (.21) | (.23) |
| Party identification | — | — | — | .98** | 1.00** |
| | | | | (.20) | (.21) |
| State | — | — | — | — | .38 |
| | | | | | (.33) |
| AUTH | — | — | — | — | .51** |
| | | | | | (.21) |
| Safety | — | — | — | — | .71* |
| | | | | | (.30) |
| Corruption | — | — | — | — | .68* |
| | | | | | (.29) |
| Democracy | — | — | — | — | 1.01** |
| | | | | | (.32) |
| SRE | — | — | — | — | .79** |
| | | | | | (.18) |
| Constant | .26* | -.17 | -.66 | -1.52** | -3.76** |
| | (.11) | (.20) | (.37) | (.42) | (.51) |
| Nagelkerke pseudo-$R^2$ | .03 | .09 | .13 | .16 | .27 |
| % correctly predicted | 72.2% | 72.4% | 72.8% | 73.9% | 76.4% |
| N | 2,401 | 2,377 | 2,080 | 1,773 | 1,639 |

**$p \leq .01$; *$p \leq .05$ (two-tailed tests). Entries are unstandardized logistic regression coefficients, with standard errors in parentheses.

TABLE A2.12. Change in Probabilities for Voting Intentions in Colombia (2008, 2010, 2012)

| | (1) | (2) | (3) | (4) | (5) |
|---|---|---|---|---|---|
| Months | .34** | .26** | .34** | .34** | .35** |
| Age | — | .11* | .02 | .00 | .07 |
| Gender | — | .05** | .04* | .03 | .04* |
| Catholic | — | .05* | .05* | .05* | .03 |
| Church attendance | — | .06 | .07* | .05 | .03 |
| Region | — | -.15** | -.10** | -.10** | -.09** |
| Race | — | .10** | .12** | .11** | .10** |
| Schooling | — | — | -.10** | -.06 | -.03 |
| Income | — | — | -.06 | -.05 | -.06 |
| Unemployment | — | — | .04 | .04 | .06 |
| Public sector | — | — | .14** | .15** | .15** |
| Property | — | — | -.09 | -.11 | -.07 |
| Ideology | — | — | — | .16** | .07 |
| Party identification | — | — | — | .17** | .16** |
| State | — | — | — | — | .06 |
| AUTH | — | — | — | — | .08* |
| Safety | — | — | — | — | .12* |
| Corruption | — | — | — | — | .11* |
| Democracy | — | — | — | — | .16** |
| SRE | — | — | — | — | .13** |
| N | 2,401 | 2,377 | 2,080 | 1,773 | 1,639 |

$**p \leq .01$; $*p \leq .05$ (two-tailed tests). Entries represent change in probabilities.

TABLE A2.13. Logistic Regression Models for Voting Intentions in Costa Rica (2008, 2010, 2012)

| | (1) | (2) | (3) | (4) | (5) |
|---|---|---|---|---|---|
| Months | -.44* | -.57** | -.78** | -.22 | -.09 |
| | (.22) | (.23) | (.26) | (.40) | (.43) |
| Age | — | 1.25** | .75** | -.17 | -.47 |
| | | (.21) | (.25) | (.36) | (.39) |
| Gender | — | .22* | .22* | -.03 | -.01 |
| | | (.09) | (.10) | (.14) | (.15) |
| Catholic | — | .06 | .11 | .09 | .13 |
| | | (.09) | (.10) | (.15) | (.16) |
| Church attendance | — | .39** | .48** | .37 | .36 |
| | | (.12) | (.13) | (.19) | (.20) |
| Region | — | -.37** | -.37** | -.19 | -.10 |
| | | (.09) | (.10) | (.14) | (.15) |
| Race | — | -.25 | -.23 | -.51* | -.63** |
| | | (.14) | (.15) | (.23) | (.25) |
| Schooling | — | — | -.29* | -.16 | -.11 |
| | | | (.14) | (.20) | (.22) |
| Income | — | — | .41** | .34 | .23 |
| | | | (.15) | (.21) | (.22) |
| Unemployment | — | — | .03 | .01 | -.04 |
| | | | (.20) | (.28) | (.30) |
| Public sector | — | — | .23 | -.03 | .09 |
| | | | (.20) | (.28) | (.30) |
| Property | — | — | -.30 | -1.09** | -1.11* |
| | | | (.29) | (.42) | (.45) |
| Ideology | — | — | — | .77** | .63* |
| | | | | (.23) | (.25) |
| Party identification | — | — | — | 4.16** | 4.05** |
| | | | | (.25) | (.26) |
| State | — | — | — | — | .21 |
| | | | | | (.31) |
| AUTH | — | — | — | — | .38 |
| | | | | | (.20) |
| Safety | — | — | — | — | -.40 |
| | | | | | (.31) |
| Corruption | — | — | — | — | 1.08** |
| | | | | | (.29) |
| Democracy | — | — | — | — | 1.14** |
| | | | | | (.29) |
| SRE | — | — | — | — | .31 |
| | | | | | (.20) |
| Constant | .45** | .07 | .16 | -1.44** | -2.60** |
| | (.11) | (.19) | (.39) | (.55) | (.61) |
| Nagelkerke pseudo-$R^2$ | .002 | .047 | .05 | .43 | .47 |
| % correctly predicted | 56.1% | 59.6% | 61.0% | 74.4% | 78.1% |
| $N$ | 2,451 | 2,393 | 1,936 | 1,390 | 1,299 |

**$p \leq .01$; *$p \leq .05$ (two-tailed tests). Entries are unstandardized logistic regression coefficients, with standard errors in parentheses.

TABLE A2.14. Change in Probabilities for Voting Intentions in Costa Rica (2008, 2010, 2012)

| | (1) | (2) | (3) | (4) | (5) |
|---|---|---|---|---|---|
| Months | −.11* | −.14* | −.18** | −.04 | −.01 |
| Age | — | .30** | .18** | −.03 | −.07 |
| Gender | — | .05** | .05* | −.01 | −.00 |
| Catholic | — | .02 | .03 | .02 | .02 |
| Church attendance | — | .09** | .11** | .06* | .06 |
| Region | — | −.09** | −.09** | −.03 | −.02 |
| Race | — | −.06 | −.05 | −.08* | −.10** |
| Schooling | — | — | −.07* | −.03 | −.02 |
| Income | — | — | .10** | .06 | .04 |
| Unemployment | — | — | .01 | .00 | −.00 |
| Public sector | — | — | .06 | −.01 | .01 |
| Property | — | — | −.07 | −.18** | −.17* |
| Ideology | — | — | — | .13** | .10** |
| Party identification | — | — | — | .68** | .62** |
| State | — | — | — | — | .03 |
| AUTH | — | — | — | — | .06 |
| Safety | — | — | — | — | −.06 |
| Corruption | — | — | — | — | .17** |
| Democracy | — | — | — | — | .18** |
| SRE | — | — | — | — | .05 |
| N | 2,451 | 2,393 | 1,936 | 1,390 | 1,299 |

**$p \leq .01$; *$p \leq .05$ (two-tailed tests). Entries represent change in probabilities.

TABLE A2.15. Logistic Regression Models for Voting Intentions in Dominican Republic (2008, 2010, 2012)

| | (1) | (2) | (3) | (4) | (5) |
|---|---|---|---|---|---|
| Months | −.17 | −.15 | −.37 | .33 | .83 |
| | (.20) | (.21) | (.24) | (.41) | (.46) |
| Age | — | .38* | −.32 | −.50 | −.36 |
| | | (.18) | (.22) | (.42) | (.48) |
| Gender | — | .53** | .50** | .13 | .14 |
| | | (.07) | (.08) | (.15) | (.17) |
| Catholic | — | −.05 | −.06 | −.31* | −.39* |
| | | (.08) | (.08) | (.15) | (.16) |
| Church attendance | — | .06 | −.02 | .02 | −.10 |
| | | (.10) | (.12) | (.21) | (.23) |
| Region | — | .05 | .13 | .07 | −.06 |
| | | (.07) | (.08) | (.15) | (.17) |
| Race | — | .27* | .33* | .20 | −.05 |
| | | (.14) | (.15) | (.28) | (.32) |
| Schooling | — | — | −.72** | −.82** | −.76** |
| | | | (.12) | (.22) | (.24) |
| Income | — | — | .28* | .33 | .31 |
| | | | (.14) | (.25) | (.27) |
| Unemployment | — | — | .26* | .22 | .21 |
| | | | (.12) | (.21) | (.22) |
| Public sector | — | — | −1.01** | −.33 | −.34 |
| | | | (.16) | (.32) | (.35) |
| Property | — | — | −.28 | −.09 | .24 |
| | | | (.23) | (.41) | (.45) |
| Ideology | — | — | — | 1.01** | .58* |
| | | | | (.21) | (.24) |
| Party identification | — | — | — | 6.28** | 5.91** |
| | | | | (.24) | (.26) |
| State | — | — | — | — | .85 |
| | | | | | (.43) |
| AUTH | — | — | — | — | −.22 |
| | | | | | (.25) |
| Safety | — | — | — | — | 1.03** |
| | | | | | (.36) |
| Corruption | — | — | — | — | .41 |
| | | | | | (.34) |
| Democracy | — | — | — | — | .94** |
| | | | | | (.34) |
| SRE | — | — | — | — | 1.34** |
| | | | | | (.21) |
| Constant | .53** | −.02 | 1.35** | −3.31** | −4.75** |
| | (.12) | (.17) | (.29) | (.57) | (.67) |
| Nagelkerke pseudo-$R^2$ | .0003 | .03 | .06 | .74 | .78 |
| % correctly predicted | 60.6% | 60.6% | 61.5% | 87.8% | 90.2% |
| N | 3,300 | 3,265 | 2,815 | 2,443 | 2,263 |

**$p \leq .01$; *$p \leq .05$ (two-tailed tests). Entries are unstandardized logistic regression coefficients, with standard errors in parentheses.

TABLE A2.16. Change in Probabilities for Voting Intentions in Dominican Republic (2008, 2010, 2012)

| | (1) | (2) | (3) | (4) | (5) |
|---|---|---|---|---|---|
| Months | −.04 | −.03 | −.08 | .03 | .06 |
| Age | — | .09* | −.07 | −.04 | −.03 |
| Gender | — | .12** | .11** | .01 | .01 |
| Catholic | — | −.01 | −.01 | −.03* | −.03* |
| Church attendance | — | .02 | −.01 | .00 | −.01 |
| Region | — | .01 | .03 | .01 | −.00 |
| Race | — | .06 | .07* | .02 | −.00 |
| Schooling | — | — | −.16** | −.07** | −.06** |
| Income | — | — | .06* | .03 | .02 |
| Unemployment | — | — | .06* | .02 | .02 |
| Public sector | — | — | −.23** | −.03 | −.03 |
| Property | — | — | −.06 | −.01 | .02 |
| Ideology | — | — | — | .08** | .04* |
| Party identification | — | — | — | .51** | .43** |
| State | — | — | — | — | .06* |
| AUTH | — | — | — | — | −.02 |
| Safety | — | — | — | — | .08** |
| Corruption | — | — | — | — | .03 |
| Democracy | — | — | — | — | .07** |
| SRE | — | — | — | — | .10** |
| N | 3,300 | 3,265 | 2,815 | 2,443 | 2,263 |

**p ≤ .01; *p ≤ .05 (two-tailed tests). Entries represent change in probabilities.

TABLE A2.17. Logistic Regression Models for Voting Intentions in Ecuador (2008, 2010, 2012)

| | (1) | (2) | (3) | (4) | (5) |
|---|---|---|---|---|---|
| Months | 1.12** | 1.19** | 1.26** | .76** | .53 |
| | (.24) | (.24) | (.25) | (.31) | (.35) |
| Age | — | .02 | .20 | .40 | −.12 |
| | | (.18) | (.20) | (.26) | (.29) |
| Gender | — | −.03 | .01 | −.03 | −.01 |
| | | (.07) | (.07) | (.09) | (.10) |
| Catholic | — | −.05 | −.02 | −.09 | −.08 |
| | | (.09) | (.09) | (.12) | (.14) |
| Church attendance | — | −.08 | −.05 | .06 | .13 |
| | | (.12) | (.12) | (.15) | (.17) |
| Region | — | .20** | .11 | .00 | −.02 |
| | | (.07) | (.07) | (.09) | (.10) |
| Race | — | −.19 | −.24 | −.05 | .14 |
| | | (.16) | (.17) | (.23) | (.25) |
| Schooling | — | — | .18 | .21 | .12 |
| | | | (.09) | (.12) | (.14) |
| Income | — | — | −.13 | −.25 | −.21 |
| | | | (.15) | (.18) | (.20) |
| Unemployment | — | — | −.28* | −.47** | −.53** |
| | | | (.13) | (.17) | (.19) |
| Public sector | — | — | −.11 | −.08 | −.03 |
| | | | (.14) | (.17) | (.19) |
| Property | — | — | .50** | .63** | .49* |
| | | | (.20) | (.25) | (.28) |
| Ideology | — | — | — | .73** | .76** |
| | | | | (.17) | (.19) |
| Party identification | — | — | — | 4.33** | 3.73** |
| | | | | (.26) | (.28) |
| State | — | — | — | — | .26 |
| | | | | | (.22) |
| AUTH | — | — | — | — | −.69** |
| | | | | | (.17) |
| Safety | — | — | — | — | .43 |
| | | | | | (.25) |
| Corruption | — | — | — | — | .65* |
| | | | | | (.27) |
| Democracy | — | — | — | — | 1.43** |
| | | | | | (.27) |
| SRE | — | — | — | — | 1.20** |
| | | | | | (.14) |
| Constant | .46** | .49** | .18 | −2.57** | −3.61** |
| | (.06) | (.17) | (.20) | (.31) | (.40) |
| Nagelkerke pseudo-$R^2$ | .007 | .01 | .02 | .23 | .37 |
| % correctly predicted | 66.9% | 66.9% | 67.0% | 72.0% | 77.4% |
| N | 4,464 | 4,317 | 4,066 | 2,987 | 2,833 |

**$p \le .01$; *$p \le .05$ (two-tailed tests). Entries are unstandardized logistic regression coefficients, with standard errors in parentheses.

TABLE A2.18. Change in Probabilities for Voting Intentions in Ecuador (2008, 2010, 2012)

| | (1) | (2) | (3) | (4) | (5) |
|---|---|---|---|---|---|
| Months | .25** | .26** | .28** | .14** | .08 |
| Age | — | .00 | .04 | .07 | −.02 |
| Gender | — | −.01 | .00 | −.01 | −.00 |
| Catholic | — | −.01 | −.00 | −.02 | −.01 |
| Church attendance | — | −.02 | −.01 | .01 | .02 |
| Region | — | .04** | .02 | .00 | −.00 |
| Race | — | −.04 | −.05 | −.01 | .02 |
| Schooling | — | — | .04 | .04 | .02 |
| Income | — | — | −.03 | −.05 | −.03 |
| Unemployment | — | — | −.06* | −.09** | −.08** |
| Public sector | — | — | −.03 | −.01 | −.01 |
| Property | — | — | .11** | .12* | .08 |
| Ideology | — | — | — | .14** | .12** |
| Party identification | — | — | — | .79** | .58** |
| State | — | — | — | — | .04 |
| AUTH | — | — | — | — | −.11** |
| Safety | — | — | — | — | .07 |
| Corruption | — | — | — | — | .10* |
| Democracy | — | — | — | — | .22** |
| SRE | — | — | — | — | .19** |
| N | 2,464 | 4,317 | 4,066 | 2,987 | 2,833 |

**p ≤ .01; *p ≤ .05 (two-tailed tests). Entries represent change in probabilities.

TABLE A2.19. Logistic Regression Models for Voting Intentions in El Salvador (2008, 2010, 2012)

| | (1) | (2) | (3) | (4) | (5) |
|---|---|---|---|---|---|
| Months | −2.13** | −1.97** | −2.05** | −1.08** | −.78* |
| | (.16) | (.20) | (.23) | (.30) | (.32) |
| Age | — | .14 | .21 | −.26 | −.37 |
| | | (.16) | (.21) | (.29) | (.31) |
| Gender | — | .29** | .30** | .03 | −.05 |
| | | (.08) | (.08) | (.12) | (.12) |
| Catholic | — | .36** | .44** | .50** | .42** |
| | | (.08) | (.08) | (.11) | (.12) |
| Church attendance | — | .00 | .04 | −.19 | −.15 |
| | | (.11) | (.12) | (.17) | (.18) |
| Region | — | −.18* | −.12 | −.01 | −.01 |
| | | (.08) | (.10) | (.13) | (.14) |
| Race | — | .14 | .08 | .06 | .10 |
| | | (.13) | (.13) | (.18) | (.19) |
| Schooling | — | — | −.01 | .29 | .14 |
| | | | (.12) | (.17) | (.19) |
| Income | — | — | .08 | .22 | .07 |
| | | | (.17) | (.23) | (.24) |
| Unemployment | — | — | −.18 | −.42** | −.31 |
| | | | (.11) | (.15) | (.16) |
| Public sector | — | — | .15 | −.08 | .18 |
| | | | (.14) | (.21) | (.23) |
| Property | — | — | −.18 | −.15 | −.17 |
| | | | (.27) | (.36) | (.39) |
| Ideology | — | — | — | 2.54** | 2.21** |
| | | | | (.21) | (.22) |
| Party identification | — | — | — | 4.75** | 4.38** |
| | | | | (.28) | (.29) |
| State | — | — | — | — | .61* |
| | | | | | (.30) |
| AUTH | — | — | — | — | −.05 |
| | | | | | (.20) |
| Safety | — | — | — | — | .68* |
| | | | | | (.30) |
| Corruption | — | — | — | — | .78** |
| | | | | | (.30) |
| Democracy | — | — | — | — | 1.30** |
| | | | | | (.31) |
| SRE | — | — | — | — | .69** |
| | | | | | (.19) |
| Constant | .94** | .49* | .51* | −3.23** | −4.89** |
| | (.08) | (.19) | (.24) | (.36) | (.45) |
| Nagelkerke pseudo-$R^2$ | .09 | .11 | .12 | .60 | .64 |
| % correctly predicted | 61.7% | 62.0% | 63.0% | 80.9% | 82.8% |
| N | 2,791 | 2,763 | 2,582 | 2,479 | 2,406 |

**$p \le .01$; *$p \le .05$ (two-tailed tests). Entries are unstandardized logistic regression coefficients, with standard errors in parentheses.

TABLE A2.20. Change in Probabilities for Voting Intentions in El Salvador (2008, 2010, 2012)

| | (1) | (2) | (3) | (4) | (5) |
|---|---|---|---|---|---|
| Months | −.50** | −.45** | −.47** | −.14** | −.09** |
| Age | — | .03 | .05 | −.04 | −.04 |
| Gender | — | .07** | .07** | .00 | −.01 |
| Catholic | — | .08** | .10** | .07** | .05** |
| Church attendance | — | .00 | .01 | −.02 | −.02 |
| Region | — | −.04* | −.03 | −.00 | −.00 |
| Race | — | .03 | .02 | .01 | .01 |
| Schooling | — | — | −.00 | .04 | .02 |
| Income | — | — | .02 | .03 | .01 |
| Unemployment | — | — | −.04 | −.05** | −.03 |
| Public sector | — | — | .03 | −.01 | .02 |
| Property | — | — | −.04 | −.02 | −.02 |
| Ideology | — | — | — | .33** | .26** |
| Party identification | — | — | — | .61** | .51** |
| State | — | — | — | — | .07* |
| AUTH | — | — | — | — | −.01 |
| Safety | — | — | — | — | .08* |
| Corruption | — | — | — | — | .09** |
| Democracy | — | — | — | — | .15** |
| SRE | — | — | — | — | .08** |
| N | 2,791 | 2,763 | 2,582 | 2,479 | 2,406 |

**$p \leq .01$; *$p \leq .05$ (two-tailed tests). Entries represent change in probabilities.

TABLE A2.21. Logistic Regression Models for Voting Intentions in Guatemala (2008, 2010, 2012)

| | (1) | (2) | (3) | (4) | (5) |
|---|---|---|---|---|---|
| Months | −5.05** | −5.53** | −5.42** | −5.11** | −5.18** |
| | (.26) | (.29) | (.31) | (.38) | (.44) |
| Age | — | −.08 | .20 | .15 | −.12 |
| | | (.19) | (.25) | (.30) | (.34) |
| Gender | — | −.12 | −.07 | −.08 | −.07 |
| | | (.09) | (.09) | (.11) | (.13) |
| Catholic | — | −.01 | .03 | .03 | .04 |
| | | (.09) | (.09) | (.11) | (.13) |
| Church attendance | — | .14 | .06 | .16 | .01 |
| | | (.14) | (.16) | (.20) | (.23) |
| Region | — | .22* | .05 | .00 | −.09 |
| | | (.09) | (.11) | (.14) | (.15) |
| Race | — | 1.00** | .75** | .69* | .78** |
| | | (.17) | (.20) | (.25) | (.27) |
| Schooling | — | — | .05 | −.06 | −.14 |
| | | | (.15) | (.18) | (.20) |
| Income | — | — | .06 | .17 | .03 |
| | | | (.18) | (.23) | (.26) |
| Unemployment | — | — | .01 | −.08 | −.01 |
| | | | (.15) | (.18) | (.21) |
| Public sector | — | — | .16 | .07 | .06 |
| | | | (.16) | (.19) | (.21) |
| Property | — | — | .91** | 1.04** | .96* |
| | | | (.28) | (.34) | (.38) |
| Ideology | — | — | — | .16 | .19 |
| | | | | (.21) | (.24) |
| Party identification | — | — | — | 5.59** | 5.64** |
| | | | | (.46) | (.50) |
| State | — | — | — | — | .53 |
| | | | | | (.28) |
| AUTH | — | — | — | — | .19 |
| | | | | | (.23) |
| Safety | — | — | — | — | 1.19** |
| | | | | | (.31) |
| Corruption | — | — | — | — | .80* |
| | | | | | (.35) |
| Democracy | — | — | — | — | .58 |
| | | | | | (.33) |
| SRE | — | — | — | — | .50* |
| | | | | | (.21) |
| Constant | .45** | −.09 | −.62* | −3.59** | −5.09** |
| | (.05) | (.17) | (.25) | (.40) | (.50) |
| Nagelkerke pseudo-$R^2$ | .21 | .23 | .25 | .41 | .48 |
| % correctly predicted | 66.8% | 68.3% | 68.4% | 74.2% | 76.3% |
| N | 2,693 | 2,654 | 2,359 | 1,896 | 1,707 |

**$p \leq .01$; *$p \leq .05$ (two-tailed tests). Entries are unstandardized logistic regression coefficients, with standard errors in parentheses.

TABLE A2.22. Change in Probabilities for Voting Intentions in Guatemala (2008, 2010, 2012)

| | (1) | (2) | (3) | (4) | (5) |
|---|---|---|---|---|---|
| Months | −1.05** | −1.11** | −1.08** | −.86** | −.78** |
| Age | — | −.02 | .04 | .03 | −.02 |
| Gender | — | −.02 | −.01 | −.01 | −.01 |
| Catholic | — | −.00 | .01 | .01 | .01 |
| Church attendance | — | .03 | .01 | .03 | .00 |
| Region | — | .04* | .01 | .00 | −.01 |
| Race | — | .20** | .15** | .12** | .12** |
| Schooling | — | — | .01 | −.01 | −.02 |
| Income | — | — | .01 | .03 | .00 |
| Unemployment | — | — | .00 | −.01 | −.00 |
| Public sector | — | — | .03 | .01 | .01 |
| Property | — | — | .18** | .18** | .15* |
| Ideology | — | — | — | .03 | .03 |
| Party identification | — | — | — | .94** | .86** |
| State | — | — | — | — | .08 |
| AUTH | — | — | — | — | .03 |
| Safety | — | — | — | — | .18** |
| Corruption | — | — | — | — | .12* |
| Democracy | — | — | — | — | .09 |
| SRE | — | — | — | — | .08* |
| N | 2,693 | 2,654 | 2,359 | 1,896 | 1,707 |

**$p \leq .01$; *$p \leq .05$ (two-tailed tests). Entries represent change in probabilities.

TABLE A2.23. Logistic Regression Models for Voting Intentions in Honduras (2008, 2010, 2012)

| | (1) | (2) | (3) | (4) | (5) |
|---|---|---|---|---|---|
| Months | −2.43** | −2.51** | −2.25** | −2.03** | −2.20** |
| | (.23) | (.24) | (.26) | (.37) | (.41) |
| Age | — | −.02 | .06 | −.10 | .01 |
| | | (.25) | (.28) | (.40) | (.43) |
| Gender | — | −.04 | −.10 | −.01 | .04 |
| | | (.09) | (.10) | (.13) | (.14) |
| Catholic | — | .21* | .18 | .26 | .27 |
| | | (.09) | (.10) | (.13) | (.14) |
| Church attendance | — | −.00 | .06 | .06 | .09 |
| | | (.13) | (.14) | (.20) | (.21) |
| Region | — | −.06 | .07 | .17 | .13 |
| | | (.10) | (.11) | (.16) | (.17) |
| Race | — | −.13 | −.07 | .09 | .11 |
| | | (.15) | (.16) | (.23) | (.24) |
| Schooling | — | — | −.03 | −.00 | .00 |
| | | | (.14) | (.20) | (.21) |
| Income | — | — | −.64** | −1.02** | −.90** |
| | | | (.17) | (.24) | (.26) |
| Unemployment | — | — | .02 | .13 | .14 |
| | | | (.16) | (.23) | (.24) |
| Public sector | — | — | −.13 | .00 | −.01 |
| | | | (.20) | (.29) | (.31) |
| Property | — | — | −.23 | −.21 | −.12 |
| | | | (.25) | (.36) | (.38) |
| Ideology | — | — | — | .33 | .07 |
| | | | | (.25) | (.28) |
| Party identification | — | — | — | 4.47** | 4.62** |
| | | | | (.21) | (.22) |
| State | — | — | — | — | −.82** |
| | | | | | (.29) |
| AUTH | — | — | — | — | .19 |
| | | | | | (.27) |
| Safety | — | — | — | — | −.51 |
| | | | | | (.39) |
| Corruption | — | — | — | — | −.15 |
| | | | | | (.38) |
| Democracy | — | — | — | — | .19 |
| | | | | | (.38) |
| SRE | — | — | — | — | .05 |
| | | | | | (.23) |
| Constant | .56** | .58** | 1.01** | −2.00** | −1.65** |
| | (.07) | (.16) | (.31) | (.48) | (.54) |
| Nagelkerke pseudo-$R^2$ | .06 | .07 | .09 | .57 | .57 |
| % correctly predicted | 60.9% | 61.1% | 61.2% | 83.0% | 82.7% |
| $N$ | 2,258 | 2,210 | 1,980 | 1,756 | 1,614 |

**$p \leq .01$; *$p \leq .05$ (two-tailed tests). Entries are unstandardized logistic regression coefficients, with standard errors in parentheses.

TABLE A2.24. Change in Probabilities for Voting Intentions in Honduras (2008, 2010, 2012)

| | (1) | (2) | (3) | (4) | (5) |
|---|---|---|---|---|---|
| Months | −.58** | −.59** | −.53** | −.27** | −.29** |
| Age | — | −.01 | .01 | .01 | .00 |
| Gender | — | −.01 | −.02 | −.00 | .01 |
| Catholic | — | .05* | .04 | .03 | .04* |
| Church attendance | — | −.00 | .01 | .01 | .01 |
| Region | — | −.01 | .02 | .02 | .02 |
| Race | — | −.03 | −.02 | .01 | .01 |
| Schooling | — | — | −.01 | −.00 | .00 |
| Income | — | — | −.15** | −.14** | −.12** |
| Unemployment | — | — | .00 | .02 | .02 |
| Public sector | — | — | −.03 | .00 | −.00 |
| Property | — | — | −.05 | −.02 | −.02 |
| Ideology | — | — | — | .04 | .01 |
| Party identification | — | — | — | .60** | .61** |
| State | — | — | — | — | −.11** |
| AUTH | — | — | — | — | .03 |
| Safety | — | — | — | — | −.07 |
| Corruption | — | — | — | — | −.02 |
| Democracy | — | — | — | — | .03 |
| SRE | — | — | — | — | .01 |
| N | 2,258 | 2,210 | 1,980 | 1,756 | 1,614 |

**p ≤ .01; *p ≤ .05 (two-tailed tests). Entries represent change in probabilities.

TABLE A2.25. Logistic Regression Models for Voting Intentions in Mexico (2008, 2010, 2012)

| | (1) | (2) | (3) | (4) | (5) |
|---|---|---|---|---|---|
| Months | −.35** | −.29* | −.14 | −.20 | −.26 |
| | (.12) | (.12) | (.14) | (.17) | (.18) |
| Age | — | −.35 | −.27 | −.36 | −.15 |
| | | (.20) | (.25) | (.32) | (.34) |
| Gender | — | .22** | .25** | .34** | .33** |
| | | (.08) | (.09) | (.11) | (.11) |
| Catholic | — | .16 | .16 | .07 | −.03 |
| | | (.11) | (.12) | (.15) | (.15) |
| Church attendance | — | .40** | .34* | .34 | .38* |
| | | (.13) | (.14) | (.18) | (.19) |
| Region | — | −.12 | −.11 | −.04 | .05 |
| | | (.08) | (.09) | (.11) | (.12) |
| Race | — | .14 | .04 | .05 | .00 |
| | | (.13) | (.15) | (.19) | (.20) |
| Schooling | — | — | −.37** | −.60** | −.45* |
| | | | (.13) | (.17) | (.18) |
| Income | — | — | .17 | −.01 | −.06 |
| | | | (.14) | (.17) | (.18) |
| Unemployment | — | — | .14 | .14 | .14 |
| | | | (.17) | (.21) | (.22) |
| Public sector | — | — | .11 | −.01 | −.06 |
| | | | (.18) | (.22) | (.23) |
| Property | — | — | .42 | .24 | .12 |
| | | | (.24) | (.29) | (.31) |
| Ideology | — | — | — | .87** | .56** |
| | | | | (.20) | (.21) |
| Party identification | — | — | — | 4.19** | 4.08** |
| | | | | (.22) | (.22) |
| State | — | — | — | — | .15 |
| | | | | | (.25) |
| AUTH | — | — | — | — | .05 |
| | | | | | (.18) |
| Safety | — | — | — | — | .95** |
| | | | | | (.27) |
| Corruption | — | — | — | — | .19 |
| | | | | | (.25) |
| Democracy | — | — | — | — | .67* |
| | | | | | (.27) |
| SRE | — | — | — | — | .62** |
| | | | | | (.17) |
| Constant | −.14 | −.54** | −.99** | −3.01** | −3.90** |
| | (.08) | (.18) | (.33) | (.43) | (.47) |
| Nagelkerke pseudo-$R^2$ | .004 | .02 | .02 | .37 | .41 |
| % correctly predicted | 58.8% | 59.5% | 59.1% | 72.8% | 76.0% |
| $N$ | 2,796 | 2,752 | 2,392 | 2,140 | 2,043 |

**$p ≤ .01$; *$p ≤ .05$ (two-tailed tests). Entries are unstandardized logistic regression coefficients, with standard errors in parentheses.

TABLE A2.26. Change in Probabilities for Voting Intentions in Mexico (2008, 2010, 2012)

| | (1) | (2) | (3) | (4) | (5) |
|---|---|---|---|---|---|
| Months | −.08** | −.07* | −.03 | −.04 | −.04 |
| Age | — | −.08 | −.06 | −.06 | −.02 |
| Gender | — | .05** | .06** | .06** | .06** |
| Catholic | — | .04 | .04 | .01 | −.01 |
| Church attendance | — | .10** | .08* | .06 | .06* |
| Region | — | −.03 | −.03 | −.01 | .01 |
| Race | — | .03 | .01 | .01 | .00 |
| Schooling | — | — | −.09** | −.11** | −.08** |
| Income | — | — | .04 | −.00 | −.01 |
| Unemployment | — | — | .03 | .02 | .02 |
| Public sector | — | — | .03 | −.00 | −.01 |
| Property | — | — | .10 | .04 | .02 |
| Ideology | — | — | — | .15** | .09** |
| Party identification | — | — | — | .73** | .68** |
| State | — | — | — | — | .02 |
| AUTH | — | — | — | — | .01 |
| Safety | — | — | — | — | .16** |
| Corruption | — | — | — | — | .03 |
| Democracy | — | — | — | — | .11* |
| SRE | — | — | — | — | .10** |
| N | 2,796 | 2,752 | 2,392 | 2,140 | 2,043 |

**$p ≤ .01$; *$p ≤ .05$ (two-tailed tests). Entries represent change in probabilities.

TABLE A2.27. Logistic Regression Models for Voting Intentions in Nicaragua (2008, 2010, 2012)

| | (1) | (2) | (3) | (4) | (5) |
|---|---|---|---|---|---|
| Months | -1.73** | -1.68** | -1.65** | -1.17** | -.77** |
| | (.16) | (.16) | (.17) | (.26) | (.29) |
| Age | — | -.56** | -.17 | .18 | -.18 |
| | | (.21) | (.23) | (.39) | (.44) |
| Gender | — | -.15 | -.17* | -.11 | -.19 |
| | | (.08) | (.08) | (.14) | (.15) |
| Catholic | — | .45** | .39** | .37** | .40** |
| | | (.08) | (.08) | (.13) | (.15) |
| Church attendance | — | .37** | .35** | .05 | -.09 |
| | | (.12) | (.12) | (.19) | (.21) |
| Region | — | .07 | -.07 | -.05 | -.06 |
| | | (.08) | (.09) | (.15) | (.17) |
| Race | — | -.12 | -.15 | -.16 | -.15 |
| | | (.13) | (.14) | (.22) | (.25) |
| Schooling | — | — | .43** | .67** | .55* |
| | | | (.15) | (.24) | (.26) |
| Income | — | — | -.26 | -.05 | .06 |
| | | | (.15) | (.24) | (.27) |
| Unemployment | — | — | .04 | .09 | .09 |
| | | | (.14) | (.23) | (.25) |
| Public sector | — | — | .85** | .28 | .07 |
| | | | (.20) | (.33) | (.36) |
| Property | — | — | .45 | .44 | .03 |
| | | | (.24) | (.39) | (.43) |
| Ideology | — | — | — | .41* | .24 |
| | | | | (.19) | (.22) |
| Party identification | — | — | — | 6.32** | 5.37** |
| | | | | (.27) | (.29) |
| State | — | — | — | — | -.56 |
| | | | | | (.35) |
| AUTH | — | — | — | — | -.34 |
| | | | | | (.21) |
| Safety | — | — | — | — | .45 |
| | | | | | (.33) |
| Corruption | — | — | — | — | .82* |
| | | | | | (.33) |
| Democracy | — | — | — | — | 1.40** |
| | | | | | (.33) |
| SRE | — | — | — | — | .89** |
| | | | | | (.21) |
| Constant | .71** | .87** | .27 | -4.26** | -4.12** |
| | (.06) | (.19) | (.25) | (.46) | (.59) |
| Nagelkerke pseudo-$R^2$ | .06 | .08 | .09 | .67 | .72 |
| % correctly predicted | 58.4% | 59.3% | 60.6% | 85.5% | 88.1% |
| N | 2,820 | 2,799 | 2,667 | 2,294 | 2,123 |

**$p \leq .01$; *$p \leq .05$ (two-tailed tests). Entries are unstandardized logistic regression coefficients, with standard errors in parentheses.

TABLE A2.28. Change in Probabilities for Voting Intentions in Nicaragua (2008, 2010, 2012)

| | (1) | (2) | (3) | (4) | (5) |
|---|---|---|---|---|---|
| Months | −.41** | −.39** | −.38** | −.12** | −.07** |
| Age | — | −.13** | −.04 | .02 | −.02 |
| Gender | — | −.04 | −.04* | −.01 | −.02 |
| Catholic | — | .10** | .09** | .04** | .04** |
| Church attendance | — | .08** | .08** | .01 | −.01 |
| Region | — | .02 | −.02 | −.01 | −.01 |
| Race | — | −.03 | −.03 | −.02 | −.01 |
| Schooling | — | — | .10** | .07** | .05* |
| Income | — | — | −.06 | −.01 | .01 |
| Unemployment | — | — | .01 | .01 | .01 |
| Public sector | — | — | .19** | .03 | .01 |
| Property | — | — | .10 | .05 | .00 |
| Ideology | — | — | — | .04* | .02 |
| Party identification | — | — | — | .66** | .49** |
| State | — | — | — | — | −.05 |
| AUTH | — | — | — | — | −.03 |
| Safety | — | — | — | — | .04 |
| Corruption | — | — | — | — | .07* |
| Democracy | — | — | — | — | .13** |
| SRE | — | — | — | — | .08** |
| $N$ | 2,820 | 2,799 | 2,667 | 2,294 | 2,123 |

**$p \leq .01$; *$p \leq .05$ (two-tailed tests). Entries represent change in probabilities.

TABLE A2.29. Logistic Regression Models for Voting Intentions in Panama (2008, 2010, 2012)

| | (1) | (2) | (3) | (4) | (5) |
|---|---|---|---|---|---|
| Months | −1.82** | −1.91** | −1.90** | −2.72** | −1.96** |
| | (.17) | (.18) | (.18) | (.24) | (.27) |
| Age | — | .65** | .36 | .08 | 0.10 |
| | | (.23) | (.26) | (.32) | (.34) |
| Gender | — | −.21* | −.18 | −.21 | −.18 |
| | | (.09) | (.09) | (.11) | (.12) |
| Catholic | — | .35** | .35** | .31* | .28* |
| | | (.10) | (.11) | (.13) | (.14) |
| Church attendance | — | .46** | .48** | .53** | .36 |
| | | (.14) | (.14) | (.17) | (.19) |
| Region | — | −.01 | .06 | .06 | .09 |
| | | (.09) | (.11) | (.13) | (.14) |
| Race | — | .09 | .14 | .01 | .07 |
| | | (.12) | (.13) | (.16) | (.17) |
| Schooling | — | — | −.41** | −.45* | −.49** |
| | | | (.14) | (.18) | (.19) |
| Income | — | — | .11 | .14 | .12 |
| | | | (.19) | (.23) | (.25) |
| Unemployment | — | — | .08 | .05 | .11 |
| | | | (.14) | (.17) | (.18) |
| Public sector | — | — | −.44** | −.26 | −.14 |
| | | | (.14) | (.17) | (.18) |
| Property | — | — | .01 | −.47 | −.52 |
| | | | (.27) | (.33) | (.35) |
| Ideology | — | — | — | −.13 | −.37 |
| | | | | (.21) | (.23) |
| Party identification | — | — | — | 3.97** | 3.87** |
| | | | | (.22) | (.23) |
| State | — | — | — | — | −.09 |
| | | | | | (.27) |
| AUTH | — | — | — | — | .33 |
| | | | | | (.19) |
| Safety | — | — | — | — | −.11 |
| | | | | | (.33) |
| Corruption | — | — | — | — | .75* |
| | | | | | (.32) |
| Democracy | — | — | — | — | .58 |
| | | | | | (.34) |
| SRE | — | — | — | — | .64** |
| | | | | | (.17) |
| Constant | .64** | .04 | .55** | −.89* | −1.95** |
| | (.08) | (.17) | (.27) | (.37) | (.43) |
| Nagelkerke pseudo-$R^2$ | .06 | .08 | .09 | .37 | .40 |
| % correctly predicted | 62.6% | 62.7% | 62.1% | 76.1% | 76.8% |
| N | 2,351 | 2,329 | 2,227 | 1,929 | 1,843 |

**$p \leq .01$; *$p \leq .05$ (two-tailed tests). Entries are unstandardized logistic regression coefficients, with standard errors in parentheses.

TABLE A2.30. Change in Probabilities for Voting Intentions in Panama (2008, 2010, 2012)

| | (1) | (2) | (3) | (4) | (5) |
|---|---|---|---|---|---|
| Months | −.43** | −.45** | −.44** | −.48** | −.34** |
| Age | — | .15** | .08 | .01 | −.02 |
| Gender | — | −.05* | −.04* | −.04 | −.03 |
| Catholic | — | .08** | .08** | .06* | .05* |
| Church attendance | — | .11** | .11** | .09** | .06 |
| Region | — | −.00 | .01 | .01 | .02 |
| Race | — | .02 | .03 | .00 | .01 |
| Schooling | — | — | −.10** | −.08* | −.08** |
| Income | — | — | .04 | .04 | .02 |
| Unemployment | — | — | .02 | .01 | .02 |
| Public sector | — | — | −.09** | −.04 | −.03 |
| Property | — | — | −.01 | −.09 | −.09 |
| Ideology | — | — | — | −.02 | −.06 |
| Party identification | — | — | — | .71** | .67** |
| State | — | — | — | — | −.02 |
| AUTH | — | — | — | — | .06 |
| Safety | — | — | — | — | −.02 |
| Corruption | — | — | — | — | .13* |
| Democracy | — | — | — | — | .10 |
| SRE | — | — | — | — | .11** |
| N | 2,351 | 2,329 | 2,227 | 1,929 | 1,843 |

**p ≤ .01; *p ≤ .05 (two-tailed tests). Entries represent change in probabilities.

TABLE A2.31. Logistic Regression Models for Voting Intentions in Paraguay (2008, 2010, 2012)

| | (1) | (2) | (3) | (4) | (5) |
|---|---|---|---|---|---|
| Months | -.99** | -1.20** | -1.33** | -.63 | -.61 |
| | (.18) | (.25) | (.30) | (.38) | (.41) |
| Age | — | -.27 | -.32 | -.42 | -.69 |
| | | (.22) | (.29) | (.37) | (.42) |
| Gender | — | .11 | .13 | .20 | .13 |
| | | (.09) | (.10) | (.12) | (.13) |
| Catholic | — | .04 | .07 | -.10 | -.10 |
| | | (.12) | (.15) | (.18) | (.20) |
| Church attendance | — | -.21 | -.20 | -.17 | -.11 |
| | | (.17) | (.19) | (.23) | (.25) |
| Region | — | .16 | -.03 | .01 | .10 |
| | | (.09) | (.11) | (.13) | (.14) |
| Race | — | .14 | -.08 | -.14 | -.09 |
| | | (.13) | (.15) | (.19) | (.20) |
| Schooling | — | — | -.06 | -.02 | -.09 |
| | | | (.14) | (.17) | (.19) |
| Income | — | — | .09 | -.22 | -.11 |
| | | | (.18) | (.22) | (.25) |
| Unemployment | — | — | .09 | -.37 | -.20 |
| | | | (.17) | (.21) | (.24) |
| Public sector | — | — | -.19 | -.36* | -.28 |
| | | | (.15) | (.19) | (.20) |
| Property | — | — | .99** | 1.04** | .83* |
| | | | (.28) | (.36) | (.40) |
| Ideology | — | — | — | .68** | .63** |
| | | | | (.22) | (.24) |
| Party identification | — | — | — | 2.18** | 2.08** |
| | | | | (.18) | (.20) |
| State | — | — | — | — | -.03 |
| | | | | | (.31) |
| AUTH | — | — | — | — | -.34 |
| | | | | | (.20) |
| Safety | — | — | — | — | .42 |
| | | | | | (.32) |
| Corruption | — | — | — | — | .43 |
| | | | | | (.36) |
| Democracy | — | — | — | — | .73* |
| | | | | | (.32) |
| SRE | — | — | — | — | 1.07** |
| | | | | | (.19) |
| Constant | -.04 | .12 | -.01 | -1.37** | -2.08** |
| | (.11) | (.26) | (.32) | (.43) | (.53) |
| Nagelkerke pseudo-$R^2$ | .02 | .024 | .04 | .20 | .28 |
| % correctly predicted | 65.2% | 65.0% | 66.3% | 72.2% | 75.3% |
| N | 2,386 | 2,364 | 2,011 | 1,544 | 1,422 |

**$p \le .01$; *$p \le .05$ (two-tailed tests). Entries are unstandardized logistic regression coefficients, with standard errors in parentheses.

TABLE A2.32. Change in Probabilities for Voting Intentions in Paraguay (2008, 2010, 2012)

|                     | (1)     | (2)     | (3)     | (4)     | (5)     |
|---------------------|---------|---------|---------|---------|---------|
| Months              | −.22**  | −.27**  | −.29**  | −.12*   | −.10    |
| Age                 | —       | −.06    | −.07    | .08     | −.12    |
| Gender              | —       | .02     | .03     | .04     | .02     |
| Catholic            | —       | .01     | .02     | −.02    | −.02    |
| Church attendance   | —       | −.05    | −.04    | −.03    | −.02    |
| Region              | —       | .04     | −.01    | .00     | .02     |
| Race                | —       | .03     | −.02    | −.03    | −.02    |
| Schooling           | —       | —       | −.01    | −.00    | −.02    |
| Income              | —       | —       | .01     | −.04    | −.02    |
| Unemployment        | —       | —       | .02     | −.07    | −.03    |
| Public sector       | —       | —       | −.04    | −.07*   | −.05    |
| Property            | —       | —       | .22**   | .19**   | .14*    |
| Ideology            | —       | —       | —       | .13**   | .11**   |
| Party identification| —       | —       | —       | .40**   | .35**   |
| State               | —       | —       | —       | —       | −.01    |
| AUTH                | —       | —       | —       | —       | −.06    |
| Safety              | —       | —       | —       | —       | .07     |
| Corruption          | —       | —       | —       | —       | .08     |
| Democracy           | —       | —       | —       | —       | .13*    |
| SRE                 | —       | —       | —       | —       | .18**   |
| N                   | 2,386   | 2,364   | 2,011   | 1,544   | 1,422   |

**p ≤ .01; *p ≤ .05 (two-tailed tests). Entries represent change in probabilities.

TABLE A2.33. Logistic Regression Models for Voting Intentions in Peru (2008, 2010, 2012)

| | (1) | (2) | (3) | (4) | (5) |
|---|---|---|---|---|---|
| Months | -2.89** | -3.36** | -3.45** | -3.21** | -3.34** |
| | (.22) | (.29) | (.33) | (.37) | (.41) |
| Age | — | -.06 | -.07 | .00 | -.16 |
| | | (.21) | (.26) | (.30) | (.33) |
| Gender | — | .04 | .13 | .13 | .09 |
| | | (.10) | (.10) | (.12) | (.13) |
| Catholic | — | .40** | .38** | .20 | .24 |
| | | (.11) | (.13) | (.14) | (.16) |
| Church attendance | — | -.22 | -.24 | -.36 | -.28 |
| | | (.16) | (.17) | (.19) | (.21) |
| Region | — | -.02 | -.21 | -.14 | -.12 |
| | | (.10) | (.12) | (.14) | (.15) |
| Race | — | .54** | .38 | .31 | .53 |
| | | (.20) | (.21) | (.25) | (.27) |
| Schooling | — | — | -.07 | .12 | .15 |
| | | | (.17) | (.20) | (.21) |
| Income | — | — | .58** | .53* | .61* |
| | | | (.22) | (.25) | (.27) |
| Unemployment | — | — | -.15 | -.14 | .01 |
| | | | (.16) | (.18) | (.20) |
| Public sector | — | — | .22 | .25 | .41 |
| | | | (.16) | (.18) | (.20) |
| Property | — | — | .39 | -.10 | -.27 |
| | | | (.31) | (.35) | (.38) |
| Ideology | — | — | — | .57* | .53 |
| | | | | (.25) | (.28) |
| Party identification | — | — | — | 4.27** | 4.11** |
| | | | | (.30) | (.32) |
| State | — | — | — | — | .54 |
| | | | | | (.30) |
| AUTH | — | — | — | — | .33 |
| | | | | | (.22) |
| Safety | — | — | — | — | 1.20** |
| | | | | | (.35) |
| Corruption | — | — | — | — | .53 |
| | | | | | (.35) |
| Democracy | — | — | — | — | .73* |
| | | | | | (.36) |
| SRE | — | — | — | — | 1.19** |
| | | | | | (.19) |
| Constant | -.16* | -.40 | -.72** | -3.01** | -5.12** |
| | (.08) | (.21) | (.27) | (.36) | (.49) |
| Nagelkerke pseudo-$R^2$ | .11 | .13 | .14 | .31 | .39 |
| % correctly predicted | 74.9% | 75.0% | 74.9% | 80.3% | 81.5% |
| N | 2,572 | 2,546 | 2,318 | 2,075 | 1,952 |

**$p \leq .01$; *$p \leq .05$ (two-tailed tests). Entries are unstandardized logistic regression coefficients, with standard errors in parentheses.

TABLE A2.34. Change in Probabilities for Voting Intentions in Peru (2008, 2010, 2012)

| | (1) | (2) | (3) | (4) | (5) |
|---|---|---|---|---|---|
| Months | -.50** | -.58** | -.59** | -.48** | -.45** |
| Age | — | -.01 | -.01 | .01 | -.02 |
| Gender | — | .01 | .02 | .02 | .01 |
| Catholic | — | .07** | .07** | .03 | .03 |
| Church attendance | — | -.04 | -.04 | -.05 | -.04 |
| Region | — | -.00 | -.04 | -.02 | -.02 |
| Race | — | .09** | .06 | .05 | .07 |
| Schooling | — | — | -.01 | .02 | .02 |
| Income | — | — | .10** | .08* | .08* |
| Unemployment | — | — | -.03 | -.02 | .00 |
| Public sector | — | — | .04 | .04 | .05* |
| Property | — | — | .07 | -.02 | -.04 |
| Ideology | — | — | — | .08* | .07 |
| Party identification | — | — | — | .63** | .56** |
| State | — | — | — | — | .07 |
| AUTH | — | — | — | — | .05 |
| Safety | — | — | — | — | .16** |
| Corruption | — | — | — | — | .07 |
| Democracy | — | — | — | — | .10* |
| SRE | — | — | — | — | .16** |
| N | 2,572 | 2,546 | 2,318 | 2,075 | 1,952 |

$**p \leq .01$; $*p \leq .05$ (two-tailed tests). Entries represent change in probabilities.

TABLE A2.35. Logistic Regression Models for Voting Intentions in Uruguay (2008, 2010, 2012)

| | (1) | (2) | (3) | (4) | (5) |
|---|---|---|---|---|---|
| Months | -.95** | -.75** | -.72** | -1.26** | -1.05** |
| | (.15) | (.15) | (.16) | (.28) | (.32) |
| Age | — | 1.08** | 1.04** | .91** | .96* |
| | | (.18) | (.20) | (.34) | (.39) |
| Gender | — | -.03 | -.05 | .24 | .24 |
| | | (.08) | (.08) | (.14) | (.16) |
| Catholic | — | .70** | .66** | .19 | .18 |
| | | (.08) | (.08) | (.14) | (.16) |
| Church attendance | — | .71** | .67** | .12 | .26 |
| | | (.13) | (.13) | (.22) | (.25) |
| Region | — | -.37** | -.34** | -.01 | -.06 |
| | | (.09) | (.10) | (.16) | (.18) |
| Race | — | .25 | .24 | .14 | -.13 |
| | | (.12) | (.14) | (.23) | (.26) |
| Schooling | — | — | -.19 | .42 | .12 |
| | | | (.12) | (.21) | (.25) |
| Income | — | — | -.29* | -.17 | -.26 |
| | | | (.14) | (.24) | (.27) |
| Unemployment | — | — | -.07 | .11 | .30 |
| | | | (.15) | (.24) | (.28) |
| Public sector | — | — | -.30* | -.28 | -.25 |
| | | | (.14) | (.23) | (.25) |
| Property | — | — | .34 | .33 | .00 |
| | | | (.28) | (.44) | (.50) |
| Ideology | — | — | — | 3.14** | 3.11** |
| | | | | (.29) | (.33) |
| Party identification | — | — | — | 5.74** | 5.22** |
| | | | | (.27) | (.29) |
| State | — | — | — | — | .46 |
| | | | | | (.39) |
| AUTH | — | — | — | — | -.68** |
| | | | | | (.25) |
| Safety | — | — | — | — | 1.08** |
| | | | | | (.37) |
| Corruption | — | — | — | — | 1.06** |
| | | | | | (.38) |
| Democracy | — | — | — | — | .64 |
| | | | | | (.41) |
| SRE | — | — | — | — | 1.34** |
| | | | | | (.23) |
| Constant | .85** | -.79** | -.56** | -5.07** | -6.94** |
| | (.06) | (.16) | (.19) | (.39) | (.62) |
| Nagelkerke pseudo-$R^2$ | .02 | .11 | .11 | .74 | .78 |
| % correctly predicted | 63.6% | 66.1% | 66.1% | 88.% | 90.6% |
| N | 3,215 | 3,160 | 2,819 | 2,667 | 2,494 |

**$p \leq .01$; *$p \leq .05$ (two-tailed tests). Entries are unstandardized logistic regression coefficients, with standard errors in parentheses.

TABLE A2.36. Change in Probabilities for Voting Intentions in Uruguay (2008, 2010, 2012)

| | (1) | (2) | (3) | (4) | (5) |
|---|---|---|---|---|---|
| Months | −.22** | −.16** | −.15** | −.10** | −.07** |
| Age | — | .23** | .22** | .07** | .06* |
| Gender | — | −.01 | −.01 | .02 | .02 |
| Catholic | — | .15** | .14** | .01 | .01 |
| Church attendance | — | .15** | .14** | .01 | .02 |
| Region | — | −.08** | −.07** | −.00 | −.01 |
| Race | — | .05 | .05 | .01 | −.01 |
| Schooling | — | — | −.04 | .03 | .01 |
| Income | — | — | −.06* | −.01 | −.02 |
| Unemployment | — | — | −.01 | .01 | .02 |
| Public sector | — | — | −.06* | −.02 | −.02 |
| Property | — | — | .07 | .03 | .00 |
| Ideology | — | — | — | .25** | .22** |
| Party identification | — | — | — | .46** | .36** |
| State | — | — | — | — | .03 |
| AUTH | — | — | — | — | −.05** |
| Safety | — | — | — | — | .07** |
| Corruption | — | — | — | — | .07** |
| Democracy | — | — | — | — | .04 |
| SRE | — | — | — | — | .09** |
| N | 3,215 | 3,160 | 2,819 | 2,667 | 2,494 |

$**p \leq .01$; $*p \leq .05$ (two-tailed tests). Entries represent change in probabilities.

TABLE A2.37. Logistic Regression Models for Voting Intentions in Venezuela (2008, 2010, 2012)

| | (1) | (2) | (3) | (4) | (5) |
|---|---|---|---|---|---|
| Months | .29* | −.08 | .39* | .46 | .25 |
| | (.12) | (.15) | (.18) | (.28) | (.36) |
| Age | — | −.42 | −.00 | .82 | .40 |
| | | (.23) | (.30) | (.44) | (.55) |
| Gender | — | −.02 | .10 | .11 | −.07 |
| | | (.08) | (.10) | (.15) | (.18) |
| Catholic | — | .39** | .29* | .13 | −.28 |
| | | (.11) | (.13) | (.18) | (.23) |
| Church attendance | — | .17 | −.01 | −.31 | −.31 |
| | | (.13) | (.15) | (.22) | (.27) |
| Region | — | .07 | −.12 | −.10 | −.23 |
| | | (.09) | (.10) | (.15) | (.19) |
| Race | — | .50** | .28 | .29 | −.01 |
| | | (.12) | (.14) | (.21) | (.26) |
| Schooling | — | — | .65** | .46 | −.07 |
| | | | (.16) | (.24) | (.30) |
| Income | — | — | .44* | .49 | .48 |
| | | | (.18) | (.26) | (.33) |
| Unemployment | — | — | −.53** | −.74** | −1.14** |
| | | | (.19) | (.26) | (.34) |
| Public sector | — | — | .74** | .30 | .28 |
| | | | (.15) | (.22) | (.28) |
| Property | — | — | 1.43** | 1.77** | 2.35** |
| | | | (.32) | (.46) | (.58) |
| Ideology | — | — | — | 2.42** | 1.98** |
| | | | | (.26) | (.34) |
| Party identification | — | — | — | 5.94** | 4.65** |
| | | | | (.34) | (.38) |
| State | — | — | — | — | .32 |
| | | | | | (.40) |
| AUTH | — | — | — | — | .25 |
| | | | | | (.27) |
| Safety | — | — | — | — | 1.58** |
| | | | | | (.47) |
| Corruption | — | — | — | — | 1.29** |
| | | | | | (.46) |
| Democracy | — | — | — | — | 1.16** |
| | | | | | (.40) |
| SRE | — | — | — | — | 2.27** |
| | | | | | (.28) |
| Constant | .10 | .27 | −1.16** | −6.11** | −7.16** |
| | (.08) | (.20) | (.28) | (.50) | (.71) |
| Nagelkerke pseudo-$R^2$ | .003 | .02 | .10 | .63 | .76 |
| % correctly predicted | 56.8% | 57.4% | 62.5% | 82.5% | 89.1% |
| N | 2,575 | 2,422 | 1,882 | 1,714 | 1,627 |

**p ≤ .01; *p ≤ .05 (two-tailed tests). Entries are unstandardized logistic regression coefficients, with standard errors in parentheses.

TABLE A2.38. Change in Probabilities for Voting Intentions in Venezuela (2008, 2010, 2012)

| | (1) | (2) | (3) | (4) | (5) |
|---|---|---|---|---|---|
| Months | .07* | −.02 | .09* | .05 | .02 |
| Age | — | −.10 | −.00 | .10 | .03 |
| Gender | — | −.00 | .02 | .01 | −.01 |
| Catholic | — | .09** | .07* | .02 | −.02 |
| Church attendance | — | .04 | −.00 | −.04 | −.03 |
| Region | — | .02 | −.03 | −.01 | −.02 |
| Race | — | .12** | .06* | .03 | −.00 |
| Schooling | — | — | .15** | .05 | −.01 |
| Income | — | — | .10* | .06 | .04 |
| Unemployment | — | — | −.12** | −.09** | −.09** |
| Public sector | — | — | .17** | .04 | .02 |
| Property | — | — | .33** | .21** | .19** |
| Ideology | — | — | — | .29** | .16** |
| Party identification | — | — | — | .70** | .38** |
| State | — | — | — | — | .03 |
| AUTH | — | — | — | — | .02 |
| Safety | — | — | — | — | .13** |
| Corruption | — | — | — | — | .10** |
| Democracy | — | — | — | — | .09** |
| SRE | — | — | — | — | .19** |
| N | 2,575 | 2,422 | 1,882 | 1,714 | 1,627 |

$**p \leq .01$; $*p \leq .05$ (two-tailed tests). Entries represent change in probabilities.

# Appendix 3: Logistic Regression Models with Interactive Variables

TABLE A3.1. Logistic Regression Models for Voting Intentions in 18 Latin American Countries with Interactive Variables (LAPOP 2008, 2010, 2012)

|  | (1) | (2) | (3) | (4) | (5) |
|---|---|---|---|---|---|
| Months | −1.03** | −1.10** | −1.14** | −1.02** | −.73** |
|  | (.04) | (.04) | (.05) | (.06) | (.07) |
| Age | — | .11* | .13* | .18** | .03 |
|  |  | (.04) | (.05) | (.07) | (.08) |
| Gender | — | .06** | .07** | .04 | .00 |
|  |  | (.02) | (.02) | (.03) | (.03) |
| Catholic | — | .17** | .19** | .08** | .08* |
|  |  | (.02) | (.02) | (.03) | (.03) |
| Church attendance | — | .22** | .24** | .13** | .12** |
|  |  | (.03) | (.03) | (.04) | (.04) |
| Region | — | .03 | −.06** | −.06* | −.07* |
|  |  | (.02) | (.02) | (.03) | (.03) |
| Race | — | .19** | .10* | .04 | .02 |
|  |  | (.04) | (.04) | (.06) | (.06) |
| DRACE6 | — | −.23** | −.21** | −.42** | −.40** |
|  |  | (.07) | (.07) | (.09) | (.10) |
| DRACE6*Race | — | .49** | .48** | .39** | .33** |
|  |  | (.06) | (.07) | (.09) | (.10) |
| Schooling | — | — | −.08* | −.06 | −.07 |
|  |  |  | (.04) | (.05) | (.05) |
| DLR6 | — | — | .31** | −1.11** | −.49** |
|  |  |  | (.08) | (.12) | (.13) |
| DLR6*Schooling | — | — | .17** | .31** | .25** |
|  |  |  | (.05) | (.07) | (.08) |
| Income | — | — | .04 | .02 | −.00 |
|  |  |  | (.04) | (.06) | (.06) |

| | (1) | (2) | (3) | (4) | (5) |
|---|---|---|---|---|---|
| DLR6*Income | — | — | .31** | .35** | .28** |
| | | | (.06) | (.09) | (.09) |
| Unemployment | — | — | –.10** | –.17** | –.07 |
| | | | (.03) | (.04) | (.04) |
| Public sector | — | — | –.02 | –.01 | .08 |
| | | | (.03) | (.04) | (.05) |
| Property | — | — | –.04 | –.02 | –.07 |
| | | | (.07) | (.09) | (.10) |
| DGINI6 | — | — | –1.63** | –.89** | –.40** |
| | | | (.09) | (.11) | (.12) |
| DGINI6*Property | — | — | 1.22** | 1.11** | .98** |
| | | | (.10) | (.12) | (.14) |
| Ideology | — | — | — | .49** | .27** |
| | | | | (.06) | (.07) |
| DLR6*ideology | — | — | — | 1.71** | 1.69** |
| | | | | (.10) | (.11) |
| Party identification | — | — | — | 4.57** | 4.19** |
| | | | | (.06) | (.07) |
| DFRAC6 | — | — | — | 0.30** | –.03 |
| | | | | (.10) | (.11) |
| DFRAC6*Party ID | — | — | — | –2.09** | –1.85** |
| | | | | (.11) | (.12) |
| State | — | — | — | — | .28** |
| | | | | | (.06) |
| AUTH | — | — | — | — | –.00 |
| | | | | | (.06) |
| DAUTH6 | — | — | — | — | 1.30** |
| | | | | | (.12) |
| DAUTH6*AUTH | — | — | — | — | –.67** |
| | | | | | (.10) |
| Safety | — | — | — | — | .67** |
| | | | | | (.07) |
| Corruption | — | — | — | — | .90** |
| | | | | | (.07) |
| Democracy | — | — | — | — | 1.02** |
| | | | | | (.07) |
| SRE | — | — | — | — | .75** |
| | | | | | (.05) |
| ECN6 | — | — | — | — | –1.19** |
| | | | | | (.16) |
| ECN6*SRE | — | — | — | — | .36** |
| | | | | | (.09) |
| Constant | .28** | –.13* | .12 | –2.21** | –3.78** |
| | (.05) | (.06) | (.08) | (.11) | (.13) |
| Nagelkerke pseudo-$R^2$ | .10 | .11 | .12 | .45 | .53 |
| % correctly predicted | 61.5% | 62.9% | 63.3% | 76.4% | 79.6% |
| N | 52,489 | 51,394 | 45,332 | 38,363 | 35,820 |

**$p \leq .01$; *$p \leq .05$ (two-tailed tests). Country dummies are not shown. Mexico is the reference case for country dummies. Entries are unstandardized logistic regression coefficients, with standard errors in parentheses. See appendix 4 for variable's specification.

TABLE A3.2. Change in Probabilities for Voting Intentions in 18 Latin American Countries with Interactive Variables (LAPOP 2008, 2010, 2012)

| | (1) | (2) | (3) | (4) | (5) |
|---|---|---|---|---|---|
| Months | −.24** | −.25** | −.26** | −.16** | −.10** |
| Age | — | .03* | .03* | .03** | .01 |
| Gender | — | .01** | .02** | .01 | .00 |
| Catholic | — | .04** | .04** | .01** | .01** |
| Church attendance | — | .05** | .05** | .02** | .02** |
| Region | — | .01 | −.02** | −.01* | −.01* |
| Race | — | .04** | .02* | .01 | .00 |
| DRACE6 | — | −.05** | −.05** | −.07** | −.06** |
| DRACE6*Race | — | .11** | .11** | .06** | .05** |
| Schooling | — | — | −.02* | −.01 | −.01 |
| DLR6 | — | — | .07** | −.18** | −.07** |
| DLR6*Schooling | — | — | .04** | .05** | .04** |
| Income | — | — | .01 | .00 | −.00 |
| DLR6*Income | — | — | .07** | .06** | .04** |
| Unemployment | — | — | −.02** | −.03** | −.01 |
| Public sector | — | — | −.01 | −.00 | .01 |
| Property | — | — | −.01 | −.00 | −.01 |
| Dgini06 | — | — | −.37** | −.14** | −.06** |
| DGINI6*Property | — | — | .28** | .18** | .14** |
| Ideology | — | — | — | .08** | .04** |
| DLR6*Ideology | — | — | — | .27** | .24** |
| Party identification | — | — | — | .73** | .60** |
| DFRAC6 | — | — | — | .05** | −.01 |
| DFRAC6*Party ID | — | — | — | −.33** | −.26** |
| State | — | — | — | — | .04** |
| AUTH | — | — | — | — | −.00 |
| DAUTH6 | — | — | — | — | .19** |
| DAUTH6*AUTH | — | — | — | — | −.10** |
| Safety | — | — | — | — | .10** |
| Corruption | — | — | — | — | .13** |
| Democracy | — | — | — | — | .15** |
| SRE | — | — | — | — | .11** |
| ECN6 | — | — | — | — | −.17** |
| ECN6*SRE | — | — | — | — | .05** |
| N | 52,489 | 51,394 | 45,332 | 38,363 | 35,820 |

$**p \le .01$; $*p \le .05$ (two-tailed tests). Entries represent change in probabilities. Country dummies not shown. See appendix 4 for variable's specification.

# Appendix 4: Definition of Variables

TABLE A.4.

| **Dependent Variable** | | |
| --- | --- | --- |
| Vote | Dummy | 1= Respondents would vote for the incumbent candidate or party in the next presidential election<br>0 = Respondents would vote for a candidate or party opposing the current administration<br>Abstentions, blank votes, or missing observations are coded as missing |
| **Sociodemographic Variables** | | |
| Months | Scale | Number of months from the last presidential election to the month the survey was conducted, rescaled from (0) to (1) |
| Age | Scale | Age of respondent, rescaled from (0) to (1)<br>This variable is adjusted to obtain a positive sign assuming that older people would be more likely to vote for an incumbent right-wing government |
| Gender | Dummy | 1 = Female; 0 = Male<br>This variable is adjusted to obtain a negative sign assuming that females would be less likely to vote for an incumbent right-wing government |
| Catholic | Dummy | 1 = Catholic; 0 = Otherwise<br>This variable is adjusted to obtain a positive sign assuming that Catholics would be more likely to vote for an incumbent right-wing government |

| | | |
|---|---|---|
| Church attendance | 5 point scale | Respondents indicate how often they attend religious services (0 = Never or almost never; 2 = Once or twice a year; 3 = Once a month; 4 = Once per week; 5 = More than once per week)<br>Scores are rescaled from (0) to (1)<br>This variable is adjusted to obtain a positive sign assuming that persons with a high degree of religiosity would be more likely to vote for an incumbent right-wing government |
| Region | Dummy | 1 = Respondents residing in small city or rural area<br>0 = Respondents living in medium or large cities or metropolitan areas<br>This variable is adjusted to obtain a negative sign assuming that residents in a small city or rural area would be less likely to vote for an incumbent right-wing government |
| Race | 3 point scale | 1 = White/Asian; 0.5 = Mestizos/Mulattos; 0 = Otherwise<br>This variable is adjusted to obtain a positive sign assuming that Caucasians/Asians would be more likely to vote for an incumbent right-wing government |
| DRACE6 | Dummy | 1 = Six countries where the self-reported percentages of blacks and indigenous is the highest (Bolivia, Brazil, Colombia, Dominican Republic, Guatemala, Panama)<br>0 = Otherwise |
| DRACE6*Race | Scale | Interactive DRACE6 and Race |

**Socioeconomic Variables**

| | | |
|---|---|---|
| Schooling | 3 point scale | Number of years of schooling, coded (0) from none to 6 years; (0.5) from 7 to 11 years; and (1) from 12 years and above<br>This variable is adjusted to obtain a positive sign assuming that educated people would be more likely to vote for an incumbent right-wing government |
| DLR6 | Dummy | 1 = Six countries with the highest left-right polarization (Bolivia, Chile, Ecuador, El Salvador, Uruguay, Venezuela) |
| DLR6*Schooling | Scale | Interactive DLR6 and Schooling |

| Income | 5 point scale | Respondent's income divided in quintiles from lowest income (0) to highest income (1), rescaled from 0 to 1<br>This variable is adjusted to obtain a positive sign assuming that individuals with a higher income would be more likely to vote for an incumbent right-wing government |
|---|---|---|
| DLR6*Income | Scale | Interactive DLR6 and Income |
| Unemployment | Dummy | Coded (1) for respondents mainly spending their time actively looking for a job or not working and not looking for a job, (0) Otherwise<br>This variable is adjusted to obtain a negative sign assuming that the unemployed would be less likely to vote for an incumbent right-wing government |
| Public sector | Dummy | Coded (1) when respondents are salaried employees of the government or an independent state-owned enterprise, (0) Otherwise<br>This variable is adjusted to obtain a negative sign assuming that public employees would be less likely to vote for an incumbent right-wing government |
| Property | Scale | Number of a total of 11 property items, rescaled from (0) to (1)<br>This variable is adjusted to obtain a positive sign assuming that individuals with considerable patrimony would be more likely to vote for an incumbent right-wing government |
| DGINI6 | Dummy | 1 = Six countries where the Gini coefficients have experienced the largest decreases during the five-year period before the LAPOP surveys took place, 2003–2005–2007 vs. 2008–2010–2012 (Argentina, Bolivia, Chile, Ecuador, Peru, Venezuela)<br>0 = Otherwise |
| DGINI6*Property | Scale | Interactive DGINI6 and Property |

**Anchor Variables**

| Ideology | 10 point scale | Respondents' self-placement on a 10-point left-to-right scale, rescaled between 0 (left) and 1 (right)<br>Nonresponses or missing observations are coded as missing<br>This variable is adjusted to obtain a positive sign assuming that individuals with a self-placement on the right would be more likely to vote for an incumbent right-wing government |
|---|---|---|

| | | |
|---|---|---|
| DLR6*Ideology | Scale | Interactive DLR06 and Ideology |
| Party identification | 3 point scale | Coded (1) when respondents identify with the incumbent's party or a party of the ruling coalition, coded (0) when respondents identify with a party in the opposition and coded (0.5) when respondents do not identify with a political party or do not answer |
| DFRAC6 | Dummy | 1 = Six countries with the highest degree of partisan fractionalization (Brazil, Colombia, Costa Rica, Guatemala, Panama, Venezuela)<br>0 = Otherwise |
| DFRAC6*Party id | Scale | Interactive DFRAC6 and Party identification |

**Issues**

| | | |
|---|---|---|
| State | Scale | Respondents indicate how much they disagree or agree with these three statements (1 = Strongly disagree to 7 = Strongly agree):<br>– The (Country) government, instead of the private sector, should own the most important enterprises and industries of the country<br>– The (Country) government, more than individuals, should be primarily responsible for ensuring the well-being of the people<br>– The (Country) government, more than the private sector, should be primarily responsible for creating jobs<br>Means are calculated and scores are rescaled from (0) to (1)<br>Missing observations are excluded.<br>This variable is adjusted to obtain a negative sign assuming that individuals who believe in the role of the state would be less likely to vote for an incumbent right-wing government |
| AUTH | Scale | Respondents indicate how much they disagree or agree with this statement: "It is necessary for the progress of this country that our presidents/prime ministers limit the voice and vote of opposition parties" (1 = Strongly disagree to 7 = Strongly agree)<br>This variable is adjusted to obtain a positive sign assuming that individuals with a high score would be more likely to vote for an incumbent right-wing government |

| DAUTH6 | Dummy | 1 = Six countries having recently experienced an "authoritarian shift" according to Weyland et al. (2013) (Argentina, Bolivia, Ecuador, Honduras, Nicaragua, Venezuela)<br>0 = Otherwise |
| --- | --- | --- |
| DAUTH6*AUTH | Scale | Interactive DAUTH6 and AUTH |
| Corruption | 7 point scale | Respondents say to what extent the current administration combats corruption (1 to 7). Scores are rescaled from (0) to (1)<br>Missing observations are coded (0.5) |
| Democracy | 7 point scale | Respondents indicate to what extent the current administration promotes and protects democratic principles (1 to 7). Scores are rescaled from (0) to (1)<br>Missing observations are coded (0.5) |
| Safety | 7 point scale | Respondents indicate to what extent the current administration improves citizen safety (1 to 7). Scores are rescaled from (0) to (1)<br>Missing observations are coded (0.5) |
| SRE | 3 point scale | Sociotropic retrospective economic perception, coded (1) when respondents perceive the economy is "better" than 12 months ago; (0.5) when "same" or missing; and (0) when "worse" |
| ECN6 | Dummy | 1 = Six countries that display the highest scores on the misery index (unemployment rate + inflation rate). These countries are Argentina, Colombia, Dominican Republic, Nicaragua, Uruguay, and Venezuela<br>0 = Otherwise |
| ECN6*SRE | Scale | Interactive ECN6 and SRE |

# Notes

## Chapter 1

1. Pew Research Center (2014).
2. Fernandez (2005).
3. Population Reference Bureau (2003).
4. Population Reference Bureau (2003) and UNESCO (2003).
5. United Nations (2014).
6. The AmericasBarometer was carried out under the codirection of Mitchell Seligson and Elizabeth Zechmeister, in collaboration with the national teams for most of the countries involved in the study. The authors thank the Latin American Public Opinion Project (LAPOP) and its major supporters, including the United States Agency for International Development, the United Nations Development Program, the Inter-American Development Bank, Vanderbilt University, Université Laval, Princeton University, University of Notre Dame, and the Conselho Nacional de Desenvolvimento Científico e Tecnológico for making these datasets available to us.
7. Additional information on the data can be found at www.LapopSurveys.org
8. Note that there is the possibility that opposition candidates or parties are on the same side of the ideological spectrum as the incumbents about which we ask our vote intention question. We recognize this possibility, but believe that most voters understand that voting for a candidate that *opposes* the current administration means a candidate or a party also from the opposing ideological side. As a matter of fact, viable (opposing) candidates are almost always on different (left-right) ideological sides. This observation is consistent with recent studies based on expert surveys (Wiesehomeier and Benoit 2009; Wiesehomeier 2010); also, it is consistent with the work showing that most parliamentary elites in Latin America have a clear and coherent understanding of the ideological meaning of left and right (Alacantra 2015; Rosas and Zechmeister 2000; Saiegh 2009) and that most party systems in Latin America are ideologically organized along the left-right dimension (Jones 2005; Rosas 2005; Saiegh 2009).
9. There is one notable case that deserves greater justification for its coding: Zelaya from Honduras. Zelaya was elected president of Honduras in 2006 and ran under

the Partido Liberal de Honduras, a center-right political party. During his mandate, however, Zelaya clearly moved to the left by adopting redistributive policies to help the poor (Cunha Filho, Coelho, and Flores 2013). In our analysis, we coded Zelaya on the right because, at the time of our survey (February 2008), Zelaya was still perceived as such. Indeed, the significant move of Zelaya toward the left occurred in July 2008 when Zelaya sought to incorporate Honduras into ALBA (Alianza Bolivariana para los Pueblos de Nuestra América), an intergovernmental socialist organization founded by Cuba and Venezuela in 2004. Moreover, note that our coding is supported by an expert survey conducted between 2006 and 2007 by Wiesehomeier and Benoit (2009), also prior to Zelaya's clear move to the left. We also reran our regression analyses, putting Zelaya on the left. When we do so, our findings for the whole region as a single unit remain unaffected. As for the separate regression analysis for Honduras, the expected effect initially found for ideology vanishes entirely when changing Zelaya's ideological placement from right to left. It seems that Hondurans perceived Zelaya to be on the right at the time of the survey and such perception mattered for their vote choice.

10. In table A1.1 in appendix 1, we present the mean values of the demographic and socioeconomic characteristics of our respondents for the total sample (~90,000 respondents) and that of the vote intention sample (~50,000 respondents). As the entries in the table indicate, both samples exhibit very similar mean values despite the large loss in respondents. None of these differences show a difference equal to or larger than .01, the largest being that for public sector employees at .009. Five of the 13 characteristics presented in table A1.1 do show a statistically significant difference at .01, but such a finding is not surprising given the large size of the samples. Substantively speaking, there is little practical difference between the total sample and the one used in our analysis. The tiny differences that exist are trivial, and we have no reason to believe they have any bearing on the findings presented in this book.

11. We performed the same estimations by including country-year controls instead of only country fixed-effects. Our results remain unchanged and the model fit is not improved in any significant way, in part, because there is not much year variation given the proximity of the AmericasBarometer studies (2008–2010–2012). To reduce the number of parameters to be estimated, we decided to control for the country differences with country dummies and to account for the time dynamics with the variable Months, which measures the number of months elapsed since the inauguration of incumbents at the time of the surveys.

12. On the econometric characteristics of block-recursive systems, see the excellent presentation in Kmenta (1997).

13. Note that as we move from one block of determinants to another, some observations are inevitably lost. Most of the observations lost are attributed to the income and ideology variables. We performed two tests to evaluate the robustness of our findings. First, we reestimated all blocks using the number of observations available from the estimation of the last block (i.e., the one with the lowest number of observations). Second, we performed the same regression analyses by imputing values for income and ideology. For ideology, we imputed all missing observations by the central value of the 10-point ideological scale. For income, we used a more sophisticated approach where we imputed the missing values by predicted values obtained from a regression analysis of income on a set of other determinants. The results from these additional regression

analyses are presented in appendix 1 in tables 1.2 and 1.3, respectively. A comparison of these tables with that of table A2.1 in appendix 2 (the adopted results presented in this book) clearly indicates that our findings remain unaffected by the imputation of these missing observations or by using the smaller samples.

14. In order to give each country an identical weight in the pooled sample, we used the variable "WEIGHT 1500" provided by the AmericasBarometer so that each country dataset in the merged file has an *N* of 1,500. The adopted (unweighted) results presented in table A2.1 in appendix 2 and the weighted results from applying "WEIGHT 1500" in table A1.4 in appendix 1 are nearly identical.

## Chapter 2

1. Pew Research Center (2014).

2. Fernández (2005).

3. Population Reference Bureau (2003).

4. UNESCO (2003).

5. Supplementary analyses have been conducted with age operationalized into age groups (youth, middle-aged, and old), but this operationalization of age did not show improvement over the continuous version.

6. International Labour Organization, Key Indicators of the Labour Market database.

7. United Nations Statistical Divisions (UNSTAT).

8. We acknowledged above the growth in Protestant voters, and especially that of Evangelicals (*evangélicos*) in some countries. This religious group has gained access to political offices (mostly legislative seats) and has tended to vote en masse for candidates pertaining to that group (e.g., see Bohn 2007 about Brazil). In our supplementary analyses, we have included a dichotomous variable for Evangelical and Protestant voters, but found no particular effect for membership of these religious groups.

There is one notable exception to the group of countries considered—El Salvador, where the Catholic Church supported the insurgents of the FMLN (a coalition of former guerrilla organizations and today a center-left to left-wing political party) during most of the Salvadoran Civil War (1979–92). Thus, for El Salvador only, we expect Catholics to be more supportive of left-wing incumbent candidates.

9. By significant, Madrid (2005b) means any party that reaches 5% of the national vote.

10. Guatemala represents a special case where, among the options, respondents were offered a selection between Ladino, indigenous, or something else. Those selecting the Ladino option were classified as mestizos (58% of the Guatemalan sample). Indigenous were classified as indigenous (38%), and those selecting "other" or don't know were removed from the analysis (4%).

11. In the 2010 and 2012 LAPOP studies, interviewers were asked, at the end of the interview, to classify the respondent's skin color on an 11-tone color palette. Using this color palette, instead of our trichotomous variable, does not substantially affect the findings presented below.

12. Tau is generally the leading measure for ordinal variables (Lewis-Beck 1995). A tau of 1.0 (−1.0) indicates a perfectly monotonic positive (negative) relationship. A

tau of .00 indicates no monotonic relationship. It is superior to the other rival ordinal measure of association, gamma, in that it takes into account tied pairs, and is therefore not inflated (as is gamma). There are two tau measures in common use: tau-b and tau-c. If the table is square (same number of rows and columns), then tau-b is preferred. If it is rectangular (different number of rows and columns), then tau-c is technically preferred over tau-b (because it is impossible here for the latter to theoretically reach 1.0). Substantively, the differences between the two are small. That is to say, if one runs a tau-b on a rectangular table it will generally yield a number very similar to tau-c. Thus, throughout this book tau-b is reported. The consistency in use also facilitates comparison across tables.

13. Separate models were estimated to evaluate the contribution of the country dummies and our Months variable. In a regression equation where only the country dummies are included, we find, not surprisingly, that all countries except Guatemala are statistically different from the reference category, Mexico. The Nagelkerke pseudo-$R^2$ for this equation is .08, and 60.6% of the cases are predicted correctly. Now, when we regress vote intentions on the Months variable only, we find the estimated coefficient of the latter to be negative and strongly statistically significant, as expected. The Nagelkerke pseudo-$R^2$ is low at .01, and only 53.8% of the cases are correctly predicted. Finally, when we add the Months variable to the regression equation containing only the country dummies, we observe an increase in the Nagelkerke pseudo-$R^2$ of .02, from .08 to .10, and an increase in the number of cases correctly predicted from 60.6% to 61.5%. These results indicate an important, although limited, role for our Months variable. Still, it indicates the importance of controlling for country-specific characteristics through the inclusion of the country dummies, at least at this point in our analysis.

## Chapter 3

1. Honduras is excluded from our analysis in this section because the questions about clientelism were not asked in that country.

2. At first sight, the fact that better educated citizens appear to be significantly more exposed to clientelism seems to be counterintuitive. One would expect candidates and parties to target less educated voters, who should be less likely to detect the fraudulent nature of the offer. Yet the analysis suggests that more educated voters are more likely to report having been offered material benefits for their vote, everything else being equal.

3. In order to calculate the aggregate predicted probability of incumbent support, we use the "predict" command in Stata after running the full logit model. We then average individual predicted probabilities in order to generate aggregate estimates.

4. Here are the country-specific results (in alphabetical order): Argentina +0.3, Bolivia +0.2, Brazil +1.6, Chile +0.4, Colombia +0.2, Costa Rica +0.3, Dominican Republic +1.7, Ecuador –0.4, El Salvador –0.7, Guatemala 0.0, Mexico +0.7, Nicaragua 0.0, Panama +5.1, Paraguay +1.0, Peru +0.6, Uruguay –0.3, Venezuela –1.6.

## Chapter 4

1. The wording for the two variables is as follows: Party identification: "Do you currently identify with a political party?" (If yes) "Which political party do you identify with [List]?" Ideology: "Now, to change the subject. . . . On this card there is a 1–10 scale that goes from left to right. The number one means left and 10 means right. Nowadays, when we speak of political leanings, we talk of those on the left and those on the right. In other words, some people sympathize more with the left and others with the right. According to the meaning that the terms 'left' and 'right' have for you, and thinking of your own political leanings, where would you place yourself on this scale? Tell me the number." The variable measuring ideology is adjusted to obtain a positive sign assuming that individuals with a self-placement on the right would be more likely to vote for an incumbent right-wing government.

2. One advantage of merging the three surveys is to reduce the amount of largely unexplained variation in the data within a country. This is particularly true for respondents' ideological orientation. For example, the percentage of respondents able to place themselves on a left-right scale drops 13 percentage points in Honduras between 2010 and 2012. During the same period, we also note a decline of 8 percentage points for Venezuela and an increase of 12 and 10 percentage points for Panama and Nicaragua, respectively. Such sharp fluctuations in a country over such a short period of time cannot be easily explained. Therefore, the advantage of merging the surveys is to give a clearer reading of the situation in each country, one less subject to variation across individual surveys. This is apparent when we examine the average values for the three variables in the table. For example, average party identification across the 18 countries lies at 31%, 30.5%, and 30.1% for the 2008, 2010, and 2012 surveys, respectively. With regard to percentage of those who state an ideological position/preference, these figures are at 79.4%, 79.5%, and 81% for the three years. We even find the same stability in relation to ideological orientation, with mean values of .50, .51, and .50 for 2008, 2010, and 2012. Thus, these figures underline the advantages of aggregation in order to describe the actual situation in various countries. The very noticeable fluctuations in ideological orientation from one year to the next provide yet another indication of how the idea of a left-right scale is less embedded in the minds of Latin American voters when it comes to politics.

3. The distribution of Ideology for the 18 countries and the three surveys (2008, 2010, 2012) on the original 1 to 10 scale goes as follows: 1 (extreme-left) = 8%, 2 = 4%, 3 = 7%, 4 = 8%, 5 = 26%, 6 = 15%, 7 = 9%, 8 = 9%, 9 = 4%, 10 = 11%. This distribution means that roughly 40% of respondents (41%) place themselves at the center of the scale (5 and 6). It also shows that the percentage of right-wing identifiers (7 to 10) is a bit higher at 33% than the proportion of left-wing identifiers (1 to 4), which stands at 27%. The relative balance between left-wing and right-wing identifiers in Latin America parallels what is usually observed in advanced democracies (Lewis-Beck et al. 2012). Two differences stand out however. First, the proportion of "centrists" seems a bit higher in Latin America than in other well-established democracies (it stands at about 30% in countries like France and Denmark for instance; part of

this difference however may be due to the fact that surveys tapping ideology generally use an 11 (0 to 10) rather than a 10 (1 to 10) point scale (see Nadeau et al. 2012 and Nadeau 2015). Second, as previously noticed, the percentage of respondents unable to self-classify themselves on the left-right scale is higher in Latin America. Both differences underline the fact that the idea of a left-right scale is less embedded in the minds of Latin American voters.

4. As shown in appendix 1, imputing the mean value to the missing cases for Ideology (.50) leave our results virtually intact. The same is true when we delete the missing cases for Ideology in models estimating the impact of the demographics and socioeconomic determinants of the vote.

## Chapter 6

1. The regression coefficients in the figure have been recoded from 0 to 1, where 0 corresponds to the smallest coefficient (for Brazil) and 1 to the largest coefficient (for the Dominican Republic).

2. Given that this outcome was expected, we reversed the sign for the religious variable in El Salvador (see the appendix).

3. The data used to create this variable were taken from the LAPOP surveys. The countries forming DRACE6 and the other interactive terms in this section belong (with one exception, see below) to the first tercile of the distribution of key contextual variables (for an analysis of class polarization in the United States based on this idea, see Nadeau et al. 2004). Not surprisingly, the results are stronger when the selection is limited to the first three countries of these distributions and weaker when it is extended to nine countries. It is also clearly weaker when continuous versions of the contextual variables are used. It should also be noted that the results for the interactive variables remain nearly identical whether these variables are included one at a time or simultaneously. For instance, Model 5 in table 6.4 includes eight interactive variables. The effect of all of them is basically the same whether it is estimated with eight different models including one interaction at a time or with the full model including the eight interactions simultaneously. All in all, using the first tercile of the distribution of key contextual variables appears to be a simple and sensible strategy to account for intracountry differences in voting behavior within Latin American countries.

4. The countries where the Gini coefficients increased were few and the changes were small. The data for the Gini coefficients come from the Human Development Report of the United Nations (various years). We also performed analyses using the decade (98–00–02 vs. 08–10–12) before the LAPOP surveys as our period of reference. The results from these estimations are strong, significant, and point in the same direction as the ones reported in the text.

5. It should be recalled that the effect of schooling is significant when income and property are excluded from the models (see chapter 3).

6. One may argue that Brazil and Nicaragua should be included in this group. Expert surveys point in the opposite direction. First, Lula's positioning on the left-

right scale could be more aptly depicted as center-left than radical left (Weisehomeier 2010, 5–6). Second, according to Weisehomeier (2010, 6), "the Sandinista leader Daniel Ortega . . . is actually ranked as being the most moderate representative of the left-wing leaders." The inclusion of El Salvador appears justified based on the radical attitudes of the parliamentary representatives of the main left-wing party in this country, the Farabundo Marti National Liberation Front (Alcántara and Rivas 2006). The political history of this party, its rhetoric inspired from socialism and Marxism, as well as the extreme contrast between its positions and that of its right-wing opponent, ARENA (Alianza Republicana Nacionalista), also justify its inclusion (Alancantra and Rivas 2006; Wiesehomeier and Benoit 2009; Wiesehomeier 2010). Finally, substituting El Salvador for Nicaragua or Brazil in the list of the most polarized countries leaves our results basically intact.

7. The fractionalization index measures the probability that two deputies picked at random from the legislature of a given country will be of different parties (source: Data Bank of Political Institutions, 2012. World Bank, available at http://econ.world bank.org/; see also Beck et al. 2001).

8. The exclusion of Brazil appears even more justified. Not only is Lula's positioning on the left-right scale rather moderate, but the extreme party fragmentation in Brazil limits the utility for voters of left-right placement in their decision making (Sulmont 2014), and elite rhetoric in Brazil appears to be loosely tied to left-right thinking (Tarouco and Madeira 2012). Additional evidence suggests that ideological politics is more pronounced in Chile, El Salvador, and Uruguay than in Brazil and Nicaragua. Zechmeister and Corral (2010), for instance, have neatly shown that voters' ideological positioning is structured around the expected dimension of the role of the State in Chile, El Salvador, and Uruguay, but not in Brazil and Nicaragua. Furthermore, political parties in Chile and Uruguay rank much higher on the Rosas (2005) index of ideological organization, compared to other Latin American countries. These results are consistent with those obtained by Jones (2005), who has developed an index to capture to extent to which parties are programmatic. According to this index, Chile and Uruguay exhibit the most programmatic party systems.

9. The conclusions about the impact of authoritarianism on the vote are based on Weyland and colleagues' (2013) characterization (rather than forming the first tercile of a distribution like the proportion of nonwhites, for instance), and should for this reason be considered more tentative.

10. The data used to create this index were taken from the World Bank (2008, 2010, 2012).

11. Though overall it cannot be said that demographic characteristics are strong determinants of vote choice in the region.

## Conclusion

1. These countries are Costa Rica, the Dominican Republic, El Salvador, Honduras, Mexico, Nicaragua, Panama, Uruguay, and Venezuela.

2. They are Bolivia, Chile, Guatemala, and Peru.

3. They are Argentina, Brazil, Colombia, Ecuador, and Paraguay. Although note that in the cases of Brazil and Colombia, anchors (block 3)—especially party identification—have an impact that is more negligible than usual in comparison with their other blocks of variables (see chapter 4).

4. In its latest complete module (Module 3), the CSES covers five Latin American countries: Brazil, Chile, Mexico, Peru, and Uruguay.

# References

Abzug, Bella S. 1984. *Gender Gap*. Boston: Houghton Mifflin.

Achen, Christopher H. 2002. "Parental Socialization and Rational Partisan Identification." *Political Behavior* 24:151–70.

Adelson, Joseph. 1980. *Handbook of Adolescent Psychology*. New York: Wiley.

Agüero, Felipe, and Jeffrey Stark, eds. 1998. *Fault Lines of Democracy in Post-Transition Latin America*. Boulder: Lynne Rienner.

Alcántara, Manuel (dir.). 1994–2011. Proyecto de Elites Parlamentarias Latinoamericanas (PELA). Universidad de Salamanca.

Alcántara, Manuel, and Cristina Rivas. 2006. "The Left-Right Dimension in Latin America Party Politics." Paper prepared for delivery at the Annual Meeting of the American Political Science Association, Philadelphia, August 30–September 6.

Ames, Barry. 1994. "The Reverse Coattails Effect: Local Party Organization in the 1989 Brazilian Presidential Election." *American Political Science Review* 88:95–111.

Ames, Barry. 2001. *The Deadlock of Democracy in Brazil*. Ann Arbor: University of Michigan Press.

Anderson, Leslie, Michael S. Lewis-Beck, and Mary Stegmaier. 2003. "Post-Socialist Democratization: A Comparative Political Economy Model of the Vote for Hungary and Nicaragua." *Electoral Studies* 22:469–84.

Ansolabehere, Stephen, Nathaniel Persily, and Charles Stewart. 2010. "Race, Religion, and the Vote Choice in the 2008 Election: Implications for the Future of the Voting Rights Act." *Harvard Law Review* 123:1–52.

Arana, Rubi Esmeralda, and María L. Santacruz Giralt. 2005. *Opinión pública sobre el sistema político del país y la participación de la mujer en la política*. Colección Género No. 2. San Salvador: La Fundación Dr. Guillermo Manuel Ungo.

Arce, Moisés. 2003. "Political Violence and Presidential Approval in Peru." *Journal of Politics* 65:572–83.

Arce, Moisés E., and Julio F. Carrion. 2010. "Presidential Support in a Context of Crisis and Recovery in Peru, 1988–2008." *Journal of Politics in Latin America* 2:31–51.

Baker, Andy, Barry Ames, and Lucio Rennó. 2006. "Social Context and Campaign Volatility in New Democracies: Networks and Neighborhoods in Brazil's 2002 Election." *American Journal of Political Science* 50:382–99.

Baker, Andy, Barry Ames, and Lucia R. Rennó. 2008. "The Quality of Elections in Brazil: Policy, Performance, Pageantry, or Pork?" In *Democratic Brazil Revisited*, edited by Peter Kingstone. Pittsburgh: University of Pittsburgh Press.

Baker, Andy, and Kenneth F. Greene. 2011. "The Latin American Left's Mandate: Free-Market Policies and Issue Voting in New Democracies." *World Politics* 63:43–77.

Baker, Andy, and Kenneth F. Greene. 2015. "Positional Issue Voting in Latin America." In *The Latin American Voter*, edited by Ryan E. Carlin, Matthew M. Singer, and Elizabeth J. Zechmeister. Ann Arbor: University of Michigan Press.

Bartels, Larry M. 1993. "Messages Received: The Political Impact of Media Exposure." *American Political Science Review* 87:267–85.

Bateson, Regina. 2012. "Crime and Political Participation." *American Political Science Review* 106:570–87.

Baxter, Sandra, and Marjorie Lansing. 1983. *Women and Politics: The Visible Majority*. Ann Arbor: University of Michigan Press.

Beck, Thorsten, George Clarke, Alberto Groff, Philip Keefer, and Patrick Walsh. 2001. "New Tools in Comparative Political Economy: The Database of Political Institutions." *World Bank Economic Review* 15:165–76.

Beirne, Piers. 1997. *Issues in Comparative Criminology*. Brookfield, VT: Dartmouth Publishing.

Bélanger, Éric, Richard Nadeau, Mathieu Turgeon, Michael S. Lewis-Beck, and Martial Foucault. 2014. "Patrimony and French Presidential Vote Choice: Evidence from the 2012 Election." *French Politics* 12:59–68.

Bengtsson, Asa, Kasper M. Hansen, Ólafur P. Haroarson, Hanne Marthe Narud, and Henrik Oscarsson. 2013. *The Nordic Voter*. Colchester: ECPR Press.

Benton, Allyson Lucinda. 2005. "Dissatisfied Democrats or Retrospective Voters? Economic Hardship, Political Institutions, and Voting Behavior in Latin America." *Comparative Political Studies* 38:417–42.

Berelson, Bernard R., Paul F. Lazarsfeld, and William N. McPhee. 1954. *Voting: A Study of Opinion Formation in a Presidential Election*. Chicago: University of Chicago Press.

Blais, André, Elisabeth Gidengil, Richard Nadeau, and Neil Nevitte. 2002. *Anatomy of a Liberal Victory: Making Sense of the Vote in the 2000 Canadian Election*. Peterborough, Ontario: Broadview Press.

Blais, André, Simon Labbé-St-Vincent, Jean-François Laslier, Nicolas Sauger, and Karine Van der Straeten. 2011. "Strategic Vote Choice in One-Round and Two-Round Elections: An Experimental Study." *Political Research Quarterly* 64:637–45.

Boas, Taylor. 2005. "Television and Neopopulism in Latin America: Media Effects in Brazil and Peru." *Latin American Research Review* 40:27–49.

Boas, Taylor. 2015. "Voting for Democracy: Campaign Effects in Chile's Democratic Transition." *Latin American Politics and Society* 57:67–90.

Boas, Taylor. 2016. *Presidential Campaigns in Latin America: Electoral Strategies and Success Contagion*. Cambridge: Cambridge University Press.

Boas, Taylor C., and F. Daniel Hidalgo. 2011. "Controlling the Airwaves: Incumbency Advantage and Community Radio in Brazil." *American Journal of Political Science* 55:869–85.

Boas, Taylor, and Amy E. Smith. 2015. "Religion and the Latin American Voter." In *The Latin American Voter*, edited by Ryan Carlin, Matthew Singer, and Elizabeth Zechmeister. Ann Arbor: University of Michigan Press.

Bohn, Simone R. 2007. "Contexto politico eleitoral, minorias religiosas e voto em pleitos presidenciais (2002–2006)." *Opinião Pública* 13:366–87.

Box-Steffensmeier, Janet M., and Suzanna De Boef. 1996. "Partisanship and Ideology: A Subgroup Analysis over Time." Paper presented at the Annual Meeting of the American Political Science Association, San Francisco, September 1–4.

Brader, Ted, and Joshua A. Tucker. 2001. "The Emergence of Mass Partisanship in Russia, 1993–1996." *American Journal of Political Science* 45:69–83.

Brader, Ted, and Joshua A. Tucker. 2008. "Pathways to Partisanship: Evidence from Russia." *Post-Soviet Affairs* 24:263–300.

Braungart, Richard G., and Margaret M. Braungart. 1986. "Life-Course and Generational Politics." *Annual Review of Sociology* 12:205–31.

Broughton, David, and Hans-Martien ten Napel. 2000. *Religion and Mass Electoral Behavior in Europe*. London: Routledge/European Consortium of Political Research.

Brusco, Valeria, Marcelo Nazareno, and Susan Stokes. 2004. "Vote Buying in Argentina." *Latin American Research Review* 39:66–88.

Budge, Ian, Ivor Crewe, and Dennis Fairlie. 1976. *Party Identification and Beyond*. London: Wiley.

Butler, David, and Donald Stokes. 1969. *Political Change in Britain: Forces Shaping Electoral Choice*. London: Macmillan.

Calvo, Ernesto, and Maria Victoria Murillo. 2004. "Who Delivers? Partisan Clients in the Argentine Electoral Market." *American Journal of Political Science* 48:742–57.

Cameron, Maxwell A., and Eric Hershberg, eds. 2010. *Latin America's Left Turns: Politics, Policies, and Trajectories of Change*. Boulder: Lynne Rienner.

Camp, Ai Roedrick, ed. 1996. *Democracy in Latin America, Patterns and Cycles*. Wilmington, DE: SR Books.

Campbell, Angus, Phillip E. Converse, Warren E. Miller, and Donald E. Stokes. 1960. *The American Voter*. New York: John Wiley & Sons.

Cardoso, Fernando Henrique, and Enzo Faletto. 1979. *Dependency and Development in Latin America*. Berkeley: University of California Press.

Carlin, Ryan E., Matthew M. Singer, and Elizabeth J. Zechmeister, eds. 2015. *The Latin American Voter*. Ann Arbor: University of Michigan Press.

Carmines, Edward G., and James A. Stimson. 1980. "The Two Faces of Issue Voting." *American Political Science Review* 74:78–91.

Carreras, Miguel. 2013. "The Impact of Criminal Violence on Regime Legitimacy in Latin America." *Latin American Research Review* 48:85–107.

Castaneda, Jorge G., and Marco A. Morales, eds. 2008. *Leftovers: Tales of the Latin American Left*. New York: Routledge.

Cataife, Guido. 2011. "An Integrated Model of Vote Choice in Argentina, 2009." *Latin American Politics and Society* 53:115–40.

Center for the American Woman and Politics (CAWP). 2011. "CAWP Fact Sheet." Eagleton Institute of Politics, Rutgers, The State University of New Jersey, New Brunswick, NJ.

Center for the American Woman and Politics (CAWP). 2012a. "CAWP Fact Sheet." Eagleton Institute of Politics, Rutgers, The State University of New Jersey, New Brunswick, NJ.

Center for the American Woman and Politics (CAWP). 2012b. "CAWP Fact Sheet." Eagleton Institute of Politics, Rutgers, The State University of New Jersey, New Brunswick, NJ.

Center for the American Woman and Politics (CAWP). 2013. "CAWP Fact Sheet." Eagleton Institute of Politics, Rutgers, The State University of New Jersey, New Brunswick, NJ.

Chesnut, R. Andrew. 2003. *Competitive Spirits: Latin America's New Religious Economy.* New York: Oxford University Press.

Chesnut, R. Andrew. 2009. "Charismatic Competitors: Protestant Pentecostals and Catholic Charismatics in Latin America's New Religious Marketplace." In *Religion and Society in Latin America*, edited by Lee M. Penyak and Walter J. Petry. Maryknoll, NY: Orbis Books.

Clarke, Harold D., David Sanders, Marianne C. Stewart, and Paul Whiteley. 2004. *Political Choice in Britain.* Oxford: Oxford University Press.

Clarke, Harold D., David Sanders, Marianne C. Stewart, and Paul Whiteley. 2009. *Performance Politics and the British Voters.* Cambridge: Cambridge University Press.

Clarke, Harold D., David Sanders, Marianne C. Stewart, and Paul Whitely. 2012. *Campaigning for Change: The Dynamics of Politics in Britain.* Cambridge: Cambridge University Press.

Collier, David, ed. 1979. *The New Authoritarianism in Latin America.* Princeton: Princeton University Press.

Converse, Philip E., and Roy Pierce. 1986. *Political Representation in France.* Cambridge: Belknap Press of Harvard University Press.

Converse, Philip E., and Roy C. Pierce. 1992. "Partisanship and Party System." *Political Behavior* 14:239–59.

Corral, Margarita. 2011. *The State of Democracy in Latin America: A Comparative Analysis of the Attitudes of Elites and Citizens.* Salamanca: Boletin PNUD and Instituto de Ibéroamerica, University of Salamanca.

Crisp, Brian F., Daniel H. Levine, and José E. Molina. 2003. "The Rise and Decline of COPEI in Venezuela." In *Christian Democracy in Latin America: Electoral Competition and Regime Conflicts*, edited by Scott Mainwaring and Timothy Scully. Stanford: Stanford University Press.

Cruz, Cesi, and Philip Keefer. 2010. "Programmatic Political Parties and Public Sector Reform." Paper presented at the Annual Meeting of the American Political Science Association, Washington, DC, September 2–5.

Cunha Filho, C. M., A. L. Coelho, and F. I. Pérez Flores. 2013. "A Right-to-Left Policy Switch? An Analysis of the Honduran Case under Manuel Zelaya." *International Political Science Review* 34:519–42.

De Ferranti, David, Guillermo E. Perry, Francisco H. G. Ferreira, and Michael Walton. 2004. *Inequality in Latin America: Breaking with History?* Washington, DC: World Bank.

Diamond, Larry, Marc F. Plattner, and Diego Abente Brun. 2008. *Latin America's Struggle for Democracy.* Baltimore: Johns Hopkins University Press.

Di Tella, Torcuato S. 2005. *History of Political Parties in Twentieth-Century Latin America.* Newark, NJ: Transaction Publishers.

Dix, Robert H. 1989. "Cleavage Structures and Party Systems in Latin America." *Comparative Politics* 22:23–37.

Domínguez, Jorge I., and James A. McCann. 1995. "Shaping Mexico's Electoral Arena: The Construction of Partisan Cleavages in the 1988 and 1991 National Elections." *American Political Science Review* 89:34–48.

Dominguez, Jorge I., and James A. McCann. 1996. *Democratizing Mexico: Public Opinion and Electoral Choice.* Baltimore: Johns Hopkins University Press.

Dominguez, Jorge I., and James A. McCann. 1998. "Mexicans React to Electoral Fraud and Political Corruption: An Assessment of Public Opinion and Voting Behavior." *Electoral Studies* 17:483–503.

Duch, Raymond M. 2007. "Comparative Studies of the Economy and the Vote." In *The Oxford Handbook of Comparative Politics,* edited by Carles Boix and Susan C. Stokes, 805–44. Oxford: Oxford University Press.

Echegaray, Fabián. 2005. *Economic Crises and Electoral Responses in Latin America.* Lanham, MD: University Press of America.

Ellner, Steve. 2013. "Latin America's Left in Power: Complexities and Challenges in the Twentieth Century." *Latin American Perspectives* 40:5–25.

Ellner, Steve. 2014. *Latin America's Radical Left: Challenges and Complexities of Political Power in the Twenty-First Century.* Lanham, MD: Rowman & Littlefield.

Evans, Geoffrey, and Robert Andersen. 2006. "The Political Conditioning of Economic Perceptions." *Journal of Politics* 68:194–207.

Fernández, Francisco Lizcano. 2005. "Composición etnica de las tres áreas culturales del continente americano al comienzo del siglo XXI." *Convergencia* 38:185–232.

Fiorina, Morris P. 1981. *Retrospective Voting in American National Elections.* New Haven: Yale University Press.

Foucault, Martial, and Richard Nadeau. 2014. "Comparing Patrimonial Voting." Paper presented at the Annual Meeting of the American Political Science Association, Washington, DC, August 28–31.

Foucault, Martial, Richard Nadeau, and Michael S. Lewis-Beck. 2011. "La persistance de l'effet patrimoine lors des élections présidentielles françaises." *Revue française de science politique* 61:659–80.

Fox, Jonathan. 1994. "The Difficult Transition from Clientelism to Citizenship: Lessons from Mexico." *World Politics* 46:151–84.

Fraile, Marta, and Michael S. Lewis-Beck. 2010. "Economic Voting in Spain: A 2000 Panel Test." *Electoral Studies* 29:210–20.

Franklin, Mark N., Thomas T. Mackie, and Henry Valen, eds. 1992. *Electoral Change: Responses to Evolving Social and Attitudinal Structures in Western Countries.* Cambridge: Cambridge University Press.

Garrard-Burnett, Virginia. 2009. "'Like a Mighty Rushing Wind': The Growth of

Pentecostalism in Contemporary Latin America." In *Religion and Society in Latin America*, by Lee M. Penyak and Walter J. Petry. Maryknoll, NY: Orbis Books.

Gasparini, Leonardo, Guillermo Cruces, and Leopoldo Tornarolli. 2011. "Recent Trends in Income Inequality in Latin America." *Economia* 11:147–90.

Gélineau, François. 2007. "Political Context and Economic Accountability: Evidence from Latin America." *Political Research Quarterly* 69:415–28.

Gélineau, François. 2013. "Electoral Accountability in the Developing World." *Electoral Studies* 32:418–24.

Gélineau, François, and Matthew Singer. 2015. "The Economy and Incumbent Support in Latin America." In *The Latin American Voter*, edited by Ryan E. Carlin, Matthew Singer, and Elizabeth J. Zechmeister. Ann Arbor: University of Michigan.

Giles, Micheal W., and Melanie Buckner. 1993. "David Duke and Black Threat: An Old Hypothesis Revisited." *Journal of Politics* 55:702–13.

Giles, Micheal W., and Kaenan Hertz. 1994. "Racial Threat and Partisan Identification." *American Political Science Review* 88:317–26.

Gindling, Tim H., and Diego Trejos. 2013. "The Distribution of Income in Central America." Discussion Paper 7236. Bonn: Institute for the Study of Labour.

Golden, Miriam. 2003. "Electoral Connections: The Effects of the Personal Vote on Political Patronage, Bureaucracy and Legislation in Postwar Italy." *British Journal of Political Science* 33:189–212.

González, Luis E., and Rosario Queirolo. 2009. "Understanding 'Right' and 'Left' in Latin America." Paper presented at the Annual Meeting of the Latin American Studies Association, Rio de Janeiro, June 11–14.

Goren, Paul. 2005. "Party Identification and Core Political Values." *American Journal of Political Science* 49:882–97.

Graziano, Luigi. 1973. "Patron-Client Relationships in Southern Italy." *European Journal of Political Research* 1:3–34.

Green, Donald P., Bradley Palmquist, and Eric Schickler. 2002. *Partisan Hearts and Minds: Political Parties and the Social Identities of Voters*. New Haven: Yale University Press.

Haegel, Florence. 1990. "Le lien partisan." In *L'électeur français en questions*, edited by Daniel Boy and Nonna Mayer, 153–74. Paris: Presses de Sciences Po.

Hagopian, Frances, and Scott Mainwaring, eds. 2005. *The Third Wave of Democratization in Latin America: Advances and Setbacks*. Cambridge: Cambridge University Press.

Hall, Gillette, and Harry Anthony Patrinos. 2006. eds. *Indigenous Peoples, Poverty and Human Development in Latin America*. New York: Palgrave Macmillan.

Handley, Lisa, and Bernard Grofman. 1994. "The Impact of the Voting Rights Act on Minority Representation." In *Quiet Revolution in the South*, edited by Chandler Davidson and Bernard Grofman, 335–50. Princeton: Princeton University Press.

Handlin, Samuel. 2013. "Survey Research and Social Class in Venezuela: Evaluating Alternative Measures and Their Impact on Assessments of Class Voting." *Latin American Politics and Society* 55:141–67.

Hawkins, Kirk A. 2010. *Venezuela's Chavismo and Populism in Comparative Perspective*. New York: Cambridge University Press.

Heath, Oliver. 2009. "Economic Crisis, Party System Change, and the Dynamics of Class Voting in Venezuela, 1973–2003." *Electoral Studies* 28:467–79.

Hellwig, Timothy. 2010. "Context, Information, and Performance Voting." In *Citizens, Context, and Choice: How Context Shapes Citizens' Electoral Choices*, edited by Russell J. Dalton and Christopher J. Anderson, 149–75. New York: Oxford University Press.

Hicken, Allen. 2011. "Clientelism." *Annual Review of Political Science* 14:289–310.

Holbrook, Thomas M. 1996. *Do Campaigns Matter?* Thousand Oaks, CA: Sage.

Holmes, Jennifer S., and Sheila Amin Gutiérrez de Piñeres. 2003. "Sources of Fujimori's Popularity: Neoliberal Reform or Ending Terrorism?" *Terrorism & Political Violence* 14:93–112.

Howard, Gregory J., Graeme Newman, and William Alex Pridemore. 2000. "Theory, Method, and Data in Comparative Criminology." In *Criminal Justice 2000*, vol. 4, edited by David Duffee, 139–211. Washington, DC: National Institute of Justice.

Huber, John D., Georgia Kernell, and Eduardo L. Leoni. 2005. "Institutional Context, Cognitive Resources and Party Attachments among Democracies." *Political Analysis* 13:365–86.

Hunter, Wendy, and Timothy J. Power. 2007. "Rewarding Lula: Executive Power, Social Policy, and the Brazilian Elections of 2006." *Latin American Politics and Society* 49:1–30.

Inglehart, Ronald, and Pippa Norris. 2000. "The Developmental Theory of the Gender Gap: Women's and Men's Voting Behavior in Global Perspective." *International Political Science Review* 21:441–63.

Inglehart, Ronald, and Pippa Norris. 2003. *Rising Tide: Gender Equality and Cultural Change around the World.* New York: Cambridge University Press.

Iversen, Torben, and Frances Rosenbluth. 2006. "The Political Economy of Gender: Explaining Cross-National Variation in the Gender Division of Labor and the Gender Voting Gap." *American Journal of Political Science* 50:1–19.

Jackman, Simon. 2003. "Political Parties and Electoral Behavior." In *The Cambridge Handbook of the Social Sciences in Australia,* edited by Ian McAllister, Steve Doorick, and Riaz Hassan, 266–86. Cambridge: Cambridge University Press.

Jacobson, Gary C. 1978. "The Effects of Campaign Spending in Congressional Elections." *American Political Science Review* 72:469–91.

Johnson, Gregg, and Sooh-Rhee Ryu. 2010. "Repudiating or Rewarding Neoliberalism? How Broken Campaign Promises Condition Economic Voting in Latin America." *Latin American Politics and Society* 52:1–24.

Johnson, Gregg, and Leslie Schwindt-Bayer. 2009. "Economic Accountability in Central America." *Journal of Politics in Latin America* 1:33–56.

Johnson, John J. 1964. *The Military and Society in Latin America.* Stanford: Stanford University Press.

Johnston, R. J., C. J. Pattie, D. F. L. Dorling, I. MacAllister, H. Tunstall, and D. J. Rossiter. 2001. "Social Locations, Spatial Locations and Voting at the 1997 British General Election: Evaluating the Sources of Conservative Support." *Political Geography* 20:85–111.

Jones, Mark P. 2005. "The Role of Parties and Party Systems in the Policymaking

Process." Paper prepared for the Workshop on State Reform, Public Policies, and Policymaking Processes. Washington, DC: Inter-American Development Bank.

Jou, Willy. 2011. "How Do Citizens in East Asian Democracies Understand Left and Right?" *Japanese Journal of Political Science* 12:33–55.

Keefer, Philip. 2007. "Clientelism, Credibility, and the Policy Choices of Young Democracies." *American Journal of Political Science* 51:804–21.

Key, Vladimir O., Jr. 1966. *The Responsible Electorate*. New York: Vintage.

Kiewiet, D. Roderick. 1983. *Macroeconomics and Micropolitics: The Electoral Effects of Economic Issues*. Chicago: University of Chicago Press.

Kiewiet, D. Roderick, and Michael S. Lewis-Beck. 2012. "No 'Man' Is an Island: Self-Interest, the Public Interest, and Sociotropic Voting." *Critical Review* 23:303–19.

Kinder, Donald R., and D. Roderick Kiewiet. 1981. "Sociotropic Politics: The American Case." *British Journal of Political Science* 11:129–61.

Kitschelt, Herbert, Kirk Hawkins, Juan Pablo Luna, Guillermo Rosas, and Elizabeth J. Zechmeister. 2010. *Latin American Party Systems*. Cambridge: Cambridge University Press.

Kmenta, Jan. 1997. *Elements of Econometrics*. Ann Arbor: University of Michigan Press.

Kritzinger, Sylvia, Eva Zeglovits, Michael S. Lewis-Beck, and Richard Nadeau. 2013. *The Austrian Voter*. Vienna: University of Vienna Press.

Langston, Joy, and Scott Morgenstern. 2009. "Campaigning in an Electoral Authoritarian Regime: The Case of Mexico." *Comparative Politics* 41:165–81.

Lawson, Chappell, and James A. McCann. 2005. "Television News, Mexico's 2000 Elections and Media Effects in Emerging Democracies." *British Journal of Political Science* 35:1–30.

Lazarsfeld, Paul F., Bernard R. Berelson, and Hazel Gaudet. 1948. *The People's Choice*. New York: Columbia University Press.

Le Hay, Viviane, and Mariette Sineau. 2010. "'Effet patrimoine': 30 ans après, le retour?" *Revue française de science politique* 60:869–900.

Levitsky, Steven, and Maxwell A. Cameron. 2003. "Democracy without Parties? Political Parties and Regime Change in Fujimori's Peru." *Latin American Politics and Society* 45:1–33.

Levitsky, Steven, and Kenneth M. Roberts, eds. 2011. *The Resurgence of the Latin American Left*. Baltimore: Johns Hopkins University Press.

Levitsky, Steven, and Lucan Way. 2010. *Competitive Authoritarianism: The Origins and Dynamics of Hybrid Regimes in the Post-Cold War Era*. Cambridge: Cambridge University Press.

Lewis-Beck, Michael S. 1988. *Economics and Elections: The Major Western Democracies*. Ann Arbor: University of Michigan Press.

Lewis-Beck, Michael S. 1995. *Data Analysis: An Introduction*. Vol. 103 of Sage University Paper Series on Quantitative Applications in the Social Sciences. Thousand Oaks, CA: Sage.

Lewis-Beck, Michael S. 2009. "Revisiting the American Voter." *Electoral Studies* 28:521–22.

Lewis-Beck, Michael S., William G. Jacoby, Helmut Norpoth, and Harold F. Weisberg. 2008. *The American Voter Revisited*. Ann Arbor: University of Michigan Press.

Lewis-Beck, Michael S., and Richard Nadeau. 2009. "Obama and the Economy in 2008." *PS: Political Science and Politics* 42:479–83.

Lewis-Beck, Michael S., and Richard Nadeau. 2011. "Economic Voting Theory: Testing New Dimensions." *Electoral Studies* 30:288–94.

Lewis-Beck, Michael S., and Richard Nadeau. 2012. "PIGS or Not? Economic Voting in Southern Europe." *Electoral Studies* 31:472–77.

Lewis-Beck, Michael S., Richard Nadeau, and Angelo Elias. 2008. "Economics, Party, and the Vote: Causality Issues and Panel Data." *American Journal of Political Science* 52, no.1 (January): 84–95.

Lewis-Beck, Michael S., and Maria Celeste Ratto. 2013. "Economic Voting in Latin America: A General Model." *Electoral Studies* 32:489–93.

Lewis-Beck, Michael S., and Mary Stegmaier. 2000. "Economic Determinants of Electoral Outcomes." *Annual Review of Political Science* 3:183–219.

Lewis-Beck, Michael S., and Mary Stegmaier. 2007. "Economic Models of Voting." In *The Oxford Handbook of Political Behavior*, edited by Russell Dalton and Hans-Dieter Klingemann, 518–37. Oxford: Oxford University Press.

Lewis-Beck, Michael S., and Mary Stegmaier. 2008. "The Economic Vote in Transitional Democracies." *Journal of Elections, Public Opinion and Parties* 18:303–23.

Lewis-Beck, Michael S., and Mary Stegmaier. 2013. "The VP-Function Revisited: A Survey of the Literature on Vote and Popularity Functions after over 40 Years." *Public Choice* 157:367–85.

Lieuwen, Edwin. 1967. *Arms and Politics in Latin America*. New York: Frederick A. Praeger.

Lipset, Seymour M. 1960. *Political Man: The Social Bases of Politics*. New York: Doubleday.

Lipset, Seymour M., and Stein Rokkan. 1967. *Party Systems and Voter Alignments: Cross-National Perspectives*. New York: Free Press.

Loveman, Brian. 1993. *The Constitution of Tyranny: Regimes of Exception in Spanish America*. Pittsburgh: University of Pittsburgh Press.

Lupu, Noam. 2012. "Voter Partisanship in Latin America." Paper presented at the Annual Meeting of the American Political Science Association, New Orleans, August 30–September 2.

Lupu, Noam. 2015. "Partisanship in Latin America." In *The Latin American Voter*, edited by Ryan E. Carlin, Matthew Singer, and Elizabeth J. Zechmeister. Ann Arbor: University of Michigan Press.

Lupu, Noam, and Susan C. Stokes. 2009. "The Social Bases of Political Parties in Argentina, 1912–2003." *Latin American Research Review* 44:58–87.

Lupu, Noam, and Susan C. Stokes. 2010. "Democracy, Interrupted: Regime Change and Partisanship in Twentieth-Century Argentina." *Electoral Studies* 29:91–104.

Lyne, Mona M. 2007. "Rethinking Economics and Institutions: The Voter's Dilemma and Democratic Accountability." In *Patrons, Clients, and Policies: Patterns of Democratic Accountability and Political Competition*, edited by Herbert Kitschelt and Steven Wilkinson, 159–81. Cambridge: Cambridge University Press.

Madrid, Raúl L. 2005a. "Indigenous Parties and Democracy in Latin America." *Latin American Politics and Society* 47:161–79.

Madrid, Raúl L. 2005b. "Ethnic Cleavages and Electoral Volatility in Latin America." *Comparative Politics* 38:1–20.

Madrid, Raúl L. 2012. *The Rise of Ethnic Politics in Latin America*. Cambridge: Cambridge University Press.

Mainwaring, Scott. 1999. *Rethinking Party Systems in the Third Wave of Democratization: The Case of Brazil*. Stanford: Stanford University Press.

Mainwaring, Scott, Ana María Bejarano, and Eduardo Pizarro Leongómez, eds. 2006. *The Crisis of Democratic Representation in the Andes*. Stanford, CA: Stanford University Press.

Mainwaring, Scott, and Matthew Soberg Shugart, eds. 1997. *Presidentialism and Democracy in Latin America*. Cambridge: Cambridge University Press.

Mainwaring, Scott, and Mariano Torcal. 2006. "Party System Institutionalization and Party System Theory after the Third Wave of Democratization." In *Handbook of Party Politics*, edited by Richard S. Katz and William Crotty, 204–26. London: Sage.

Mainwaring, Scott, Mariano Torcal, and Nicolás M. Sommá. 2015. "The Left and the Mobilization of Class Voting in Latin America." In *The Latin American Voter*, edited by Ryan E. Carlin, Matthew M. Singer, and Elizabeth J. Zechmeister. Ann Arbor: University of Michigan Press.

Mainwaring, Scott, and Edurne Zoco. 2007. "Political Sequences and the Stabilization of Interparty Competition: Electoral Volatility in Old and New Democracies." *Party Politics* 13:155–78.

Mair, Peter. 2010. "Left-Right Orientations." In *Oxford Handbooks Online: The Oxford Handbook of Political Behavior*, edited by Russell. J. Dalton and Hans-Dieter Klingemann, 206–22. Oxford: Oxford University Press.

Malloy, James, ed. 1976. *Authoritarianism and Corporatism in Latin America*. Pittsburgh: University of Pittsburgh Press.

Manzetti, Luigi, and Carole J. Wilson. 2006. "Corruption, Economic Satisfaction, and Confidence in Government: Evidence from Argentina." *Latin Americanist* 49:131–39.

Marsh, Michael, Richard Sinnott, John Garry, and Fiachra Kennedy. 2008. *The Irish Voter: The Nature of Electoral Competition in the Republic of Ireland*. Manchester: Manchester University Press.

McAlister, Lyle N., Anthony P. Maingot, and Robert A. Potash. 1970. *The Military in Latin American Sociopolitical Evolution: Four Case Studies*. Washington, DC: Center for Research in Social Systems.

Miller, Warren E., and Merrill Shanks. 1996. *The New American Voter*. Cambridge: Harvard University Press.

Morales, Daniel E. M. 2015. "Ethnicity and Electoral Preferences in Latin America." In *The Latin American Voter*, edited by Ryan Carlin, Matthew Singer, and Elizabeth Zechmeister. Ann Arbor: University of Michigan Press.

Moreno, Alejandro M. 2003. *El Votante Mexicano: Democracia, Actitudes Politicas y Conducta Electoral*. Mexico City: Fondo de Cultura Económica.

Moreno, Alejandro. 2009. "The Activation of Economic Voting in the 2006 Campaign." In *Consolidating Mexico's Democracy: The 2006 Presidential Campaign in Comparative Perspective*, edited by Jorge Dominguez, Alejandro Moreno, and Chappell Lawsoambrin, 209–28. Baltimore: John Hopkins University Press.

Moreno Morales, Daniel E. 2015. "Ethnicity and Electoral Preferences in Latin America." In *The Latin American Voter,* edited by Ryan E. Carlin, Matthew M. Singer, and Elizabeth J. Zechmeister. Ann Arbor: University of Michigan Press.

Morgan, Jana. 2015. "Gender and the Latin American Vote." In *The Latin American Voter,* edited by Ryan Carlin, Matthew Singer, and Elizabeth Zechmeister. Ann Arbor: University of Michigan Press.

Morgan, Jana, and Melissa Buice. 2013. "Latin American Attitudes toward Women in Politics: The Influence of Elite Cues, Female Advancement, and Individual Characteristics." *American Political Science Review* 107:644–62.

Morgenstern, Scott, and Benito Nacif. 2002. *Legislative Politics in Latin America.* Cambridge: Cambridge University Press.

Nadeau, Richard. 2015. "Anchor Variables and the Vote in Denmark." Paper presented at the Annual Meeting of the Midwest Political Science Association, Chicago, April 16–19.

Nadeau, Richard, Éric Bélanger, and Thomas Didier. 2013. "The Chavez Vote and the National Economy in Venezuela." *Electoral Studies* 32:482–88.

Nadeau, Richard, Éric Bélanger, Michael S. Lewis-Beck, Bruno Cautrès, and Martial Foucault. 2012. *Le vote des Français de Mitterrand à Sarkozy.* Paris: Presses de Sciences Po.

Nadeau, Richard, Martial Foucault, and Michael S. Lewis-Beck. 2011. "Assets and Risk: A Neglected Dimension of Economic Voting." *French Politics* 9:97–119.

Nadeau, Richard, Michael S. Lewis-Beck, and Éric Bélanger. 2013. "Economics and Elections Revisited." *Comparative Political Studies* 46:551–73.

Nadeau, Richard, Richard G. Niemi, Harold W. Stanley, and Jean-François Godbout. 2004. "Class, Party and South/Non-South Differences: An Update." *American Politics Quarterly* 32:52–67.

Nadeau, Richard, Richard G. Niemi, and Antoine Yoshinaka. 2002. "A Cross-National Analysis of Economic Voting: Taking Account of the Political Context across Time and Nations." *Electoral Studies* 21:403–23.

Nadeau, Richard, María Celeste Ratto, Michael S. Lewis-Beck, Éric Bélanger, François Gélineau, and Mathieu Turgeon. 2015a. "Economía y elecciones en Argentina: Las dimensiones clásica (valence), posicional y patrimonial de la teoría del voto económico." *Revista Sociedad Argentina de Análisis Político* 9, no. 2 (November): 235–66.

Nadeau, Richard, María Celeste Ratto, Michael S. Lewis-Beck, Éric Bélanger, François Gélineau, and Mathieu Turgeon. 2015b. "Rendicion de cuentas en las democratias en desarollo: El votante latinoamericano." *Revista de Ciencia Politica* 35 (3): 463–88.

Navia, Patricio, and Rodrigo Osorio. 2015. "It's the Christian Democrats' Fault: Declining Political Identification in Chile, 1957–2012." *Canadian Journal of Political Science* 48:815–38.

Norris, Pippa. 2004. *Electoral Engineering: Voting Rules and Political Behavior.* Cambridge: Cambridge University Press.

O'Dwyer, Conor. 2006. *Runaway State-Building: Patronage Politics and Democratic Development.* Baltimore: John Hopkins University Press.

Oxhorn, Philip D., and Graciela Ducatenzeiler, eds. 1998. *What Kind of Democracy? What Kind of Market? Latin America in the Age of Neoliberalism.* University Park: Pennsylvania State University Press.

Patterson, Eric. 2004. "Different Religions, Different Politics? Religion and Political Attitudes in Argentina and Chile." *Journal for the Scientific Study of Religion* 43:345–62.

Pérez, Orlando J. 2003. "Democratic Legitimacy and Public Insecurity: Crime and Democracy in El Salvador and Guatemala." *Political Science Quarterly* 118:627–44.

Pérez, Orlando J. 2011. "Crime, Insecurity and Erosion of Democratic Values in Latin America." *Revista Latinoamericana de Opinión Pública* 1:61–86.

Persson, Torsten, Guido Tabellini, and Francesco Trebbi. 2003. "Electoral Rules and Corruption." *Journal of the European Economics Association* 1:958–89.

Peterson, Anna. 1997. *Martyrdom and the Politics of Religion: Progressive Catholicism in El Salvador's Civil War*. Albany: State University of New York Press.

Pew Research Center. 2014. *Religion in Latin America: Widespread Change in a Historically Catholic Region*. Washington, DC: Pew Research Center.

Poole, K. T., and Zeigler, L. H. 1985. *Women, Public Opinion, and Politics: The Changing Political Attitudes of American Women*. New York: Longman.

Popkin, Samuel L. 1994. *The Reasoning Voter: Communication and Persuasion in Presidential Campaigns*. Chicago: University of Chicago Press.

Population Reference Bureau. 2003. "Population Dynamics in Latin America." *Population Bulletin* 58:1–36.

Porto, Mauro. 2007. "Framing Controversies: Television and the 2002 Presidential Election in Brazil." *Political Communication* 24:19–36.

Powell, Bingham G. 2000. *Elections as Instruments of Democracy: Majoritarian and Proportional Visions*. New Haven: Yale University Press.

Powell, Bingham, and Guy D. Whitten. 1993. "A Cross-National Analysis of Economic Voting: Taking Account of the Political Context." *American Journal of Political Science* 37:391–414.

Prillaman, William C. 2003. "Crime, Democracy, and Development in Latin America." *Policy Papers on the Americas*, vol. 14. Washington, DC: Center for Strategic and International Studies.

Puddington, Arch. 2014a. "Freedom in the World 2012: Latin America." Washington, DC: Freedom House.

Puddington, Arch. 2014b. "A Conversation with Arch Puddington, Vice President at Freedom House." *SAIS Review of International Affairs* 34:35–39.

Quann, Nathalie, and Kwing Hung. 2002. "Victimization Experience and the Fear of Crime: A Cross-National Study." In *Crime Victimization in Comparative Perspective: Results from the International Crime Victims Survey, 1989–2000*, edited by Paul Nieuwbeerta, 301–16. Den Haag: Boom Juridischeuitgevers.

Remmer, Karen. 1991. "The Political Impact of Economic Crisis in Latin America in the 1980s." *American Political Science Review* 85:777–800.

Remmer, Karen. 2007. "The Political Economy of Patronage: Expenditure Patterns in the Argentine Provinces, 1983–2003." *Journal of Politics* 69:363–77.

Remmer, Karen. 2012. "The Rise of Leftist-Populist Governance in Latin America: The Roots of Electoral Change." *Comparative Political Studies* 45:947–72.

Remmer, Karen, and François Gélineau. 2003. "Subnational Electoral Choice: Economic and Referendum Voting in Argentina, 1983–1999." *Comparative Political Studies* 36:801–21.

Roberts, Kenneth M. 2002. "Social Inequalities without Class Cleavages in Latin America's Neoliberal Era." *Studies in Comparative International Development* 36:3–33.

Roberts, Kenneth M., and Erik Wibbels. 1999. "Party Systems and Electoral Volatility in Latin America: A Test of Economic, Institutional, and Structural Explanations." *American Political Science Review* 93:575–90.

Robinson, William S. 1950. "Ecological Correlation and the Behavior of Individuals." *American Sociological Review* 15:351–57.

Rosas, Guillermo. 2005. "The Ideological Organization of Latin American Legislative Parties." *Comparative Political Studies* 38:824–49.

Rosas, Guillermo, and Elizabeth Zechmeister. 2000. "Ideological Dimensions and Left-Right Semantics in Latin America." Paper prepared for the Meeting of the Latin American Studies Association, Miami, Florida, March 16–18.

Rottinghaus, Brandon, and Irina Alberro. 2005. "Rivaling the PRI: The Image Management of Vicente Fox and the Use of Public Opinion Polling in the 2000 Mexican Election." *Latin American Politics and Society* 47:143–58.

Saiegh, Sebastian M. 2009. "Recovering a Basic Space from Elite Surveys: Evidence from Latin America." *Legislative Studies Quarterly* 34:117–45.

Schmitt, Herman, and Angelika Scheuer. 2013. "Electoral Choices in Mature and Consolidating Democracies." Second European Conference on Comparative Electoral Research, Rhodes, Greece, April 11–14.

Schmitter, Philippe. 1973. *Military Rule in Latin America: Functions, Consequences, and Perspectives.* Thousand Oaks, CA: Sage.

Scully, Timothy R. 1995. *Building Democratic Institutions: Party Systems in Latin America.* Stanford: Stanford University Press.

Seligson, Mitchell A., and Daniel E. Moreno Morales. 2010. "Gay in the Americas." *Americas Quarterly* (Winter). http://www.americasquarterly.org/node/1316#1301

Silvert, Kalman H. 1961. *The Conflict Society: Reaction and Revolution in Latin America.* New Orleans: Hauser Press.

Singer, Matthew. 2009. "Buying Voters with Dirty Money: The Relationship between Clientelism and Corruption." Paper presented at the Annual Meeting of the American Political Science Association, Toronto, Ontario, September 3–6.

Singer, Matthew. 2011. "Who Says 'It's the Economy?' Cross-National and Cross-Individual Variation in the Salience of Economic Performance." *Comparative Political Studies* 44:284–312.

Singer, Matthew. 2013. "Economic Voting in an Era of Noncrisis: Economic Voting in Latin America 1982–2010." *Comparative Politics* 45:169–85.

Smith, Peter H. 2012. *Democracy in Latin America: Political Change in Comparative Perspective.* Oxford: Oxford University Press.

Soares, Gláucio A. D. 1961. "Classes sociais, strata sociais e as eleições presidenciais de 1960." *Sociologia* 23:217–38.

Stegmaier, Mary, and Michael S. Lewis-Beck. 2013. "Economic Voting." In *Oxford Bibliographies in Political Science Online,* edited by Rick Valelly. New York: Oxford University Press.

Stokes, Donald E. 1963. "Spatial Models of Party Competition." *American Political Science Review* 57:368–77.

Stokes, Susan C. 2001. *Mandates and Democracy: Neoliberalism by Surprise in Latin America*. Cambridge: Cambridge University Press.

Stokes, Susan C. 2005. "Perverse Accountability: A Formal Model of Machine Politics with Evidence from Argentina." *American Political Science Review* 99:315–25.

Studlar, Donley T., Ian McAllister, and Bernadette C. Hayes. 1998. "Explaining the Gender Gap in Voting: A Cross-National Analysis." *Social Science Quarterly* 79:779–98.

Sulmont, David. 2014. *Left-Right Voting and Party System in Latin America: Comparative Analysis of Elections in Brazil, Chile, Mexico and Peru*. Lima: Public Opinion Institute, Pontificia Universidad Catolica del Peru.

Tarouco, Gabriela da Silva, and Rafael Machado Madeira. 2012. "Left and Right in the Brazilian Political System." Paper presented at the XI Congress of the Brazilian Studies Association, University of Illinois, Urbana-Champaign, September 6–8.

Telles, Edward E. 2004. *Race in Another America: The Significance of Skin Color in Brazil*. Princeton: Princeton University Press.

Thomassen, Jacques. 1976. "Party Identification as a Cross-Cultural Concept: Its Meaning in the Netherlands." In *Party Identification and Beyond*, edited by Ian Budge, Ivor Crewe, and Dennis Farlie, 63–79. New York: Wiley.

Thomassen, Jacques. 2005. *The European Voter: A Comparative Study of Modern Democracies*. Oxford: Oxford University Press.

Torcal, Mariano, and Scott Mainwaring. 2003. "The Political Recrafting of Social Bases of Party Competition: Chile, 1973–95." *British Journal of Political Science* 33:55–84.

United Nations. 2012. *United Nations Office on Drugs and Crime*. Vienna: Vienna International Centre.

United Nations. 2014. Department of Economic and Social Affairs, Population Division. World Urbanization Prospects: The 2014 Revision, CD-ROM Edition.

United Nations Educational, Scientific and Cultural Organization (UNESCO). 2003. *Gender and Education for All: The Leap to Equality*. Paris: UNESCO.

Valenzuela, J. Samuel, Timothy R. Scully, and Nicolás Somma. 2007. "The Enduring Presence of Religion in Chilean Ideological Positionings and Voter Options." *Comparative Politics* 40:1–20.

Van Cott, Donna Lee. 2005. *From Movements to Parties in Latin America: The Evolution of Ethnic Politics*. New York: Cambridge University Press.

Van der Brug, Wouter, Mark Franklin, and Gábor Tóka. 2008. "One Electorate or Many? Differences in Party Preference Formation between New and Established European Democracies." *Electoral Studies* 27:589–600.

Vavreck, Lynn. 2009. *The Message Matters: The Economy and Presidential Campaigns*. Princeton: Princeton University Press.

Vowles, Jack. 2005. "New Zealand: Consolidation or Reform?" In *The Politics of Electoral Systems*, edited by Michael Gallagher and Paul Mitchell, 280–306. Oxford: Oxford University Press.

Weyland, Kurt. 2003. "Economic Voting Reconsidered: Crisis and Charisma in the Election of Hugo Chávez." *Comparative Political Studies* 36:822–48.

Weyland, Kurt, Raúl L. Madrid, and Wendy Hunter. 2010. *Leftist Governments in Latin America: Successes and Shortcomings*. Cambridge: Cambridge University Press.

Weyland, Kurt, Carlos de la Torres, and Miriam Kornblith. 2013. "Latin America's Authoritarian Drift." *Journal of Democracy* 24:18–32.

Wiarda, Howard J., and Hilary Collins. 2011. *Consitutional Coups? Military Intervention in Latin America*. Washington, DC: Center for Strategic and International Studies.

Widner, Jennifer. 1997. "Political Parties and Civil Societies in Sub-Saharan Africa." In *Democracy in Africa: The Hard Road Ahead*, edited by Marina Ottoway, 65–82. Boulder: Lynne Rienner.

Wiesehomeier, Nina. 2010. *The Meaning of Left-Right in Latin America: A Comparative Perspective*. Working Paper No. 370. Notre Dame, IN: Kellogg Institute for International Studies.

Wiesehomeier, Nina, and Kenneth Benoit. 2009. "Presidents, Parties, and Policy Competition." *Journal of Politics* 71:1435–47.

Wilkinson, Paul. 1986. "Maintaining the Democratic Process and Public Support." In *The Future of Political Violence*, edited by Richard Clutterbuck, 177–84. New York: St. Martin's.

Wirls, Daniel. 1986. "Reinterpreting the Gender Gap." *Public Opinion Quarterly* 50:316–30.

Wise, Carol, and Riordan Roett, eds. 2003. *Post-Stabilization Politics in Latin America: Competition, Transition, Collapse*. Washington, DC: Brookings Institution Press.

Yankelovich. Daniel. 1974. *The New Morality: A Profile of American Youth in the 70's*. New York: McGraw Hill.

Yashar, Deborah. 2005. *Contesting Citizenship in Latin America: The Rise of Indigenous Movements and the Postliberal Challenge*. New York: Cambridge University Press.

Zechmeister, Elisabeth J. 2006. "What's Left and Who's Right? A Q-Method Study of Individual and Contextual Influences on the Meaning of Ideological Labels." *Political Behavior* 28:151–73.

Zechmeister, Elizabeth J., and Margarita Corral. 2010. *The Varying Economic Meaning of "Left" and "Right" in Latin America*. AmericasBarometer Insight 38. Nashville, TN: Vanderbilt University.

Zechmeister, Elizabeth J., and Margarita Corral. 2013. "Individual and Contextual Constraints on Ideological Labels in Latin American." *Comparative Political Studies* 46:675–701.

Zechmeister, Elisabeth J., and Mitchell A. Seligson. 2011. "What Troubles Citizens of the Americas?" FOCAL Research Paper, January.

Zechmeister, Elizabeth J., and Daniel Zizumbo-Colunga. 2013. "The Varying Political Toll of Corruption in Good versus Bad Economic Times." *Comparative Political Studies* 46:1190–1218.

Zucco, Cesar. 2008. "The President's 'New' Constituency: Lula and the Pragmatic Vote in Brazil's 2006 Presidential Elections." *Journal of Latin American Studies* 40:29–49.

# About the Authors

**Richard Nadeau** is Professor of Political Science at the University of Montreal. His interests are voting behavior, public opinion, political communication, and quantitative methodology. A Fulbright Scholar and a former chief advisor to the premier of Quebec, Professor Nadeau has authored or coauthored over 180 articles (published in the most prestigious political science journals), chapters, and books. The latter include *Le vote des Français de Mitterrand à Sarkozy*, *Unsteady State*, *Anatomy of a Liberal Victory*, *Citizens*, *French Presidential Elections*, *The Austrian Voter*, *Health Care Policy and Opinion in Canada and the United States*, and *Le comportement électoral des Québécois* (Donald Smiley Award 2010).

**Éric Bélanger** is Professor in the Department of Political Science at McGill University and is a member of the Centre for the Study of Democratic Citizenship. His research interests include political parties, public opinion, and voting behavior. He has published more than 50 articles on these topics in scholarly journals such as *Comparative Political Studies*, *Political Research Quarterly*, *Electoral Studies*, *Publius: The Journal of Federalism*, the *European Journal of Political Research*, and the *Canadian Journal of Political Science*. He is also the coauthor of four books including *French Presidential Elections* and *Le comportement électoral des Québécois*.

**Michael S. Lewis-Beck** is F. Wendell Miller Distinguished Professor of Political Science at the University of Iowa. His interests are comparative elections, election forecasting, political economy, and quantitative methodology. Professor Lewis-Beck has authored or coauthored over 260 articles and books, including *Economics and Elections*, *The American Voter Revisited*, *French Presidential Elections*, *Forecasting Elections*, *The Austrian Voter*, and *Applied Regression*. He has served as Editor of the *American Journal of Political Science* and of the Sage *QASS* series (the green monographs) in quantitative methods. Currently he is Associate Editor of *International Journal of Forecasting* and of *French Politics*. In spring 2012, he held the position of Paul Lazersfeld University Professor at the University of Vienna. During the fall of 2012, he was Visiting Professor at Center for Citizenship and Democracy, University of Leuven, Belgium. In spring 2013, Professor Lewis-Beck was Visiting Scholar, Centennial Center, American Political Science Association, Washington, DC. For fall 2014, he was Visiting Professor at LUISS University, Rome.

**Mathieu Turgeon** is Assistant Professor in the Instituto de Ciência Política at the Universidade de Brasília (Brazil) and founding member of the Economics and Politics Research Group at that same institution. His research interests center on political behavior, including voting and elections, public opinion, political psychology, and experimental, statistical, and survey methodology. His work is comparative in nature, but concerns mostly Brazil, Canada, France, and the United States. His work has appeared in refereed journals that include the *British Journal of Political Science*, *Political Behavior*, *Political Psychology*, and *Electoral Studies*.

**François Gélineau** is Professor and Research Chair of Democracy and Parliamentary Institutions at the Université Laval (Canada). His research focuses on voter choice and accountability. His research has appeared in *Electoral Studies*, the *Journal of Elections, Public Opinion and Parties*, the *Political Research Quarterly*, the *British Journal of Political Science*, and *Comparative Political Studies*, among others.

# Index